POSTCARD HISTORY SERIES

Atlantic City

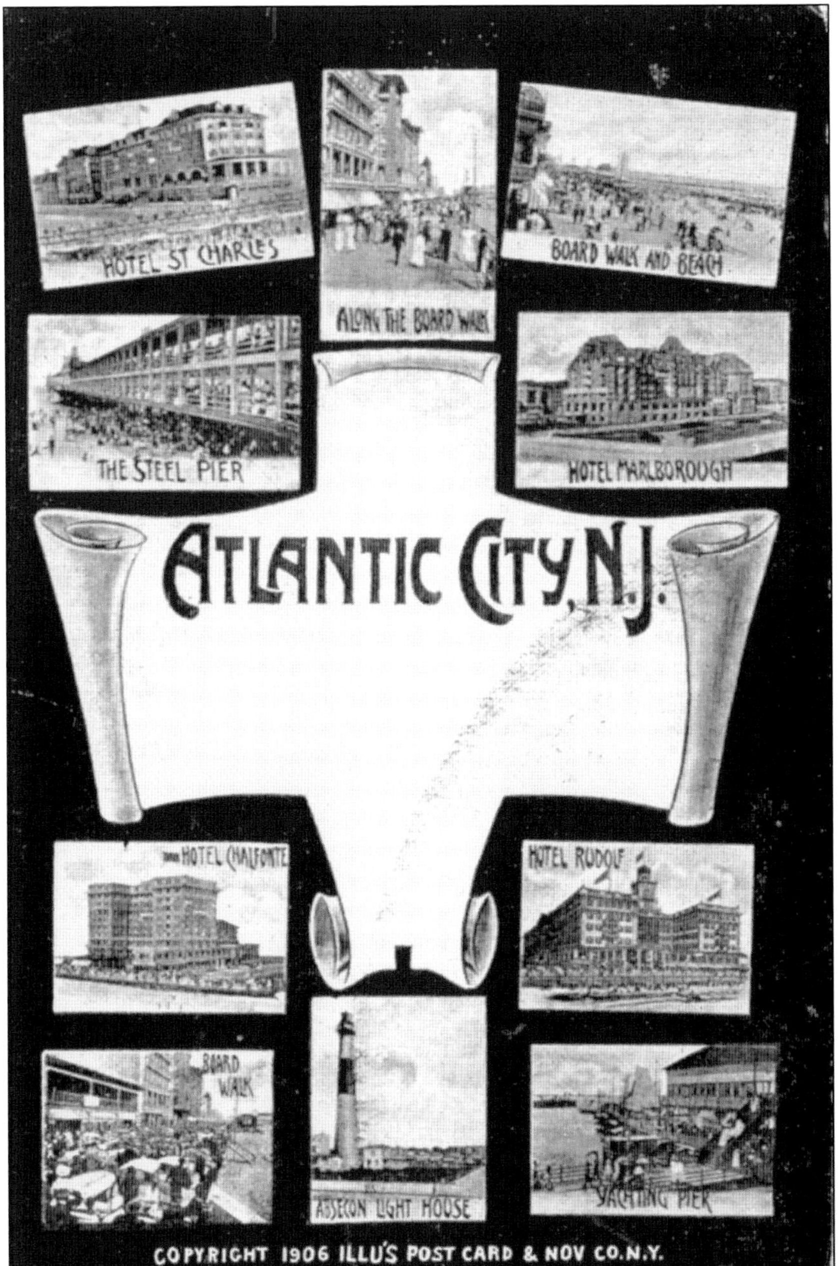

ATLANTIC CITY. Atlantic City, the "Queen of Resorts," has from its earliest days offered much to see and experience. This multiview postcard shows some of the many places of interest, in and around the city, which awaited visitors. A trip to Atlantic City was always sure to leave lasting memories. (Illustrated Post Card Company, 1906.)

On the front cover: Please see page 71. (Author's collection.)

On the back cover: Please see page 58. (Author's collection.)

POSTCARD HISTORY SERIES

Atlantic City

James D. Ristine
Foreword by Allen Pergament

ARCADIA
PUBLISHING

ISBN 978-0-7385-5704-5

Published by Arcadia Publishing
Charleston SC, Chicago IL, Portsmouth NH, San Francisco CA

Printed in the United States of America

Library of Congress Catalog Card Number: 2007939271

For all general information contact Arcadia Publishing at:
Telephone 843-853-2070
Fax 843-853-0044
E-mail sales@arcadiapublishing.com
For customer service and orders:
Toll-Free 1-888-313-2665

Visit us on the Internet at www.arcadiapublishing.com

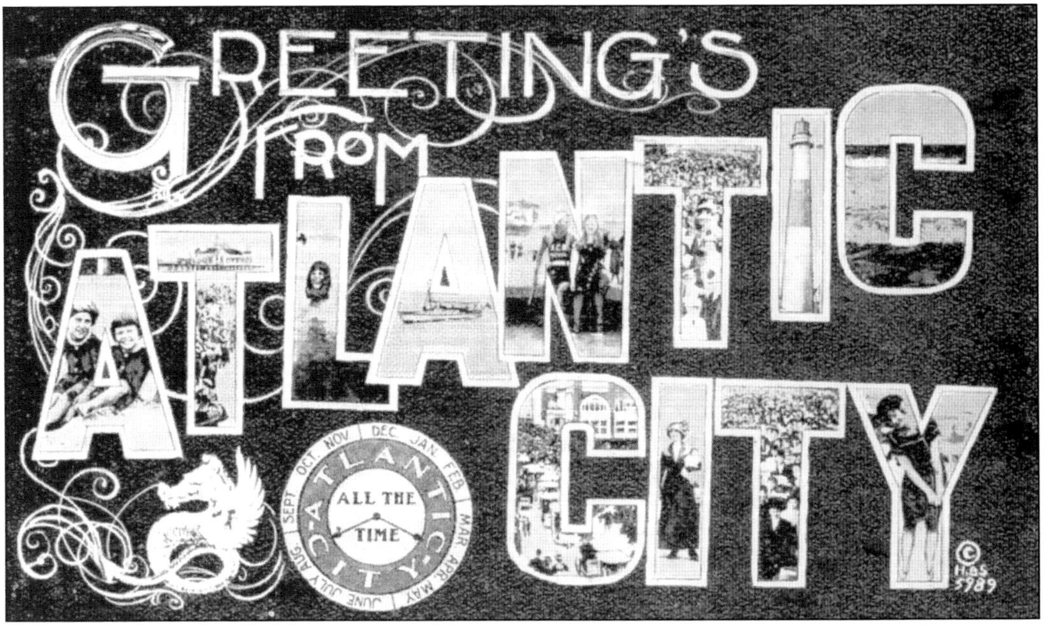

Greetings From Atlantic City. This large-letter postcard offers multiple views of sights in and around Atlantic City. Also seen on the card is the city's official slogan and emblem that was adopted in May 1914. It is a clocklike design proclaiming, "Atlantic City All The Time," any month of the year. (P. Sander, c. 1924.)

Contents

Acknowledgments

In writing this book on the history of Atlantic City I was fortunate to have the assistance of several individuals whose contributions I would like to acknowledge.

First and foremost I would like to thank Allen "Boo" Pergament, who so graciously and willingly gave of his time and allowed me to tap into his vast knowledge of the history of this remarkable city. He also kindly consented to writing the foreword to this book. Another major source of information for this book was the Atlantic City Free Public Library and its Heston Collection of local history. Thanks go out to archivist Heather Halpin, who helped guide me through the library's wealth of resources. I also wish to recognize the contributions of my wife, Deborah, who helped proofread this book and who supported me in this project.

Lastly, recognition is due to the many photographers and publishers of the postcard views found in this book. Without them, this visual history of Atlantic City as it once was would be incomplete. For the benefit of the postcard collector, each image has been identified as to publisher (when known) and estimated date of publication. All postcards in this book are from my personal collection.

FOREWORD

America, even the world, has a special love and fascination with postcards. In its infancy, back in the mid-1890s, it was simply an unusual novelty struggling for an existence. People had not yet established a useful purpose for this new means of communication. It did not take long for their acceptance, about 10 years, when it just seemed to come on like a dramatic explosion. After interest in postcards started, and over the long term, it maintained a wide diversity of interest for both the sender and receiver.

Initially its interest was for a quick means of sending a very brief message to family, loved ones, and friends, showing them they were being thought about. They were most popular at resorts or recreational sites where people were too busy enjoying themselves to want to take too much time to write a letter. It also, in some cases, allowed the senders to show off their status a bit. Here they were, on vacation and enjoying themselves, while the receiver was likely toiling hard in the big, hot city.

Up until March 1907, only the address could be written on the back of a postcard. Most cards had a thin white strip across the bottom of the front or along the side. This only allowed for the briefest of messages. After that the back had half the space for the message and half for the address. They have become known as divided backs in collectors' lingo. The previous ones are undivided backs.

Basically, postcards were created for advertising purposes, whether simply a picture, written information, or both; for a view or scene of a particular place or site; or for fun, enjoyment, or entertainment.

Jim Ristine has tried to take us through the decades on a journey into Atlantic City's past in postcards. Let's enjoy that which we remember or that which we did not know about.

Allen "Boo" Pergament
Atlantic City historian
Assistant Curator, Atlantic Heritage Center
Board member, Atlantic City Historical Museum

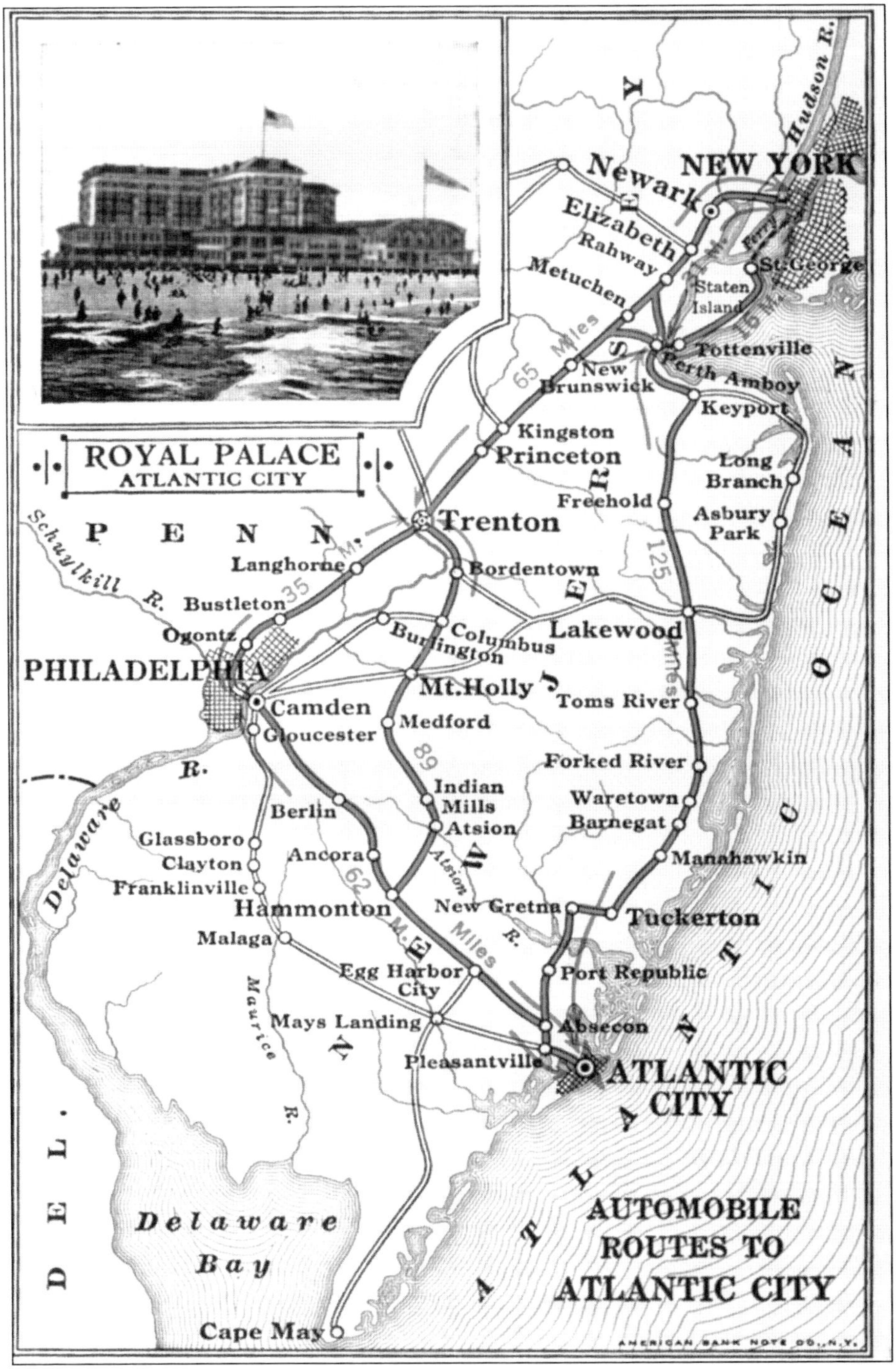

AUTOMOBILE ROUTES TO ATLANTIC CITY. Atlantic City was founded in 1854 with the intention of becoming a major seaside resort. First railroads and then the automobile transported most visitors to the city. Only 62 miles from Philadelphia and approximately 125 from New York City, major roadways have long provided easy access to the "Queen of Resorts." (American Bank Note Company, *c.* 1920.)

Introduction

Atlantic City, New Jersey, home of dazzling gambling casinos, the birthplace of the Miss America Pageant, possessor of grand beaches and famed boardwalk, and the subject of the world's best-selling board game Monopoly, is an American institution. The name Atlantic City is well known and recognizable around the world.

Occupying about 12 square miles on the northern end of Absecon Island, the city was founded in March 1854. It was created when land developers and railroads purchased land with the purpose of setting up a seaside resort to rival and surpass Cape May and Asbury Park, two already-well-established vacation destinations. Visionaries such as Dr. Jonathan Pitney and others obtained a railroad charter in 1852, creating the Camden and Atlantic Railroad, which then constructed rail lines connecting the island to Philadelphia by way of Camden. A civil engineer by the name of Richard Osborne laid out the city's design and even proposed the name Atlantic City for this new venture.

At first the city was promoted as a resort where people could enjoy the healthy benefits of ocean waters and sea breezes. This focus soon changed as promoters successfully lured visitors in vast numbers to this city by the sea. And people, arriving by the trainloads, wanted more. Since those early days, Atlantic City has attracted many tens of millions of visitors from far and wide, enticing them with its beaches, boardwalk, luxurious hotels, and myriad of entertainment attractions.

This book takes the reader on a journey back to the early 20th century, the years 1900 to 1930, when Atlantic City was truly the "Queen of Resorts." Those halcyon days were probably best captured by images utilized on the picture postcards of the time. The picture postcard itself is often attributed to local newspaperman Carl Voelker, whose wife brought back the idea from a trip to Germany in 1893. The first cards were used as souvenirs to help promote Atlantic City as a tourist attraction.

And a great tourist attraction it became. During the early 1900s, the beaches offered a place to promenade in one's finest attire, to cavort in the sand, bathe in the ocean, ride on horseback, have one's picture taken, or gaze upon sculptures carved in the sand. On June 26, 1870, the first official boardwalk, one mile in length, was opened. The boardwalk was officially designated a street on August 17, 1896. It would become a street like no other in the world. After several rebuildings, this wooden esplanade would eventually stretch for almost four miles. Before long the boardwalk evolved into Atlantic City's number one attraction. With its multitude of varied businesses, amusements, eating establishments, theaters, rolling chairs, and much more, it offered visitors all they could wish for and beyond. Strolling the boards became a summertime ritual for those visiting the shore. Amusement piers were built extending outward from the boardwalk toward the ocean as a means of increasing the space available for all forms of entertainment and diversion. Band concerts, vaudeville acts, dancing, thrill rides, fish net hauls, diving horses, human cannonballs, educational and commercial exhibits, and countless other wonders made the piers magical places. It would also be here that the top names in the entertainment world would come to perform.

Accommodating the enormous number of people coming to the city meant providing lodging on a large scale. To meet the demand for rooms, majestic hotels were constructed, some among the finest in the world. Names such as the Seaside, Ambassador, Traymore, Brighton, Chalfonte, Haddon Hall, and Marlborough-Blenheim are etched into the city's history. These and other architectural wonders provided elegant places to stay for awhile, to enjoy the most modern conveniences of the day, and to avail oneself of the stately dining rooms and grand ballrooms that were offered. Sadly, most of these former landmarks have been demolished over the years to make way for new development.

One needs to keep in mind that Atlantic City is more than a resort; it is also a true city. This book also explores some of the streets, rail lines, businesses, public buildings, schools, and churches that have existed to serve the needs of its citizens. At the northern end of the city lie the inlet and the Absecon lighthouse. This area of maritime importance has also played its role in the history of the "Queen of Resorts." All in all, this book is a trip back in time to when Atlantic City was truly America's premier seaside resort.

One

City by the Sea

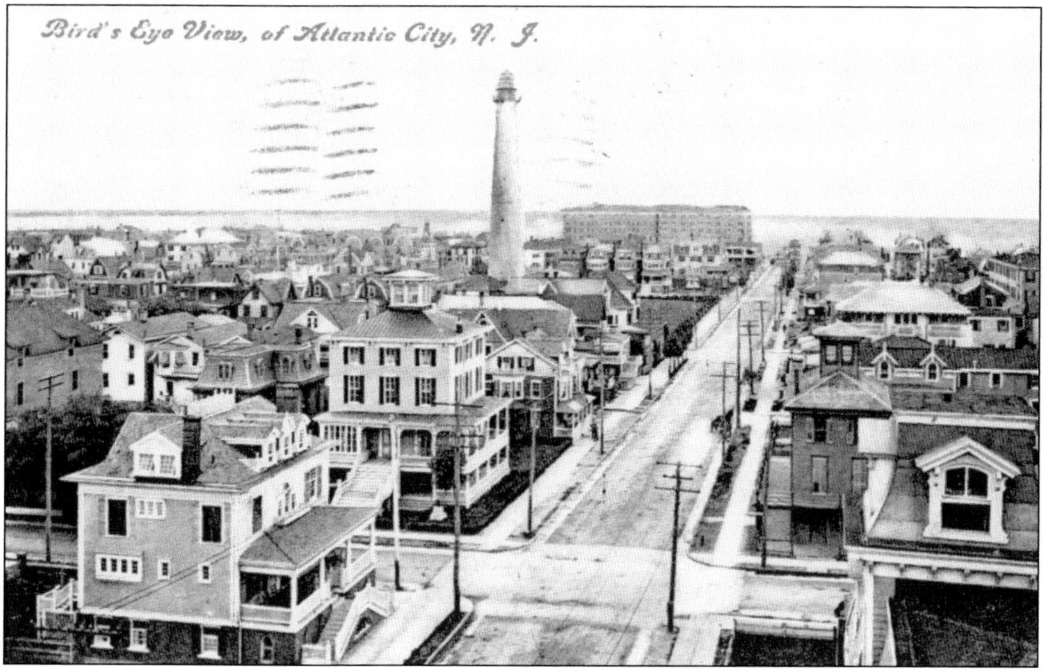

Bird's-Eye View of Atlantic City. Founded in 1854 with the intention of becoming a major seaside resort, it was civil engineer Richard Osborne who laid out the city's design and proposed its name. Streets running parallel to the ocean were named after the world's oceans while the cross streets where named for the nation's states. Here is a view looking northeast toward the Absecon Inlet. (P. Sander, *c.* 1910.)

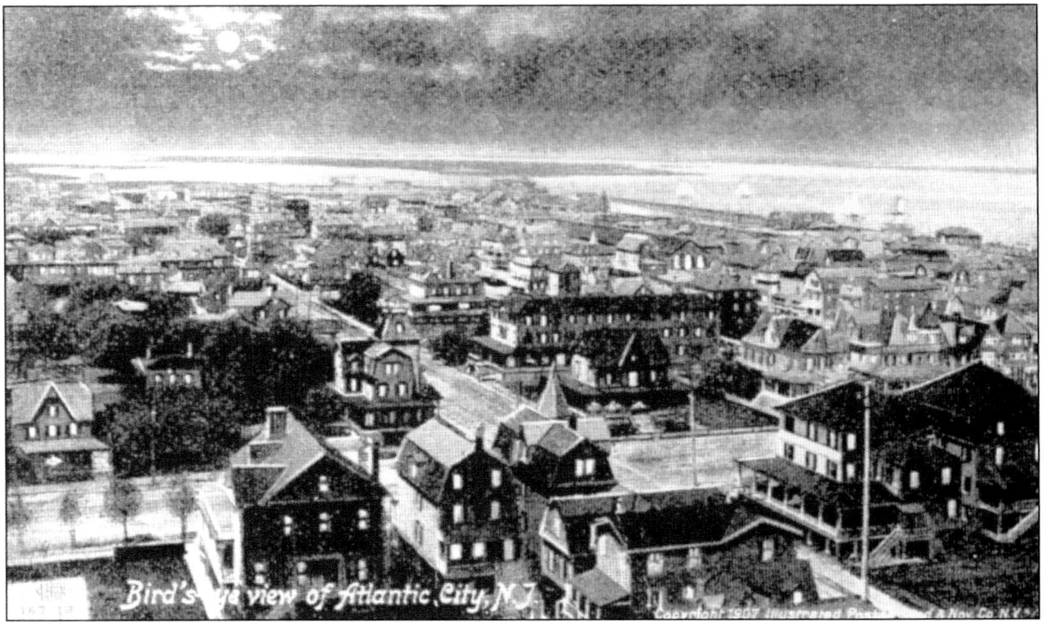

VIEW OF ATLANTIC CITY. It was in 1852 that Dr. Jonathan Pitney obtained a charter to create the Camden and Atlantic Railroad, which linked Philadelphia to the new resort. The railroad helped Atlantic City quickly grow into a sizable community. By 1910 the year-round population totaled 46,150. During the summer this number swelled enormously as visitors flocked to the "Queen of Resorts." (Illustrated Postal Card Company, 1907.)

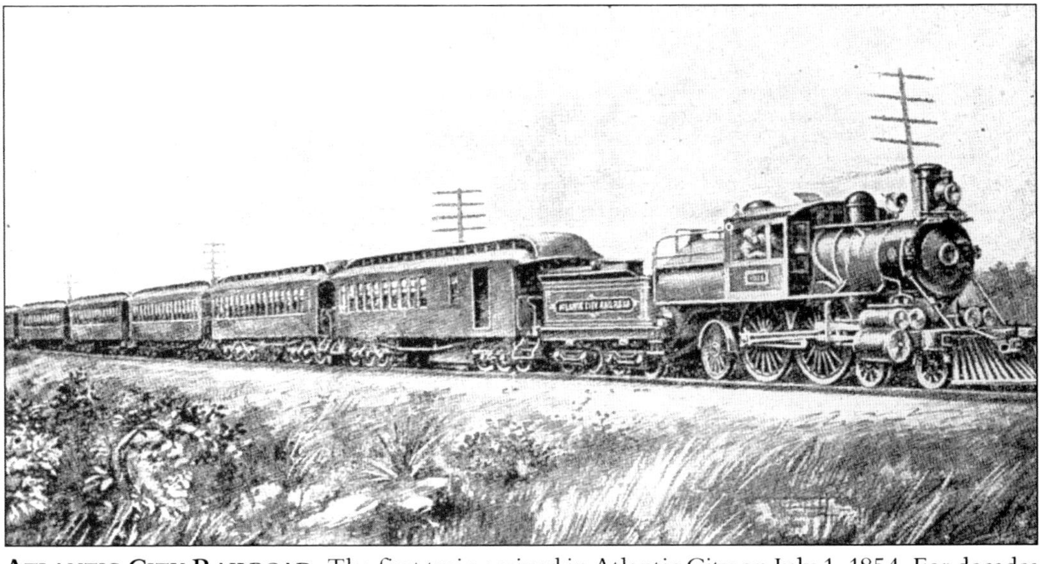

ATLANTIC CITY RAILROAD. The first train arrived in Atlantic City on July 1, 1854. For decades it was the railroad that brought most people to the resort. In the early 1900s, trains like this one, pulled by a 4-4-2 camelback engine, routinely made the 55.5-mile trip from Camden in less than one hour. One of these "Atlantic City flyers," number 343, ran the trip in only 41 minutes in June 1907. (Publisher unknown, *c.* 1904)

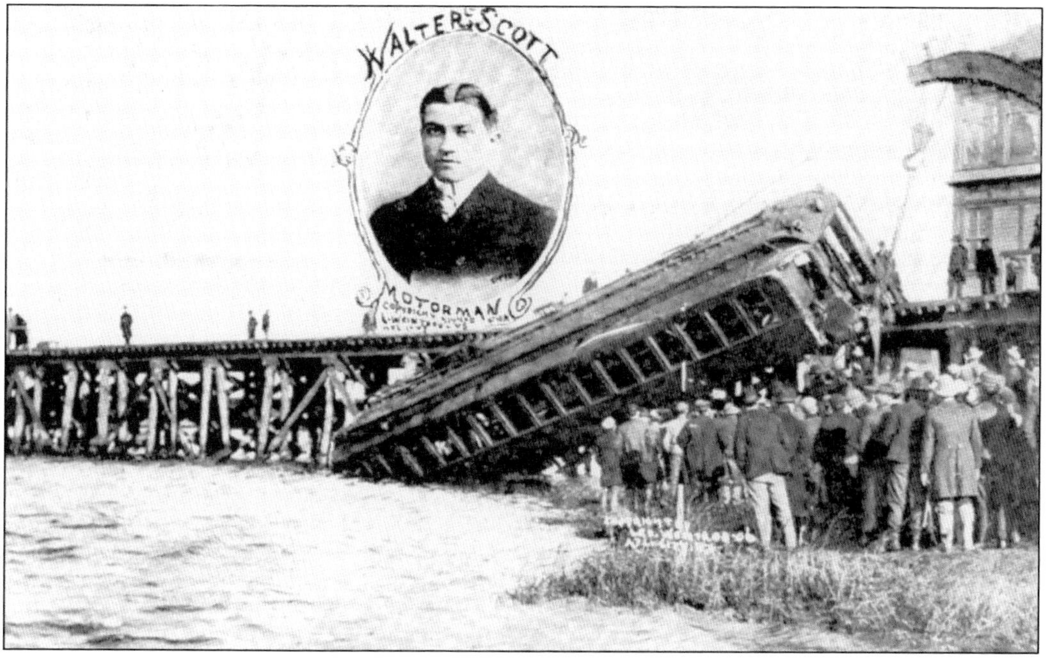

First Car Out of the Water. On October 28, 1906, around 2:30 a.m., a three-car electric train from Camden struck a partially opened drawbridge just outside Atlantic City. The accident, often referred to as the "Thoroughfare Wreck," resulted in the death of 53 passengers and motorman Walter Scott. This postcard view shows one of the cars being removed from the water. (Weintrob, 1906.)

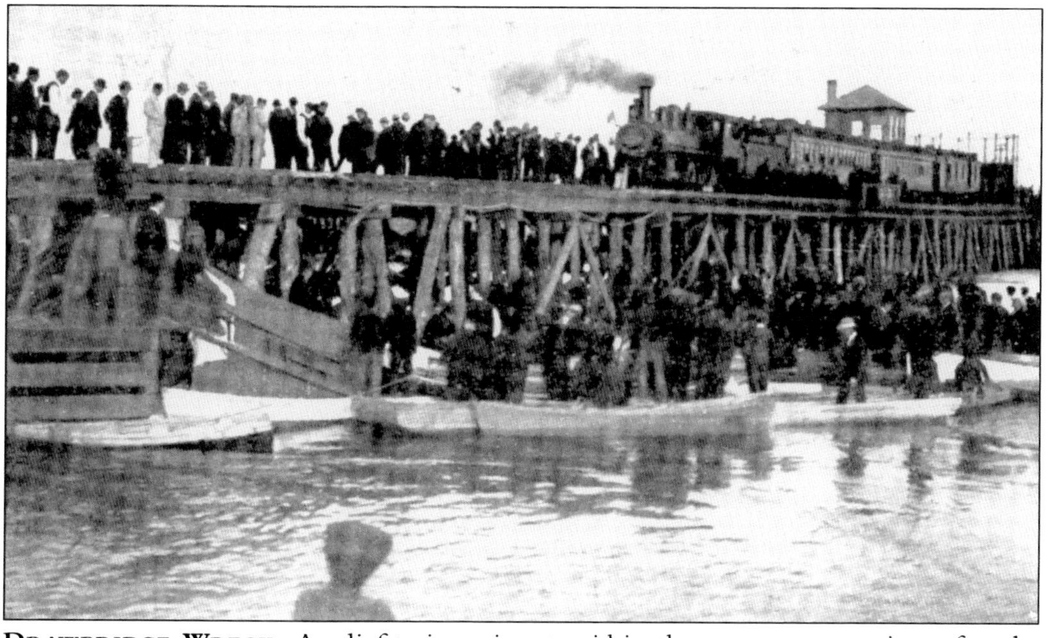

Drawbridge Wreck. A relief train arrives to aid in the recovery operations after the October 28, 1906, drawbridge wreck. Besides those killed, there were 32 passengers who were injured in the tragedy. This accident occurred only one month after the electrified trains were put into operation. (Wilbur R. Downs, 1906.)

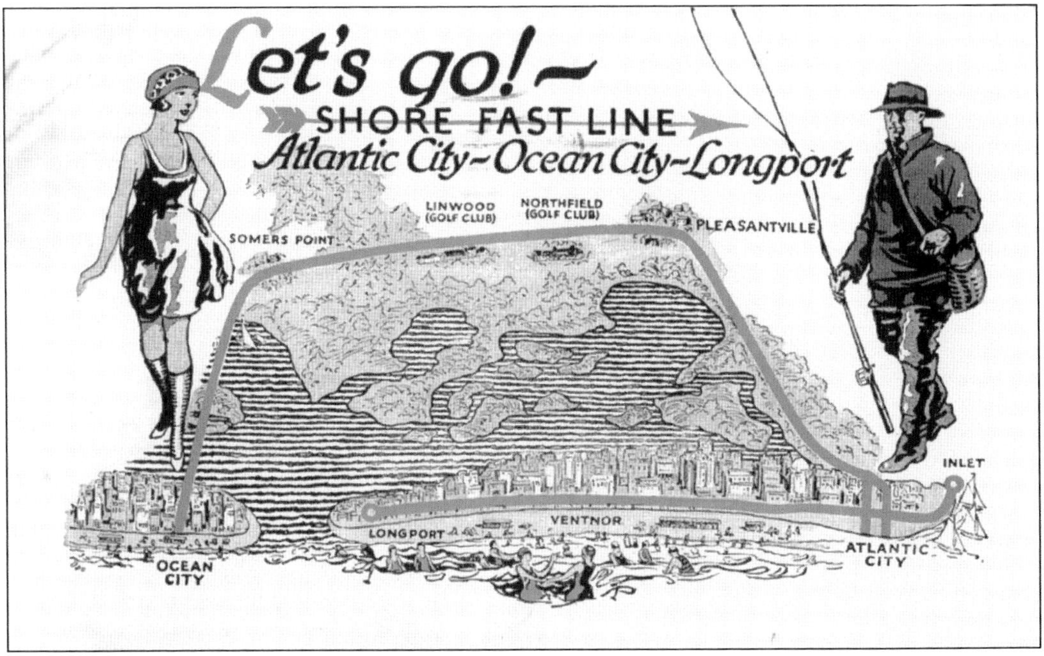

LET'S GO! The Shore Fast Line trolley system connected Atlantic City to its neighboring communities. It ran the length of Absecon Island as well as through many of the small towns on the mainland until reaching Ocean City. Trolleys provided a quick and inexpensive mode of transportation. This postcard shows a map of the route taken by this very popular rail system. (Publisher unknown, *c.* 1920.)

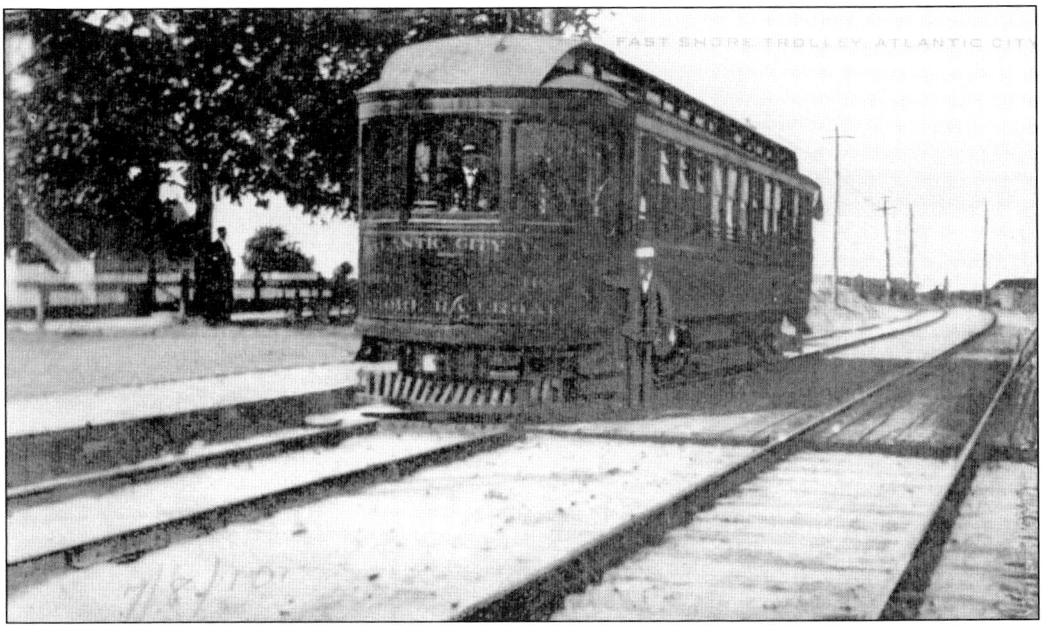

FAST SHORE TROLLEY. The motorman stands at his controls while a conductor poses beside a Shore Fast Line trolley sitting on one of the double tracks. These electric-powered trolleys, which ran from 1903 until 1948, were said to be the inspiration for the fictional Short Line Railroad in the game of Monopoly. (L. Beard, *c.* 1909.)

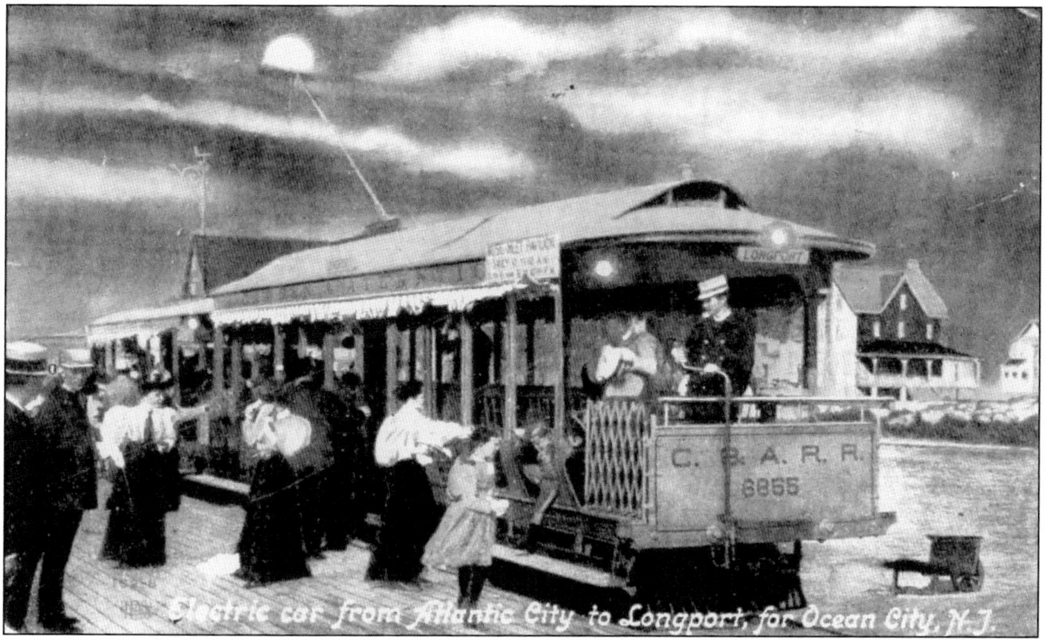

ELECTRIC CAR FROM ATLANTIC CITY TO LONGPORT. Electric trolleys began running to Longport from Atlantic City in 1893. During the summer months, open-air cars such as this were a popular means of transportation. The fares to Margate and Longport were 14¢ until reduced to 7¢ in 1929. Atlantic City was the first in the state of New Jersey to have overhead-powered electric trolleys. (Publisher unknown, *c.* 1909.)

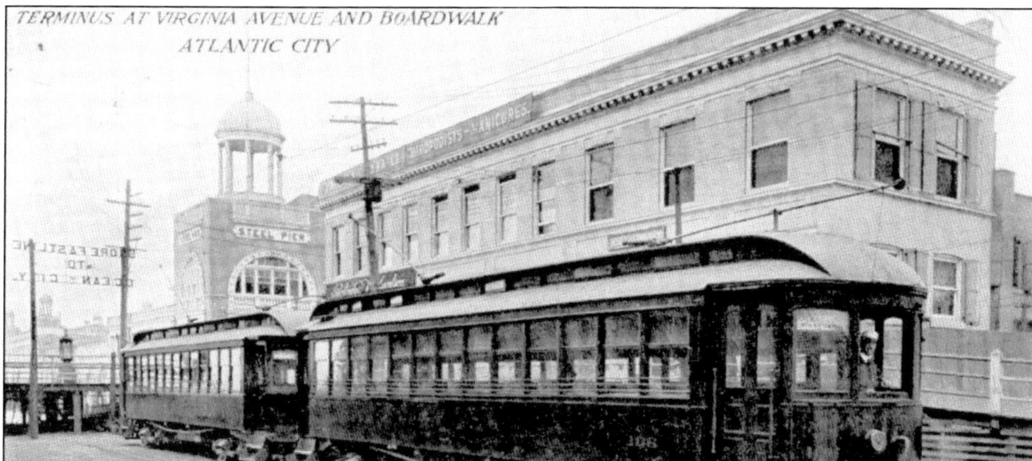

TROLLEY TERMINUS. Situated at Virginia Avenue and the boardwalk, this trolley terminal was close to Steel Pier (visible in the distance) and other popular attractions. It served as a convenient means of transportation for passengers arriving or departing for the mainland and south to Ocean City. (Publisher unknown, *c.* 1910.)

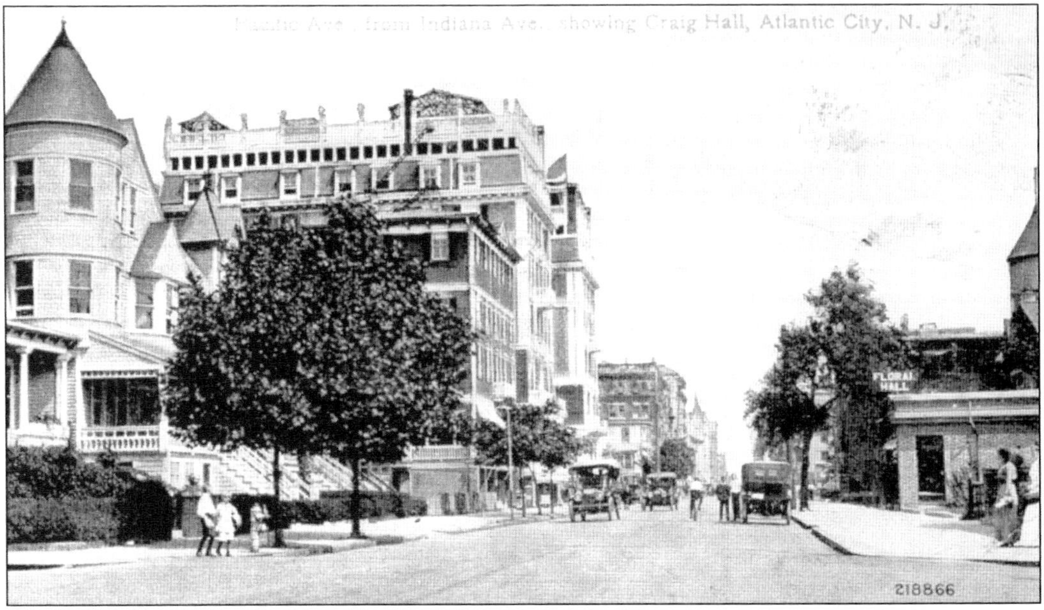

PACIFIC AVENUE FROM INDIANA AVENUE. Pacific Avenue is the closest street to the ocean and runs the length of the city. As one of the city's major streets, it was first paved with macadam in 1898 and then repaved with more modern materials in 1906. Looking north from the intersection with Indiana Avenue, Craig Hall is visible on the left at the next corner, which is Illinois Avenue. (Post Card Distribution Company, *c.* 1915.)

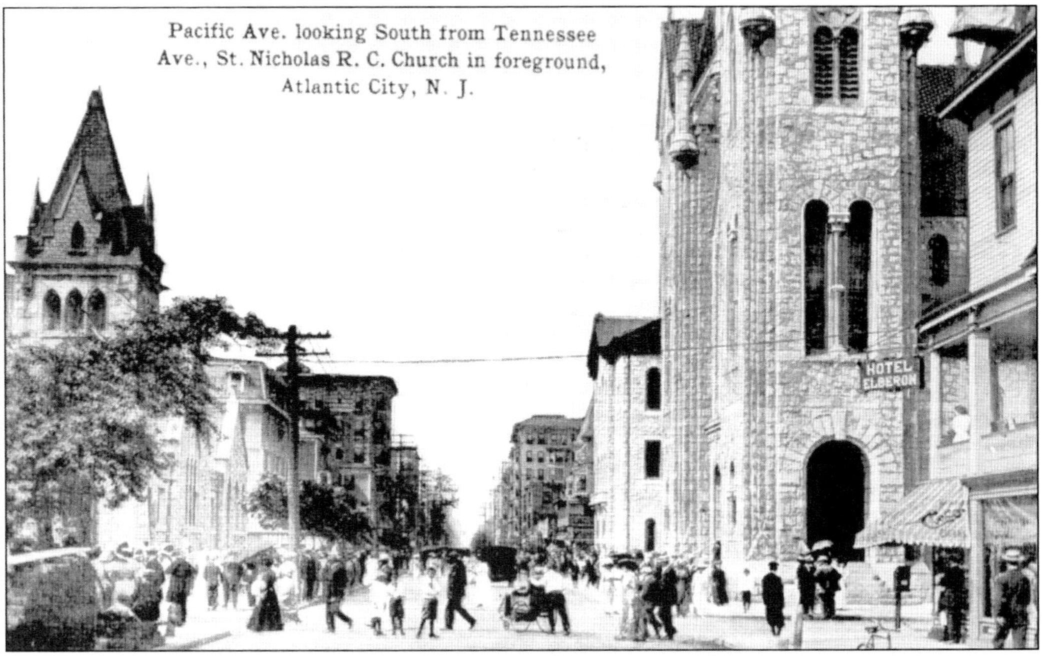

PACIFIC AVENUE LOOKING SOUTH. The intersection of Tennessee and Pacific Avenues is shown bustling with activity, people crossing the street and walking the sidewalks. On the right-hand corner stands St. Nicholas Catholic Church, while directly across the street, a sign identifies the Hotel Elberon. (Post Card Distribution Company, *c.* 1913.)

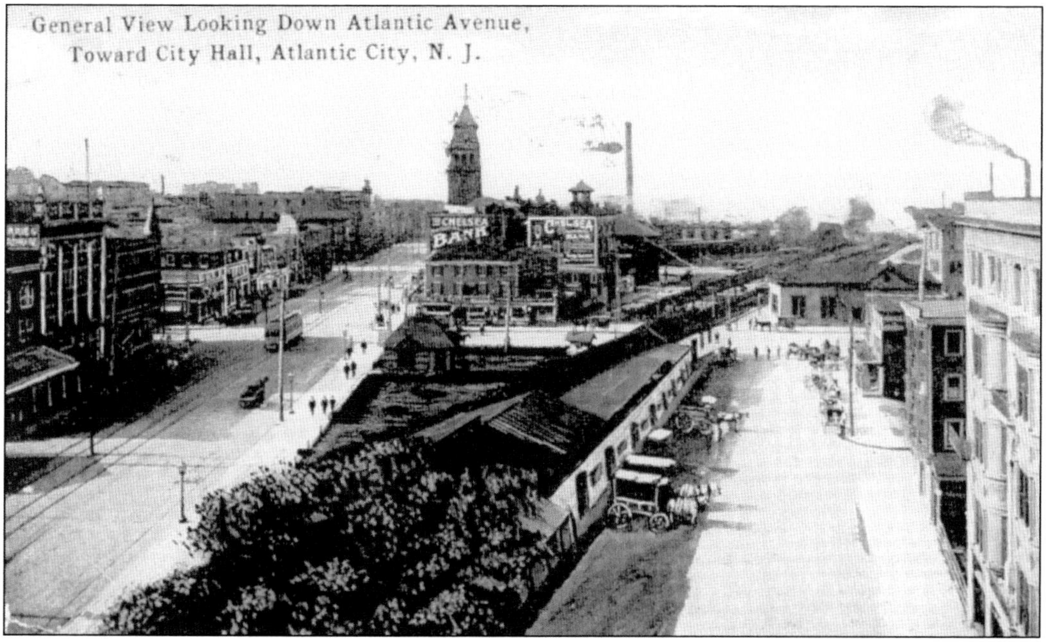

ATLANTIC AVENUE. Stretching the entire length of the city, Atlantic Avenue runs in a northeast-southeast direction parallel to, and just one block inland, from Pacific Avenue. At Boston Avenue the street bends and becomes the first avenue in from the beach as it runs down the island. From this vantage point the tower of city hall can be seen in the distance. (Sithens Post Card Company, *c.* 1915.)

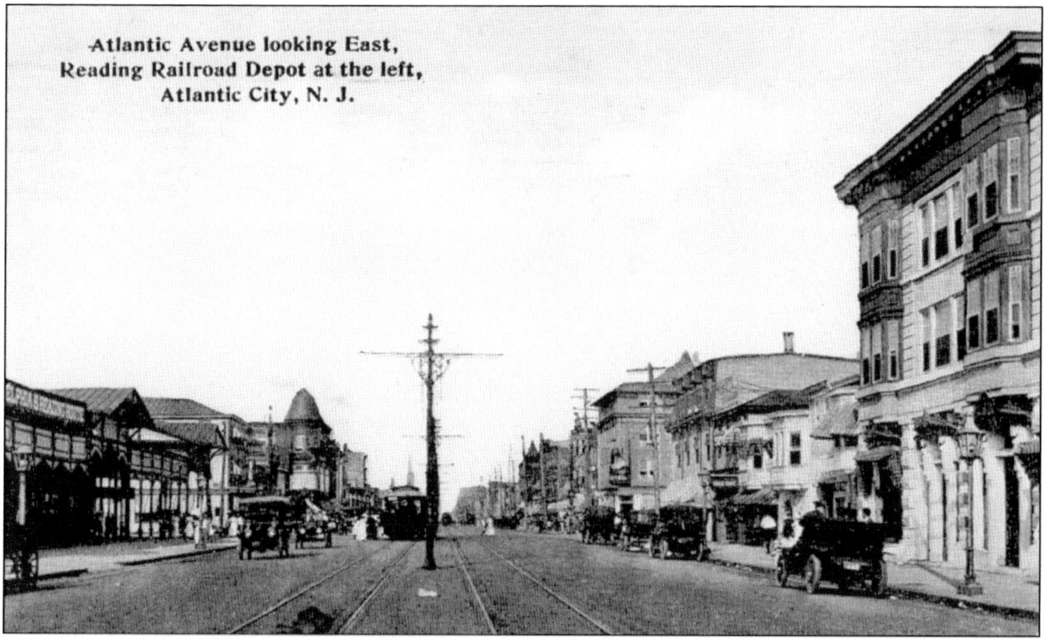

ATLANTIC AVENUE LOOKING EAST. A major commercial street, Atlantic Avenue was lined with hotels and businesses of all kinds. With a width of 100 feet, the street had ample room for two sets of trolley tracks while still allowing space for automobile traffic. In this view the Reading Railroad depot can be seen on the left. (Post Card Distribution Company, *c.* 1912.)

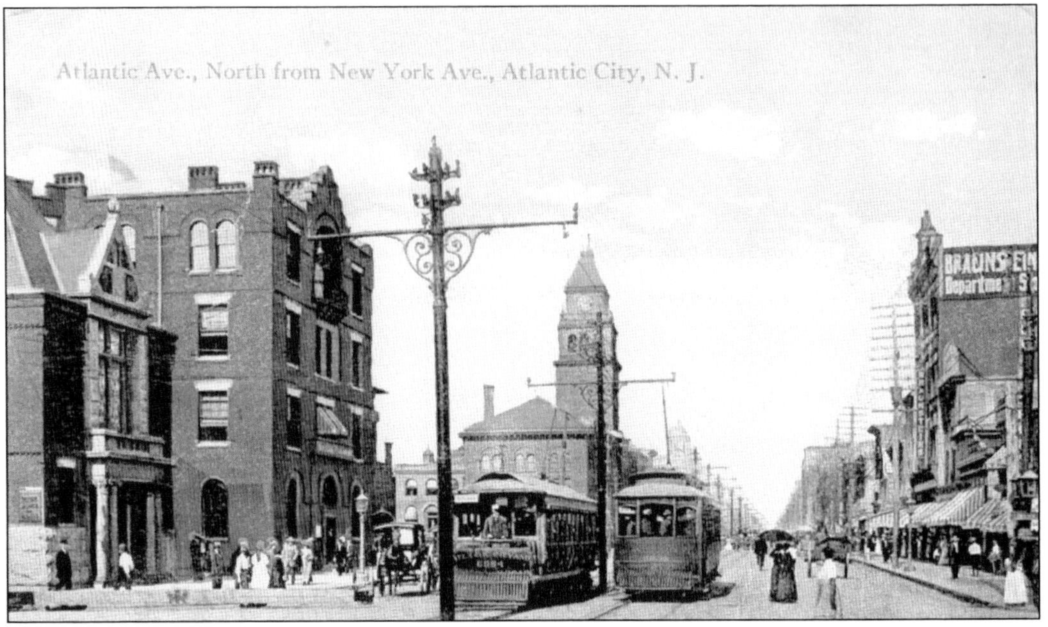

ALONG ATLANTIC AVENUE. Two electric trolley cars pass each other as they proceed along the busy thoroughfare. Looking northeast from New York Avenue, the city hall building is visible on the next corner, which is Tennessee Avenue. Braunstein's Department Store, one of many businesses located on Atlantic Avenue, sits on the right-hand side of the street. (Post Card Distribution Company, *c.* 1910.)

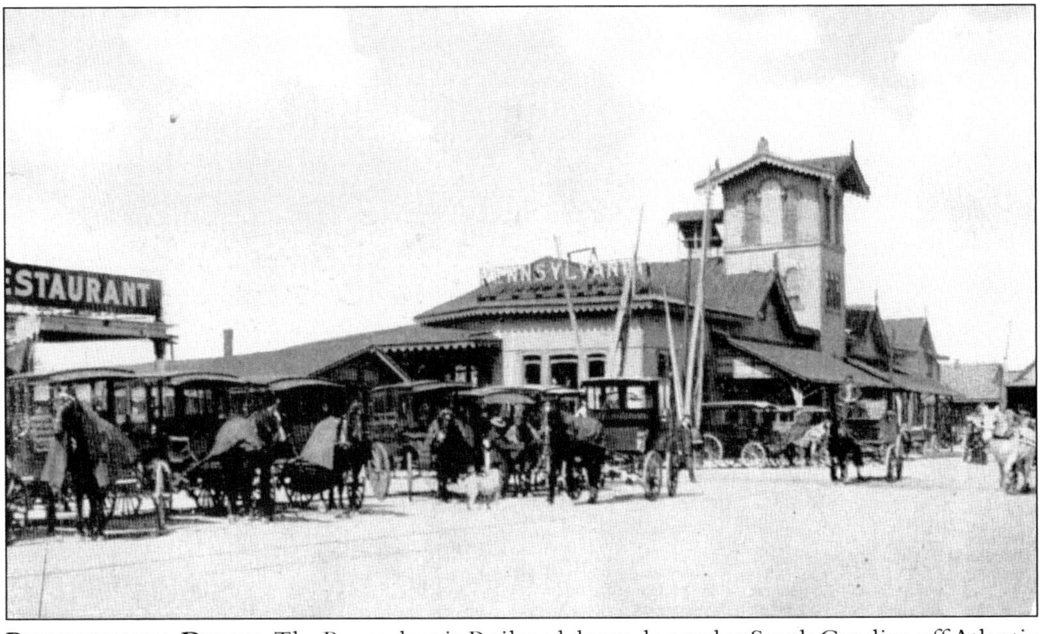

PENNSYLVANIA DEPOT. The Pennsylvania Railroad depot, located at South Carolina off Atlantic Avenue, was generally a busy place. Opened on July 1, 1876, this station finally closed down in September 1934. The building was demolished, and one mile of track leading to it was removed. In the early years, horse-drawn carriages like these waited to convey arriving train passengers to their hotels. (L. Beard, *c.* 1910.)

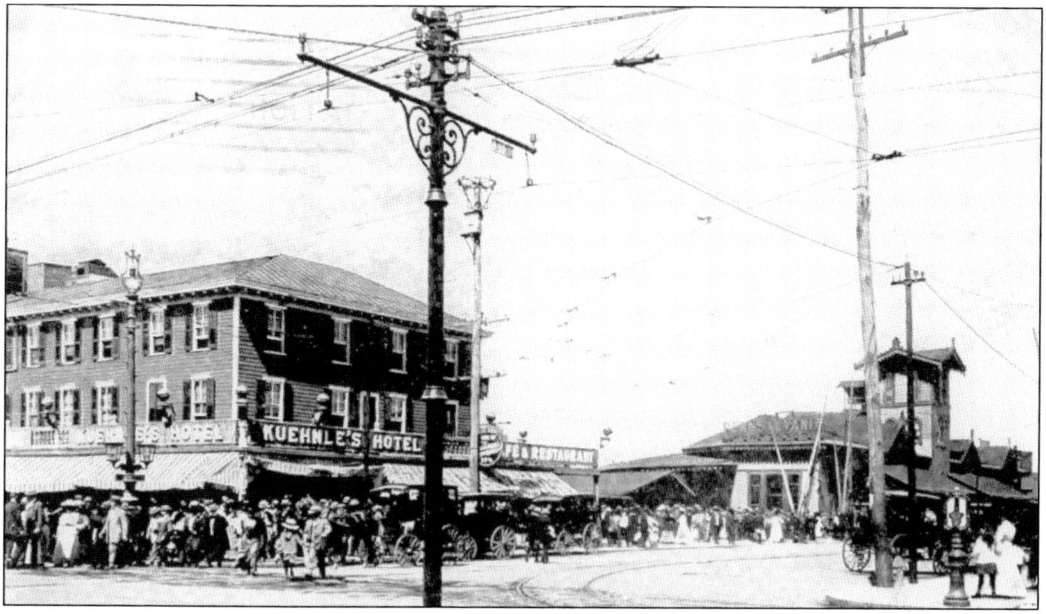

PENNSYLVANIA STATION AND KUEHNLE'S HOTEL. Situated on the corner of South Carolina and Atlantic Avenues was Kuehnle's Hotel. Opening for business in 1874, this hotel had a prime location to provide lodging for visitors arriving and departing from the nearby railroad depot. The owner of the hotel was "Commodore" Louis Kuehnle, an infamous Republican political boss of the era. (The American News Company, *c.* 1912)

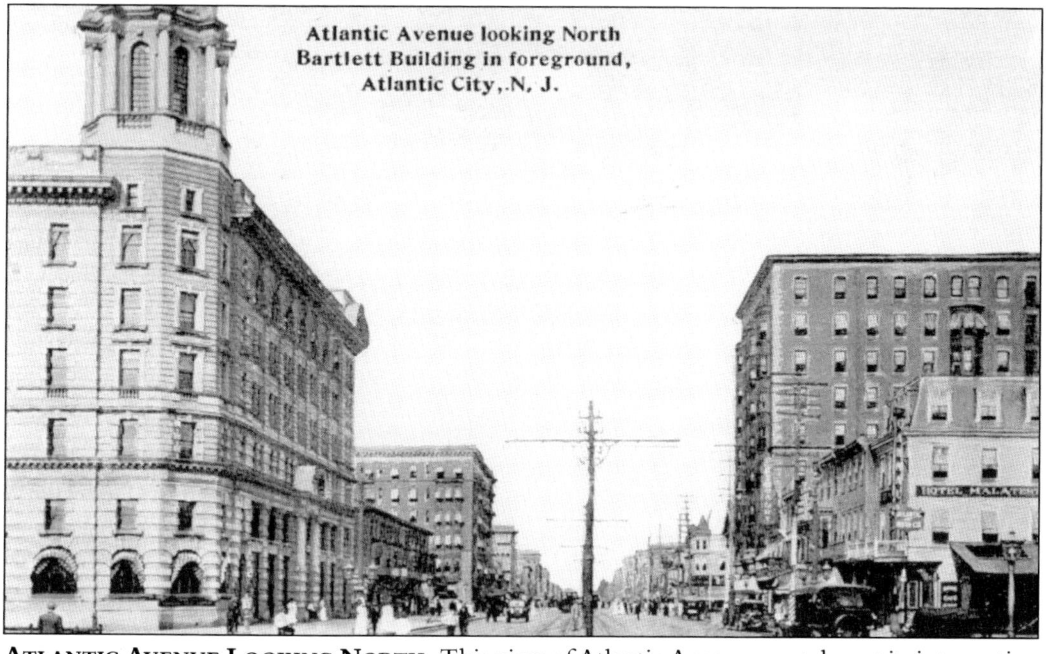

ATLANTIC AVENUE LOOKING NORTH. This view of Atlantic Avenue was taken at its intersection with North Carolina Avenue. On the corner stands the new Bartlett Building, which opened for occupancy on August 10, 1903. It was later renamed the Guarantee Trust Building when that company purchased the structure in 1913. A seventh floor was added in 1927. The building is still standing today. (Post Card Distribution Company, *c.* 1912.)

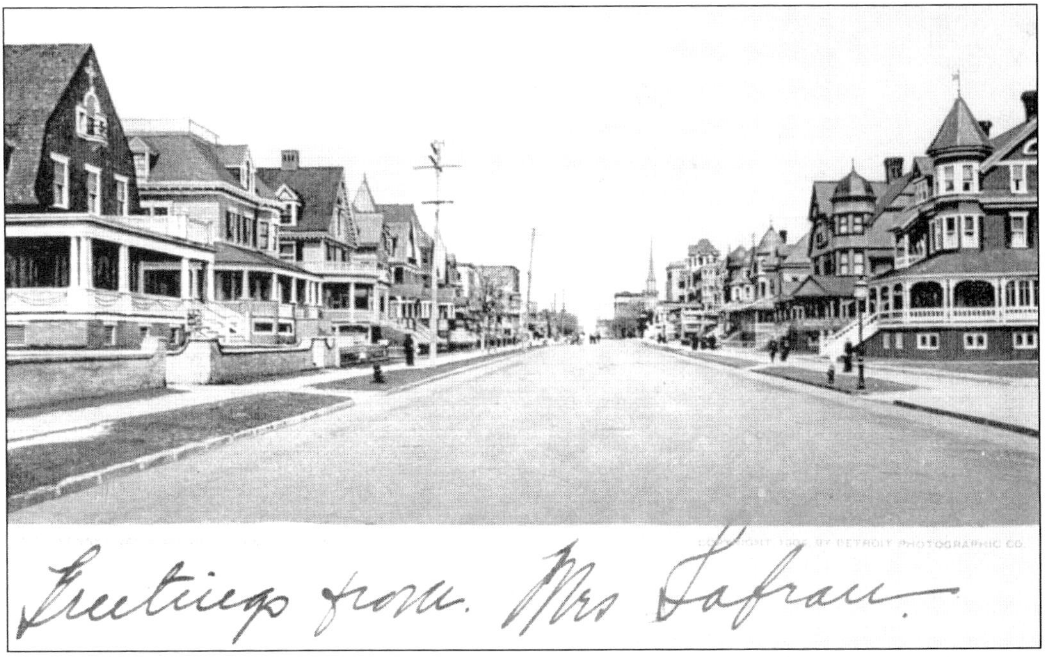

Pennsylvania Avenue. Along with North Carolina Avenue, Pennsylvania Avenue is among the widest of the city's cross streets. In the early part of the 20th century, the street was lined with elegant homes like those seen here. Visible in the far distance is the tall spire of the old First Presbyterian Church, on the corner of Pacific Avenue. (Detroit Publishing, 1904.)

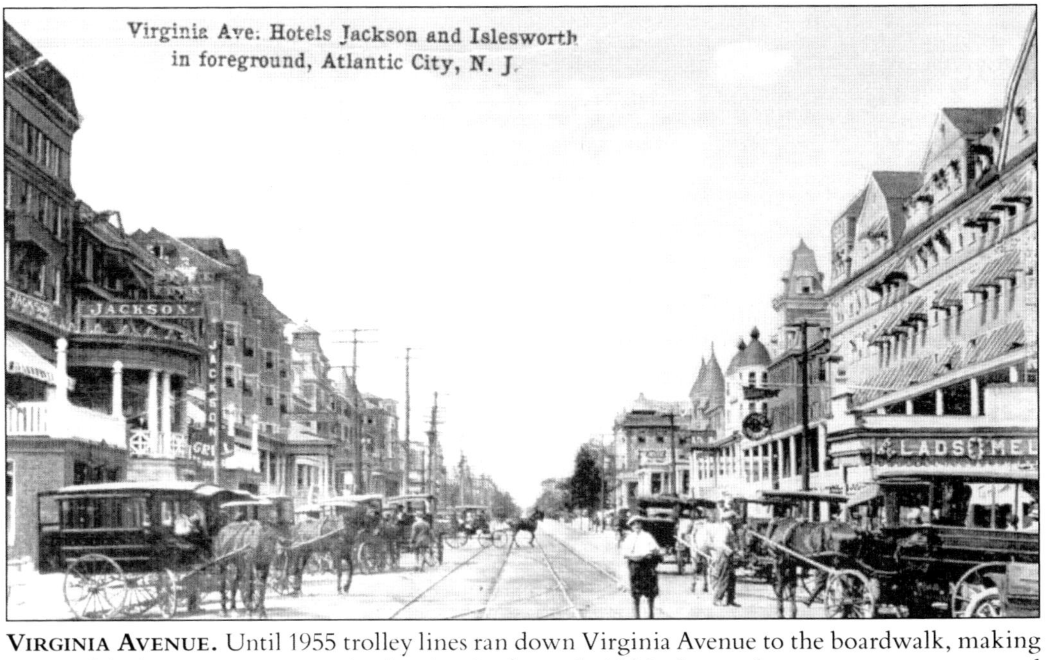

Virginia Avenue. Until 1955 trolley lines ran down Virginia Avenue to the boardwalk, making it one of the busiest cross streets in the city. In the early 1900s, horse-drawn wagons transported patrons from the train station to the many hotels and rooming houses that lined the avenue. Restaurants and small businesses often operated on the ground floor of these establishments. (Post Card Distribution Company, *c.* 1914.)

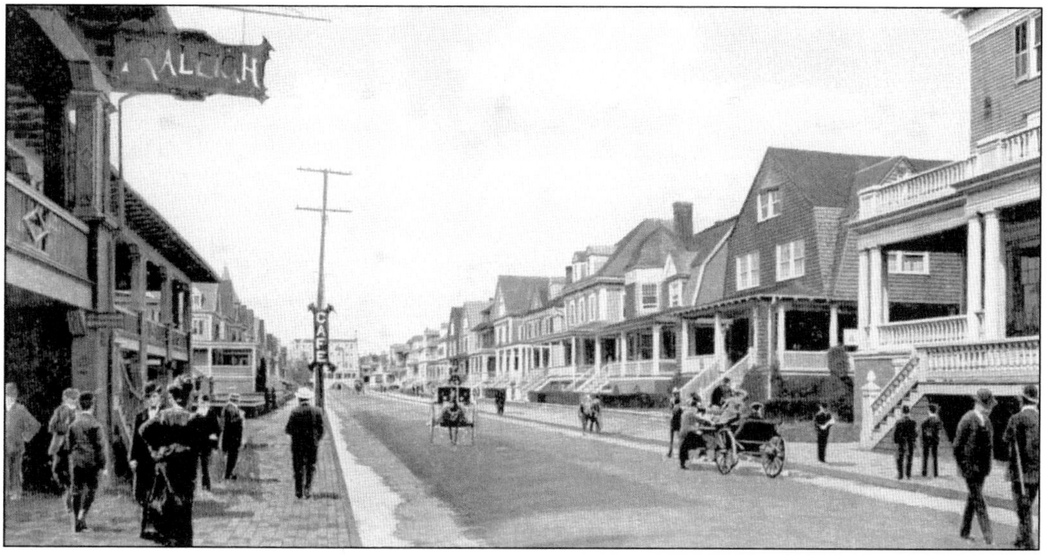

St. Charles Place. Probably best known today because of its name being associated with the game of Monopoly, St. Charles Place no longer exists. Located between New Jersey and Delaware Avenues from the boardwalk to Pacific Avenue, it was once a sector of beautiful homes and a few smaller hotels. Today the land is being utilized as a parking area. (Raphael Tuck and Sons, *c.* 1905.)

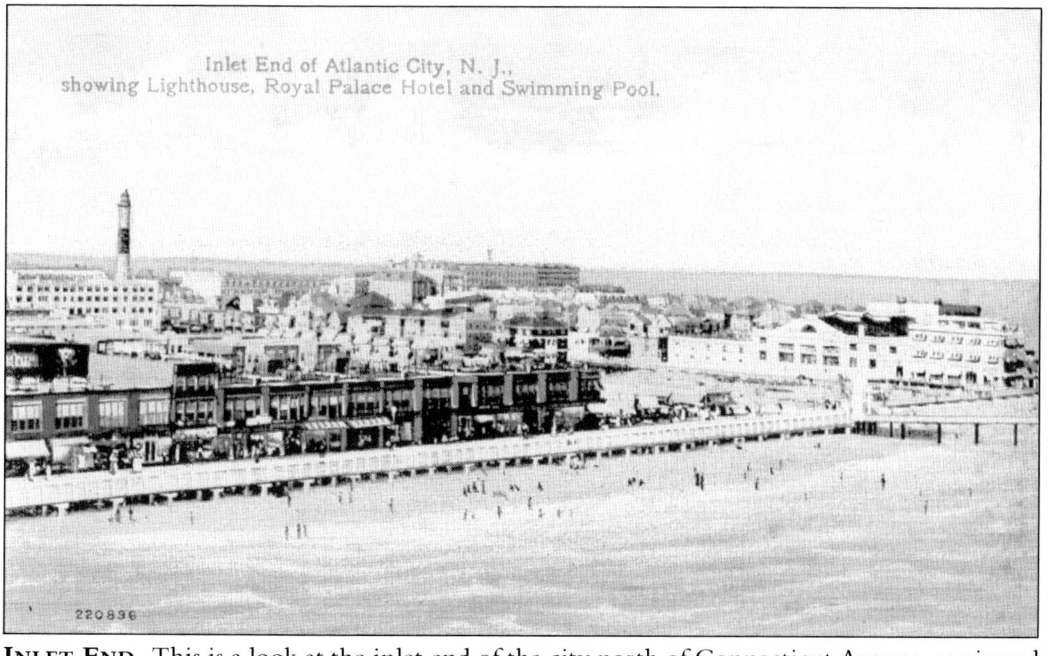

Inlet End. This is a look at the inlet end of the city north of Connecticut Avenue, as viewed from the ocean. In the distance, to the left, is the lighthouse with the Lelande Hotel seen just in front of it. Off in the distance to the north is the Royal Palace Hotel, while at Rhode Island Avenue and the boardwalk was the famous Hygeia Pool. (Post Card Distribution Company, *c.* 1912.)

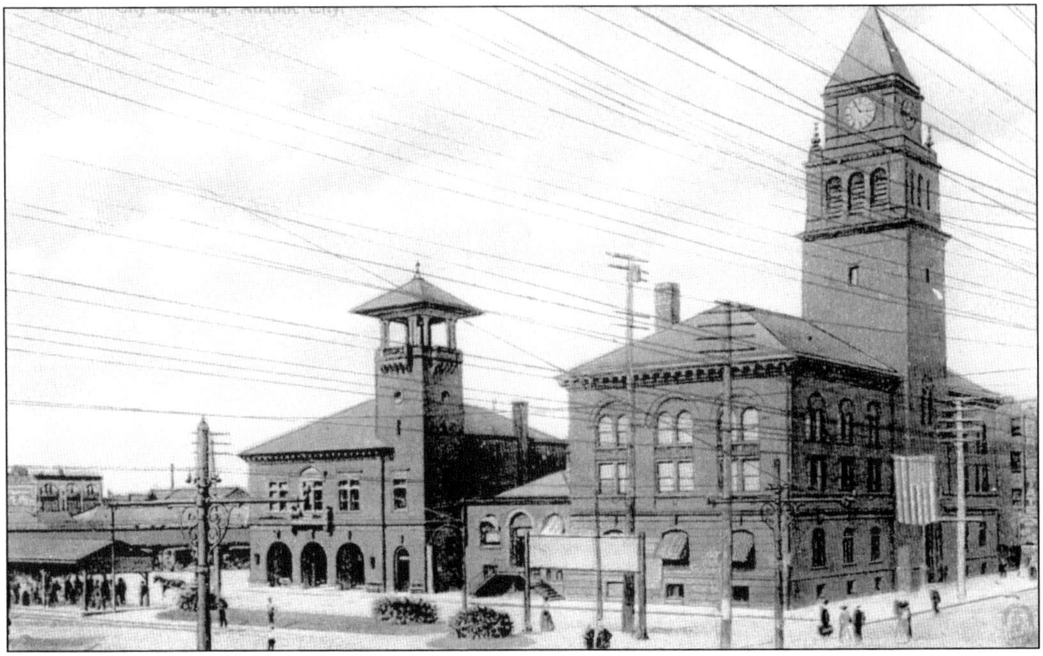

City Hall. Built in 1900–1901 at a cost of $90,000, this was the city's second city hall. A four-story building next door was later purchased in 1918 for an additional $75,000 and connected by passageways to make an annex. Situated at Tennessee and Atlantic Avenues, the brick building was in operation until 1969 when the current city hall was dedicated. On the left is one of the city's fire stations. (Osborne, *c.* 1905.)

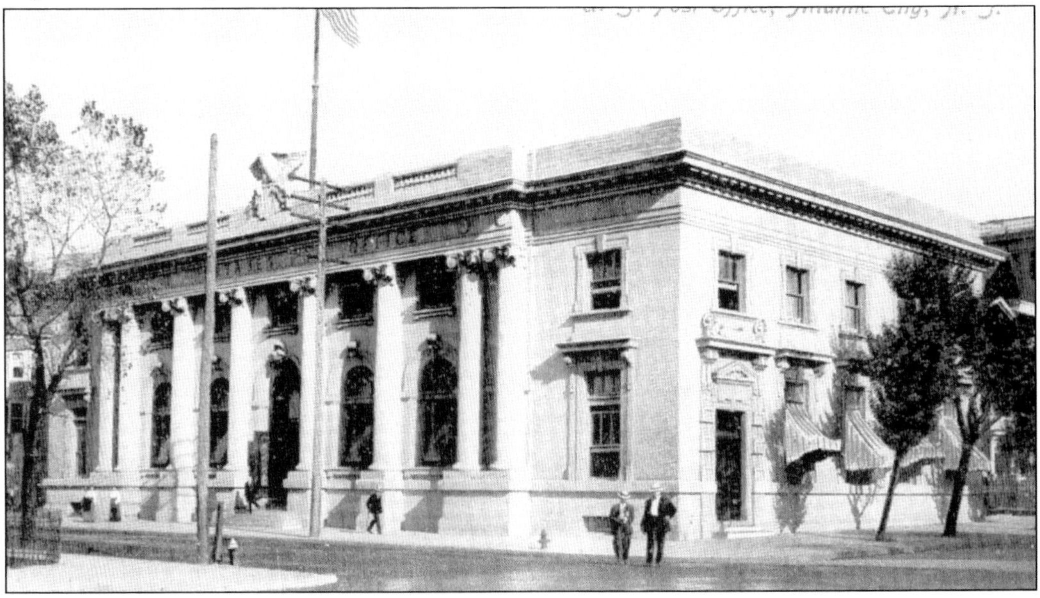

Post Office. This post office, on the southeast corner of Pennsylvania and Pacific Avenues, opened to the public on August 13, 1905. The postmaster at the time was Harry Bacharach. Many millions of postcards, including some used in this book, passed through this facility. In 1937, a new post office was erected at Illinois and Pacific Avenues, the former site of Craig Hall. (Illustrated Post Card Company, *c.* 1910.)

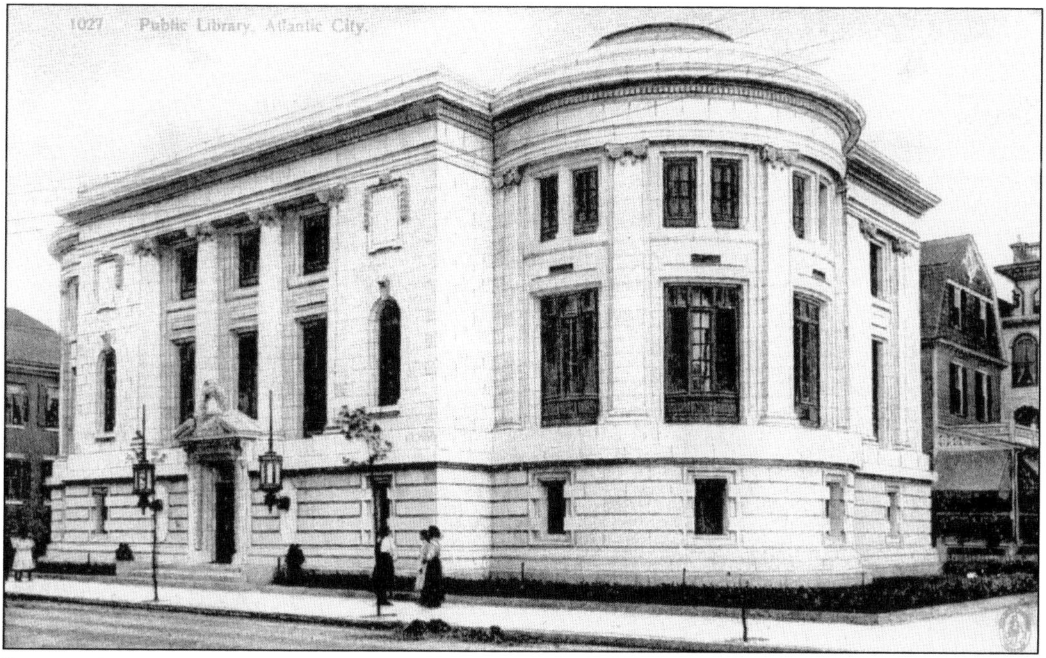

PUBLIC LIBRARY. On January 1, 1905, approximately 2,000 people attended the dedication of the public library on the corner of Illinois and Pacific Avenues. Built with $71,000 in funding donated by Andrew Carnegie, this building served the city for 80 years. It was replaced when the current library was opened in 1985 at Tennessee and Atlantic Avenues. (Osborne, *c.* 1906.)

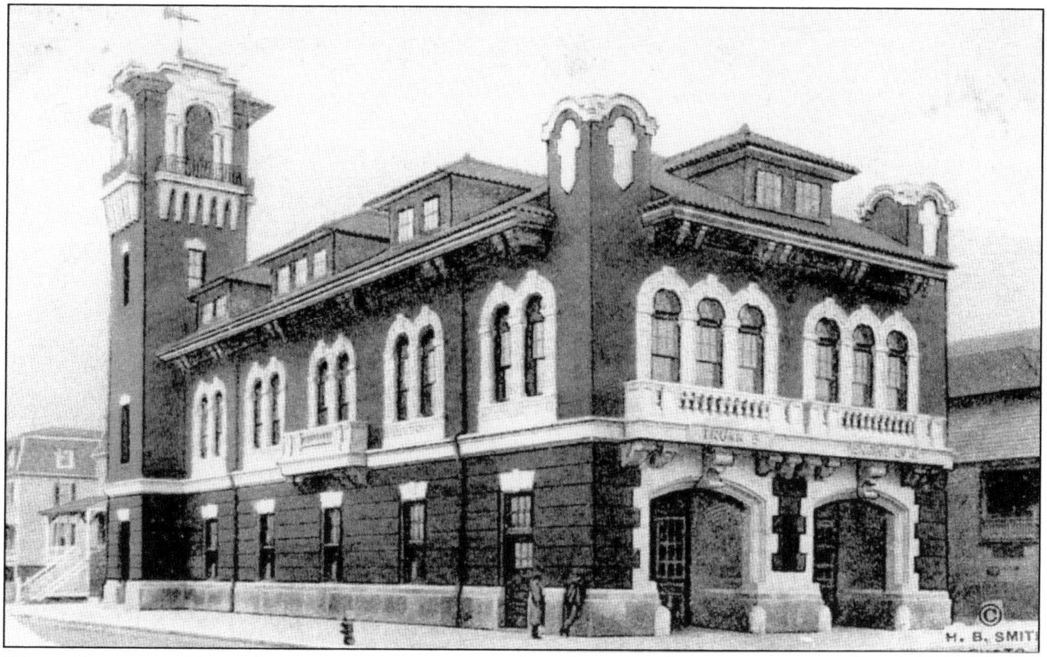

NEW CHELSEA FIRE COMPANY. In April 1904, the city established a paid fire department to replace a system of volunteer stations. The Chelsea Fire Company building located on the corner of California and Atlantic Avenues was built in 1912–1913. This station, which is still in active service, is home to engine No. 4. (Publisher unknown, *c.* 1914.)

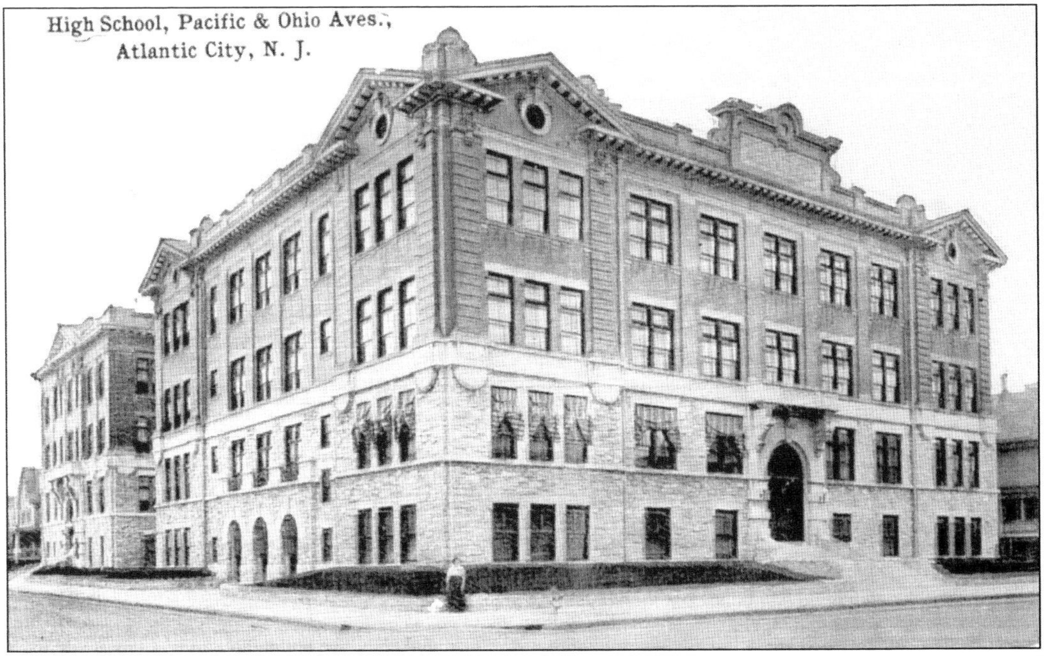

HIGH SCHOOL. Located on the corner of Ohio and Pacific Avenues, this building was dedicated on September 14, 1901, as the Atlantic City High School. It served this purpose until a newer high school was opened on Albany Avenue in 1923. The building then served as a junior high school. (Post Card Distribution Company, *c.* 1914.)

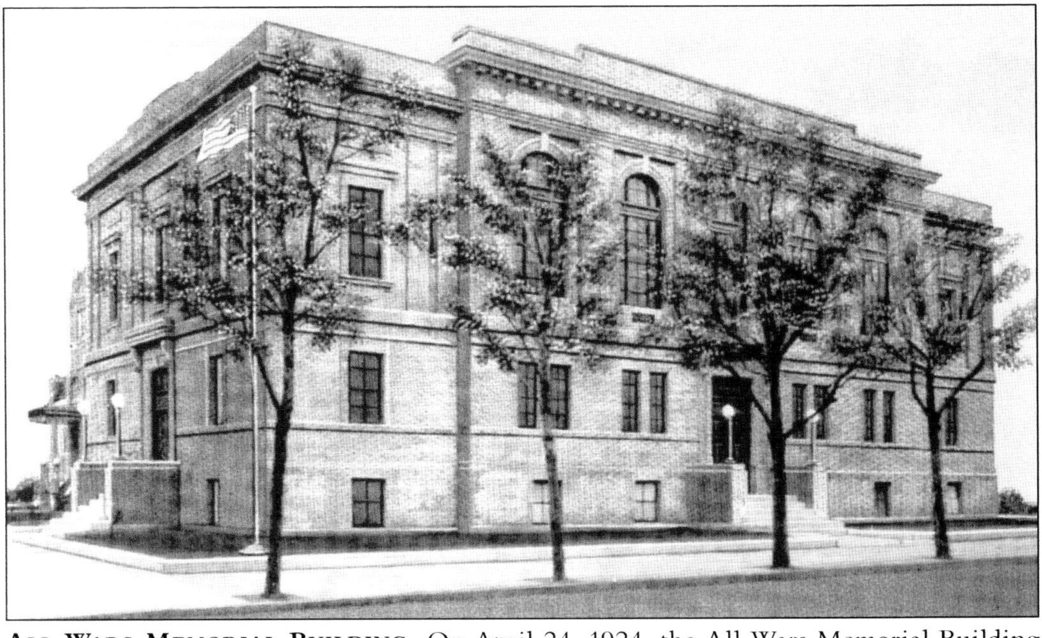

ALL WARS MEMORIAL BUILDING. On April 24, 1924, the All Wars Memorial Building was opened at the corner of States and Pacific Avenues. It was built by the city to function as a center of operations for all veterans' activities. The building had an auditorium on the second floor that seated 600 people and a basement dining room that could accommodate 280. (Saltzburg, 1924.)

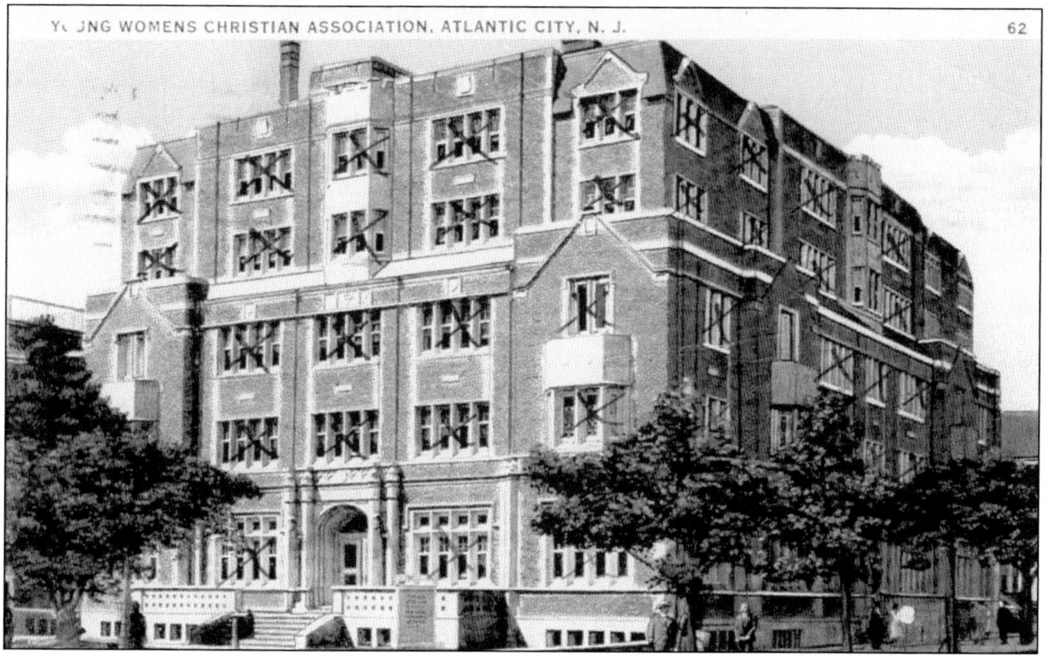

YWCA. Home to the local YWCA, this five-story Gothic-style building stood at North Carolina and Pacific Avenues. Dedicated on January 4, 1929, the structure contained sleeping quarters, meeting rooms, an auditorium, a gymnasium, a library, and a cafeteria. In the early 1970s, the building changed ownership and was eventually demolished in 1978. (Tichnor, *c.* 1929.)

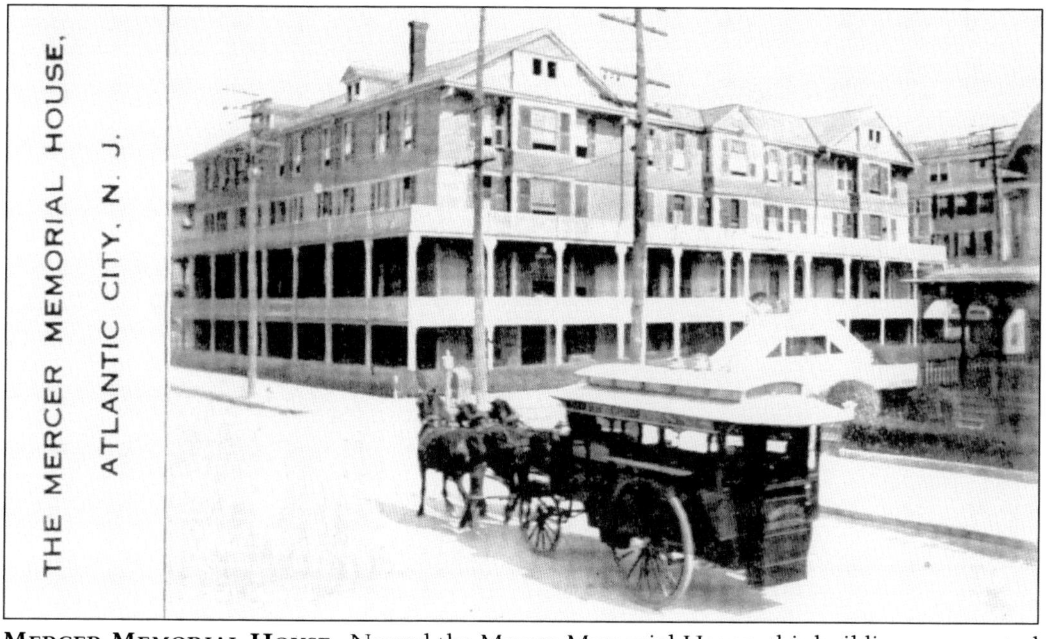

MERCER MEMORIAL HOUSE. Named the Mercer Memorial House, this building was erected in 1884 at Ohio and Pacific Avenues. Started in 1878 by Dr. William H. Bennett as the Seaside House for Invalid Women, this institution served women 18 years of age or older who needed to rest and recuperate near the ocean. Operations continued here until 1959, when the facility was moved to another location. (Publisher unknown, *c.* 1908.)

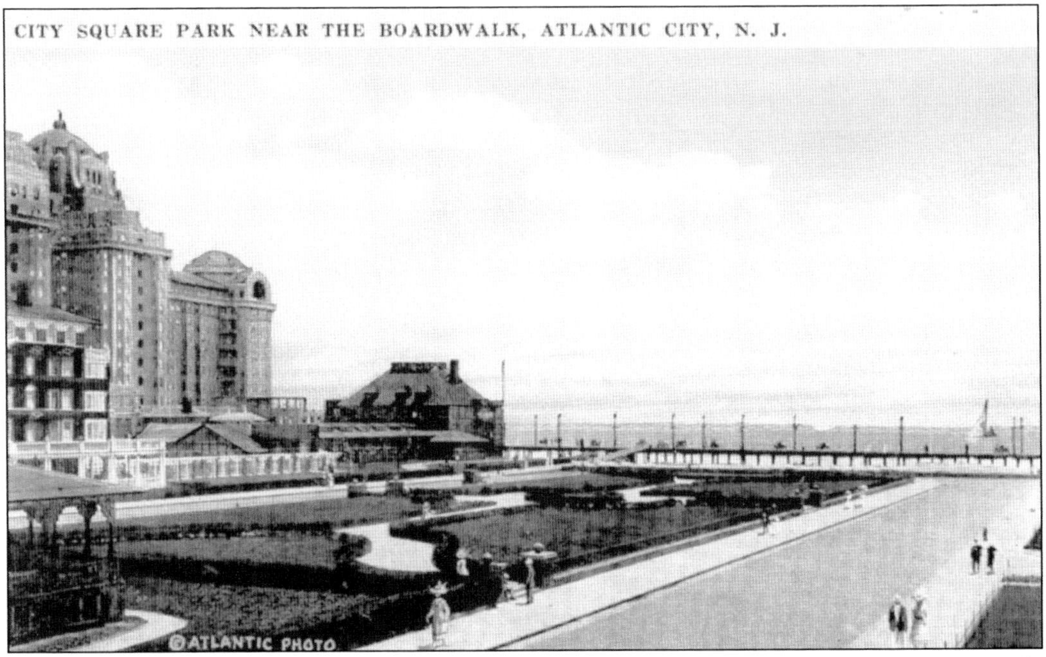

City Square Park. At the ocean end of Indiana Avenue is a park known as Brighton Park. Sometimes called Park Place by locals, it was made famous in the game of Monopoly. In 1879, George F. Lee and Hamilton Disston donated this land to the city with the stipulation that it would remain "open and unbuilt upon" forever. The park is still being maintained for public use. (Sithens, *c.* 1918.)

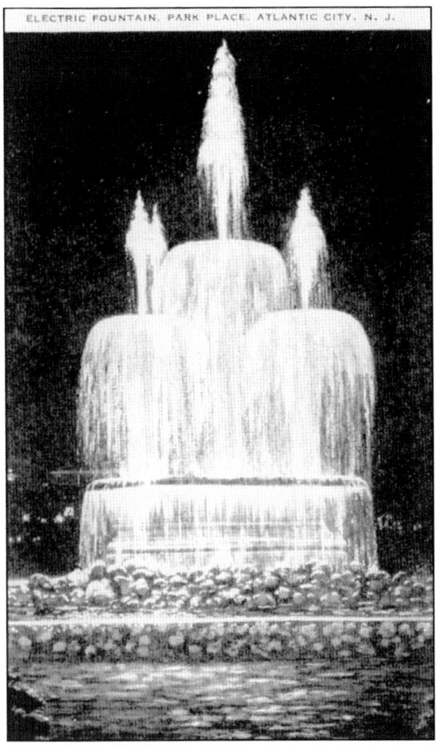

Electric Fountain. This beautiful fountain, 18 feet wide and 10 feet high, was capable of spraying water up to 30 feet into the air. At its base were 30 electric lamps capable of producing 70 different color combinations at night. It was erected in 1929 in Brighton Park by the General Electric Company to commemorate the 50th anniversary of the invention of Edison's incandescent lightbulb. (Sithens, *c.* 1930.)

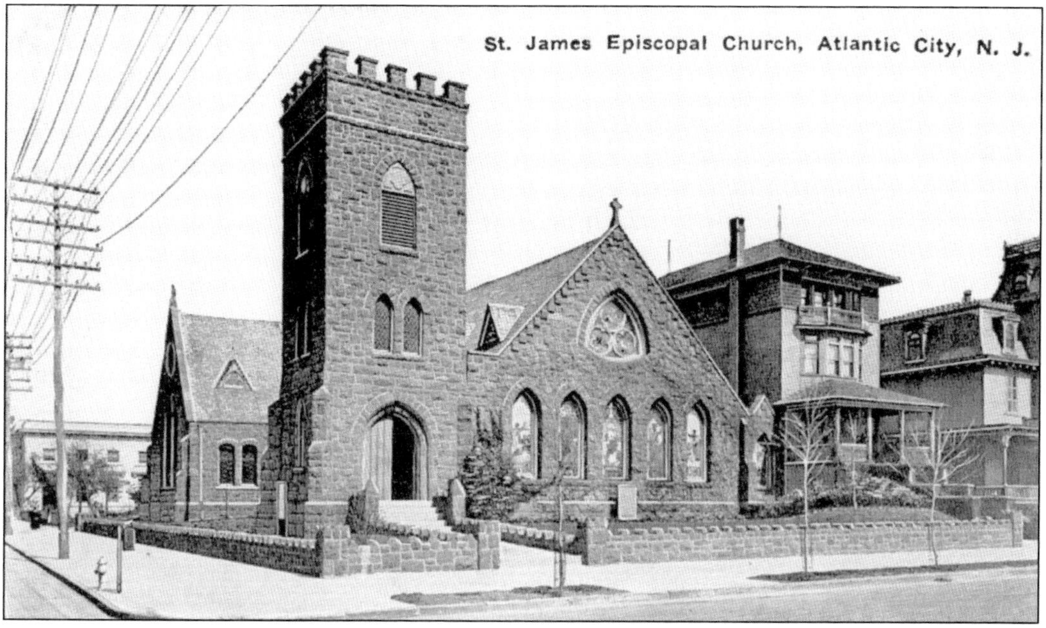

ST. JAMES EPISCOPAL CHURCH. In 1910, there were 34 churches in Atlantic City serving the spiritual needs of the community. One of these was St. James Episcopal Church located on the corner of North Carolina and Pacific Avenues. This beautiful stone church, with its large stained-glass windows, was severely damaged by fire on March 15, 1912. (Koffman, *c.* 1910.)

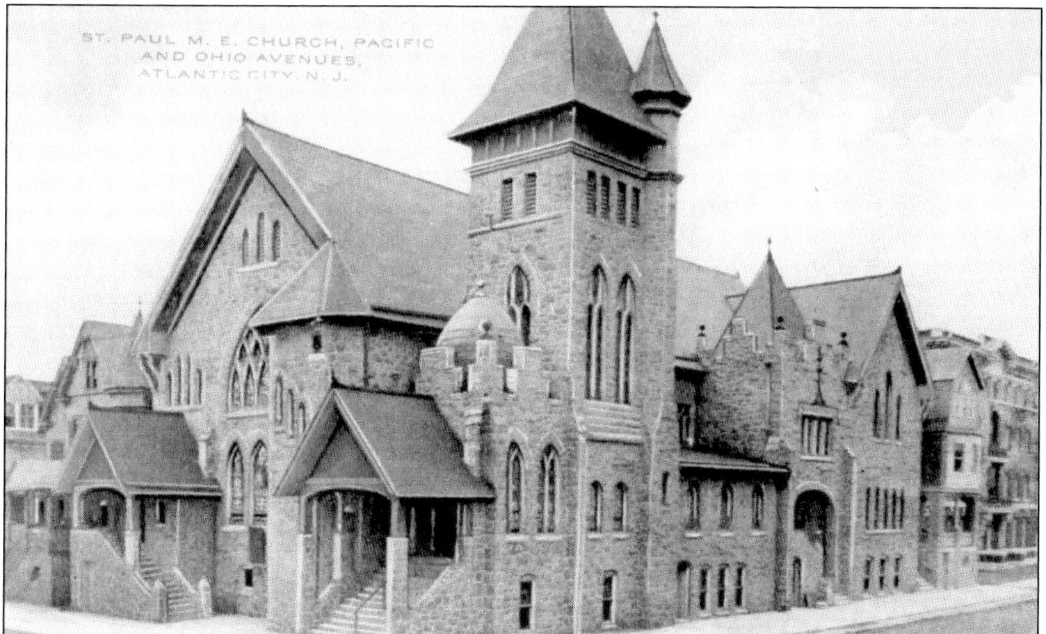

ST. PAUL METHODIST CHURCH. The site of many denominational conferences, the St. Paul Methodist Church was erected in 1898. This relatively large church was established on the corner of Ohio and Pacific Avenues. Houses of worship such as this offered religious services to permanent residents and vacationers alike and played an important role in the life of the city. (L. Beard, *c.* 1910.)

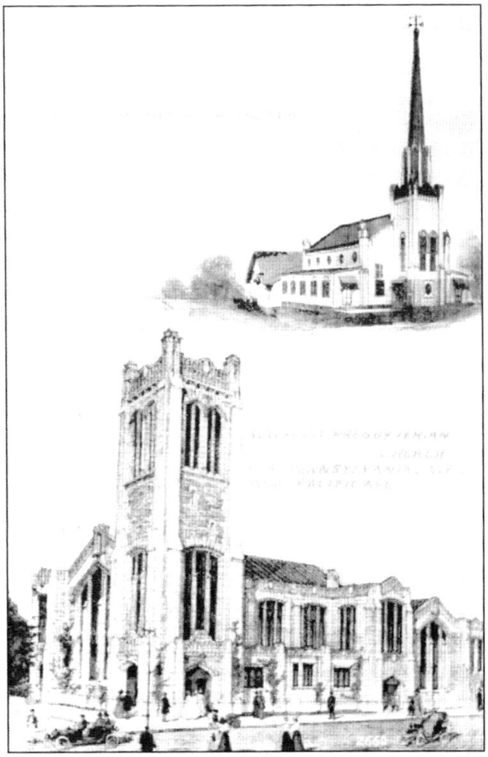

First Presbyterian Church. Founded in 1856, the First Presbyterian Church was located at Pennsylvania and Pacific Avenues. This postcard shows the original church along with the "new" church, which was constructed in the English Norman architectural style. The church was involved in helping to establish four daughter churches in the city, as well as assisting in the organization of 50 other Presbyterian churches in southern New Jersey. (Chilton Company, *c.* 1910.)

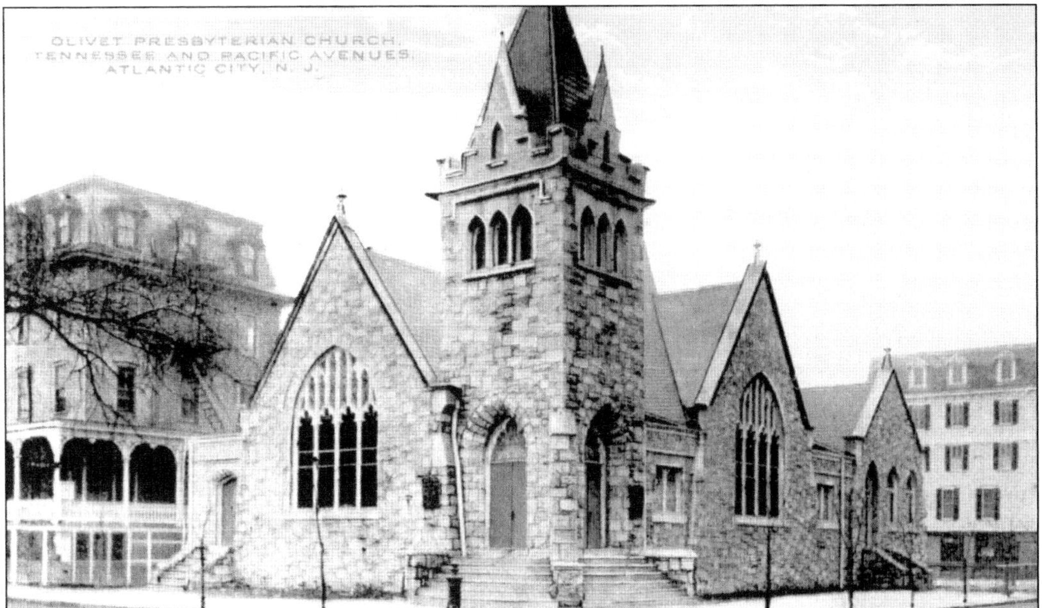

Olivet Presbyterian Church. This beautiful house of worship, dedicated in 1898, once stood at the corner of Tennessee and Pacific Avenues, where it served its parishioners for many years. The church underwent a dramatic change when it was renovated and converted into a nightclub in 1976. It was only a short time later that the building was torn down. (Post Card Distribution Company, *c.* 1912.)

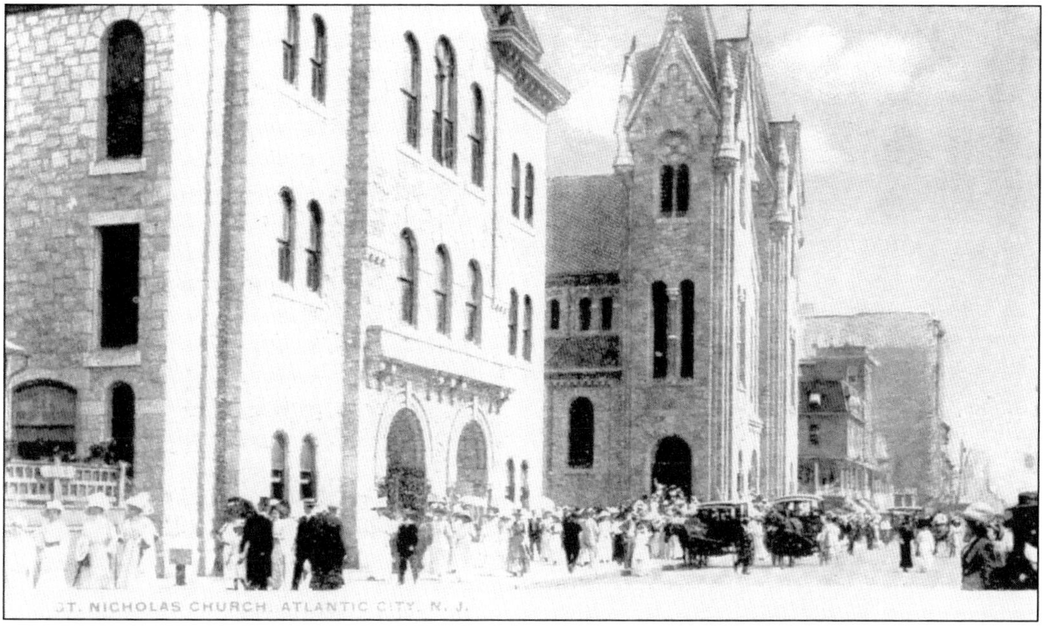

St. Nicholas Church. Worshippers begin to stream out of St. Nicholas Roman Catholic Church on a Sunday morning. This impressive place of worship, constructed in the Romanesque style in 1906, is found at Tennessee and Pacific Avenues. Its interior includes white marble altars, beautiful stained-glass windows, and a ceiling painted with the images of each of the apostles. The church still actively serves the Catholic community. (National Post Card Company, *c.* 1915.)

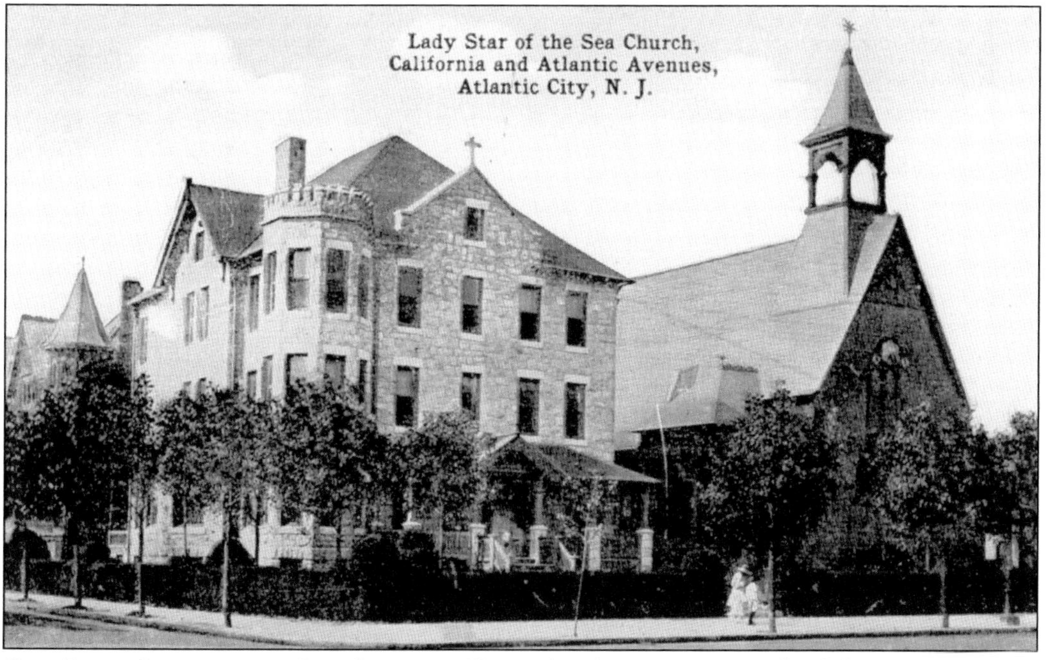

Our Lady Star of the Sea Church. Situated at the intersection of California and Atlantic Avenues is one of several Catholic churches serving the population of Atlantic City. Begun in 1897, this church is still functioning today. In this view, the church school can be seen on the corner, while the house of worship stands next to it. (Post Card Distribution Company, *c.* 1918.)

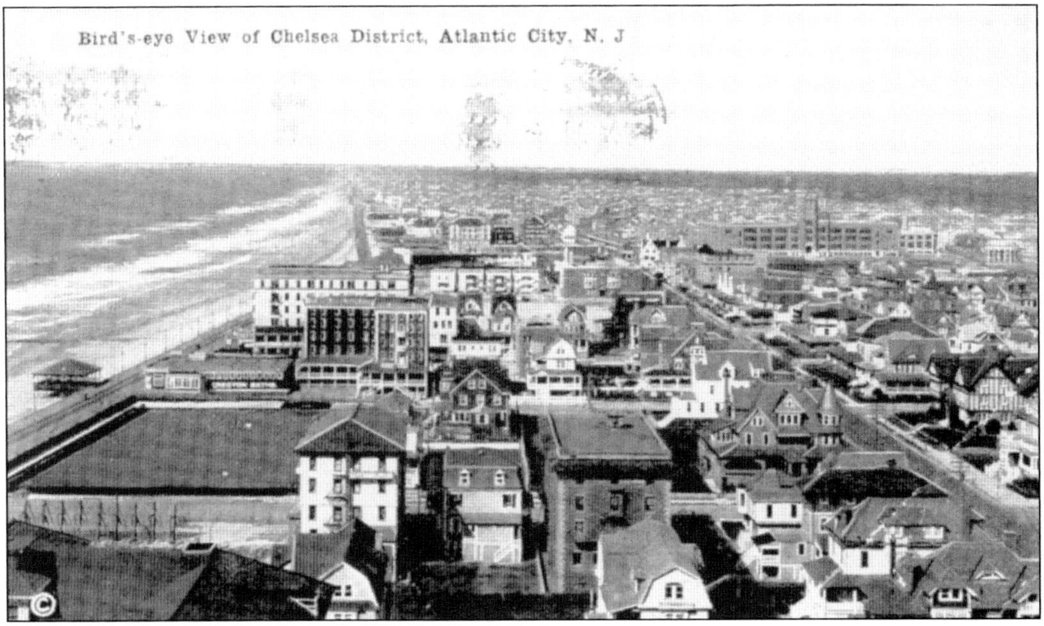

BIRD'S-EYE VIEW OF CHELSEA DISTRICT. Looking south, the lower section of the city known as Chelsea is visible. Chelsea begins at Brighton Avenue and runs southward. The first serious development of this part of the city began in 1883 with the Chelsea Beach Company building houses in the area. By 1889 trolley service connected Chelsea to the rest of Atlantic City. (Sithens, *c.* 1925.)

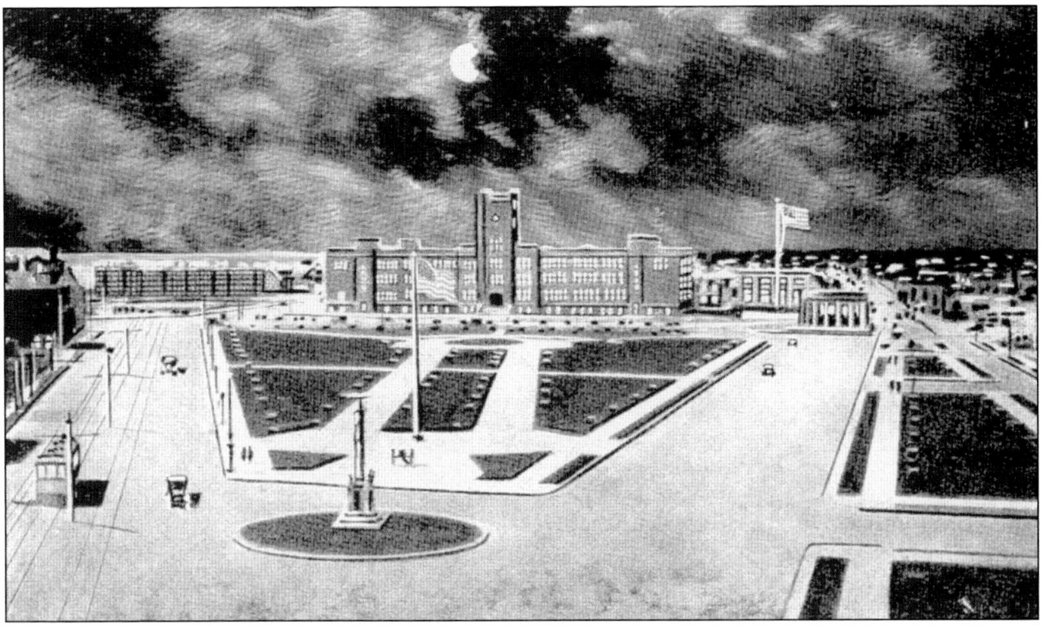

CHELSEA PARK. On the southern end of the city, bordered by Albany, Ventnor, Pacific, and Atlantic Avenues, is the triangular area of land known as Chelsea Park. In this nighttime view, the old high school can be seen in the distance, while the Soldiers and Sailors Monument is in the foreground. On the far right stands the World War Memorial. (Sithens, *c.* 1923.)

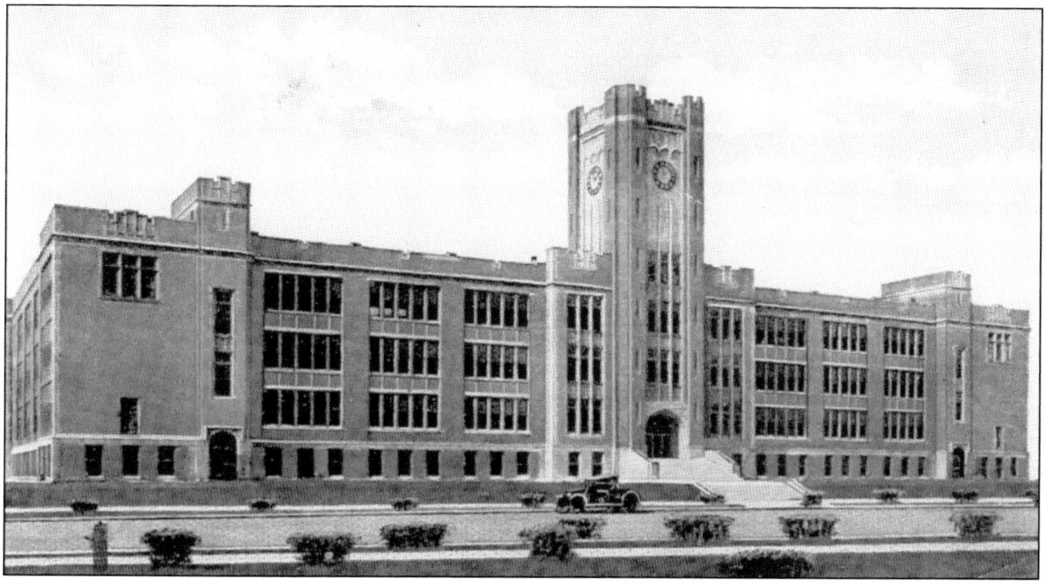

HIGH SCHOOL BUILDING. This high school building on Albany Avenue was situated across from the war memorial. Costing $2.5 million to construct, it had the capacity to serve 2,100 students. Dedicated on September 22, 1923, it was especially proud of its huge pipe organ, which at the time was said to have been the fourth largest in the world. The building was eventually demolished in 1999. (Saltzburg, *c.* 1925.)

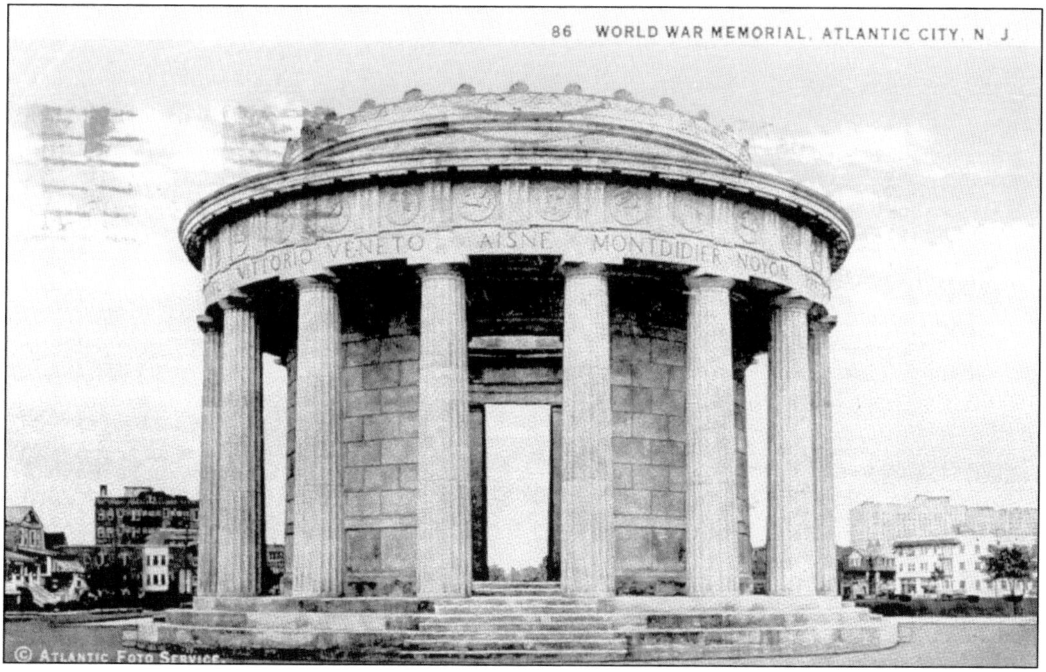

WORLD WAR MEMORIAL. Designed by the architects Carrere and Hastings in the style of a Greek temple, this monument, complete with 16 Doric columns, was erected in 1922 at a cost of $126,000. Honoring World War I veterans, the memorial served as a traffic circle for many years before the intersection where it stands was redesigned. In 1928, the statue *Liberty in Distress* was placed inside (not present in this early view). (Saltzburg, *c.* 1923.)

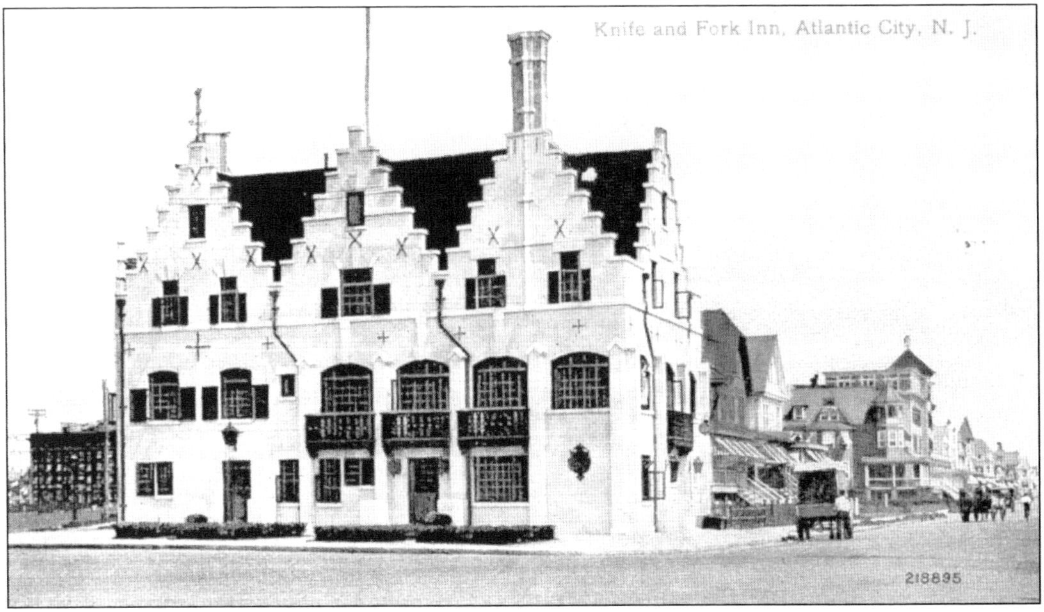

KNIFE AND FORK INN. Situated on the corner where Atlantic, Pacific, and Albany Avenues converge, the Knife and Fork Inn is an interesting example of Flemish architecture. Established as an exclusive men's club in 1912, it later became a restaurant. It was well known for the many famous entertainers and celebrities who dined there when in town. The establishment is still an operating restaurant today. (Post Card Distribution Company, *c.* 1914.)

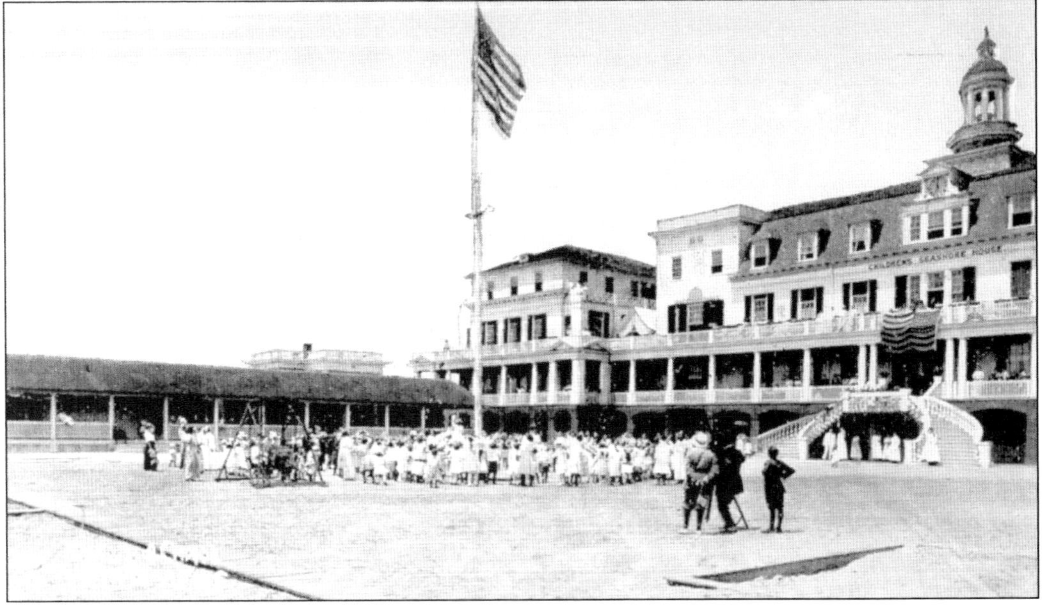

CHILDREN'S SEASHORE HOME. Founded in 1872 as a summer getaway for sick children, the Seashore Home moved to the Chelsea District in 1902. Known also as the Whitney House, it occupied the entire beachfront block between Richmond and Annapolis Avenues. In 1910, the home began offering year-round services and at one time was an accredited 104-bed pediatric hospital. In 1990, the organization moved to Philadelphia. (National Post Card Company, *c.* 1915.)

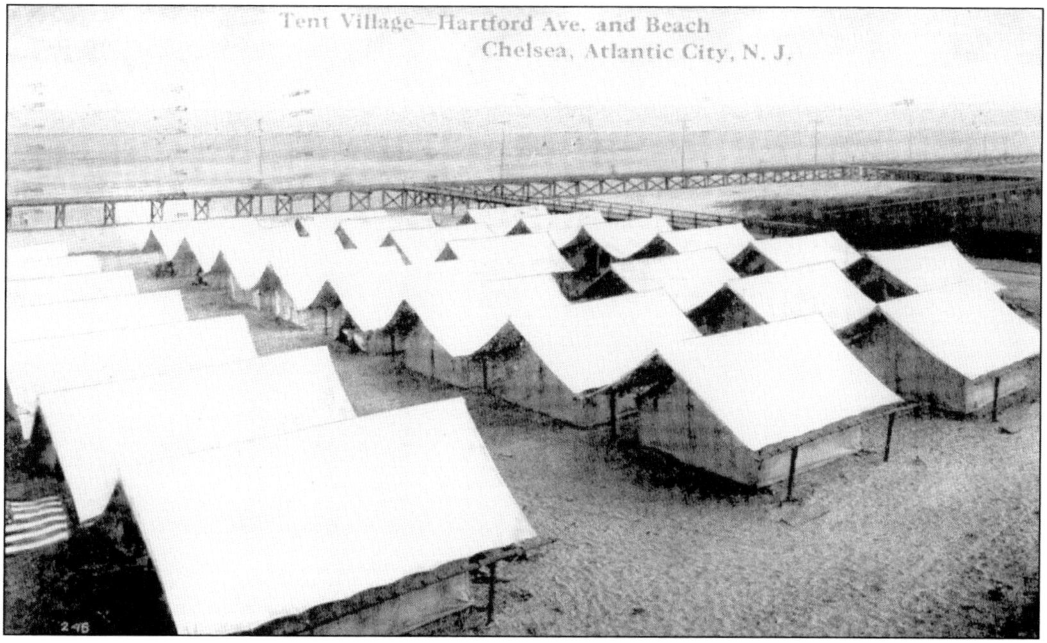

TENT VILLAGE. For many years during the early 1900s, rows of tents comprised Tent City located at Hartford Avenue and the beach in the Chelsea district. These tents provided visitors an inexpensive lodging alternative to the city's hotels, cottages, and guesthouses. The tents were available furnished and could even be taken with or without pots and pans. (Chilton, *c.* 1908.)

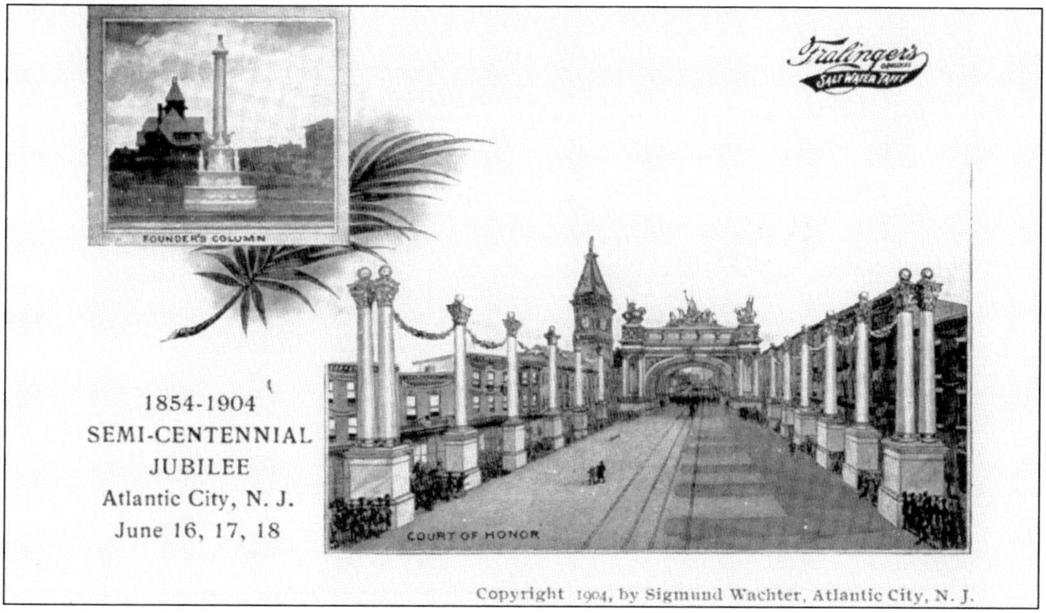

SEMI-CENTENNIAL JUBILEE. To honor the 50th anniversary of the city's founding, a three-day event called the Semi-Centennial Jubilee was held in 1904. A large arch was built straddling Atlantic Avenue near South Carolina Avenue, while tall columns flanked the street down to Tennessee Avenue. Large parades and numerous festivities took place. There was even a parade of decorated boats, which sailed the ocean within view of crowds on the boardwalk. (Sigmund Wachter, 1904.)

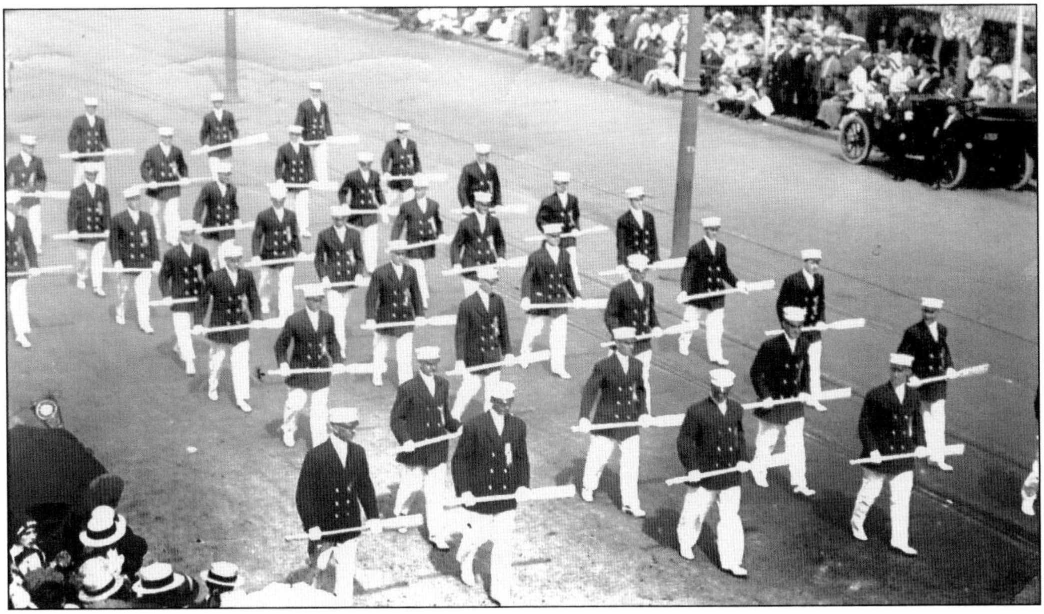

INDUSTRIAL PARADE. This Industrial Parade, as it was named, was held on May 27, 1914, as part of a weeklong celebration designed to attract visitors to the start of the summer season. Proudly marching down the street, each carrying a small wooden oar, are members of the Atlantic City Beach Patrol in formal uniform. The annual baby parade was held the following day. (Harper B. Smith, 1914.)

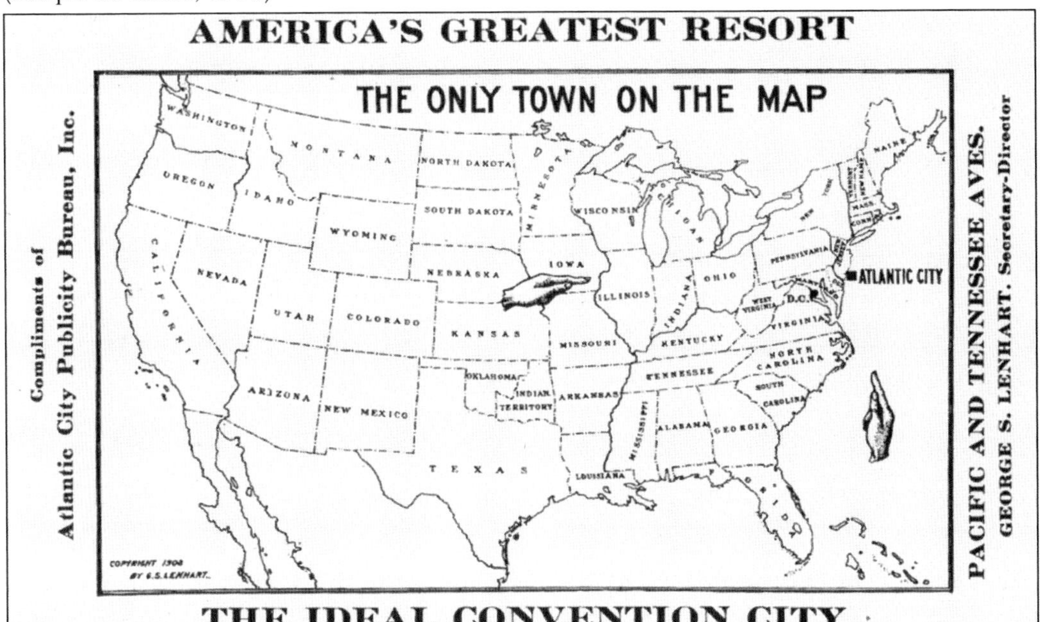

AMERICA'S GREATEST RESORT. In 1908, the Convention and Publicity Bureau was established by the city's hotels and businesses to help attract visitors. With an initial budget of $8,000, it promoted the city in many ways. Printing postcards such as this one helped market Atlantic City as America's greatest resort and convention city. Over the years the city would go on to host some of the largest convention gatherings in the nation. (G. S. Lenhart, 1908.)

Two

THE GRAND HOTELS

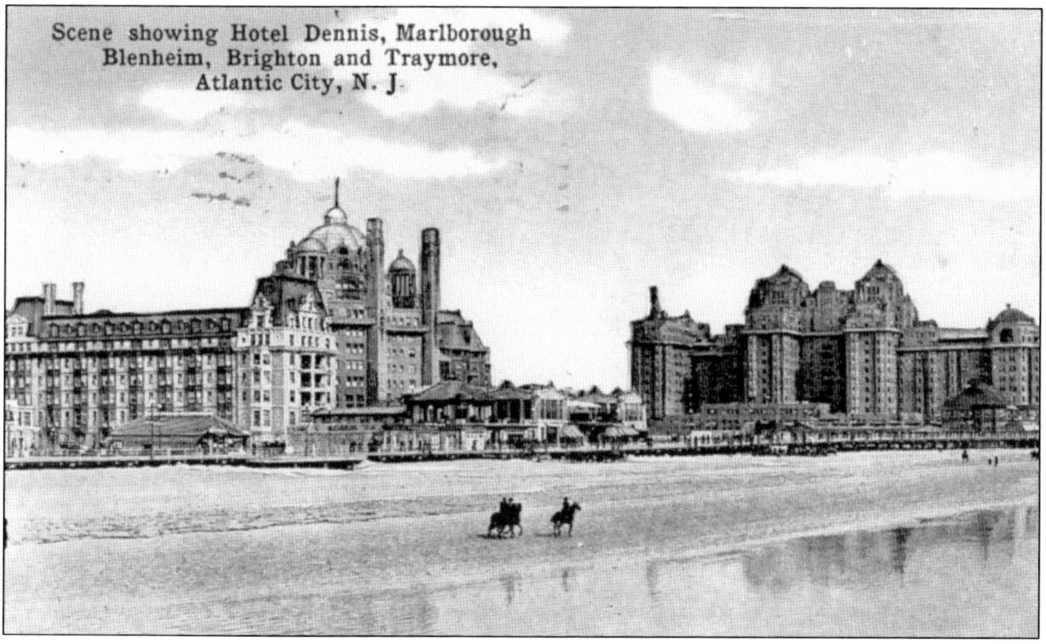

HOTEL DENNIS, MARLBOROUGH-BLENHEIM, BRIGHTON, AND TRAYMORE. When this postcard was mailed in 1918, there were approximately 1,200 hotels in Atlantic City. The city was said to lead every resort in the world in their number and splendor. However, there were never more than about 30 with a prestigious boardwalk address at any one time. The older grand hotels are now gone, having been replaced for the most part by modern casino complexes. (Virginia Post Card Company, *c.* 1918.)

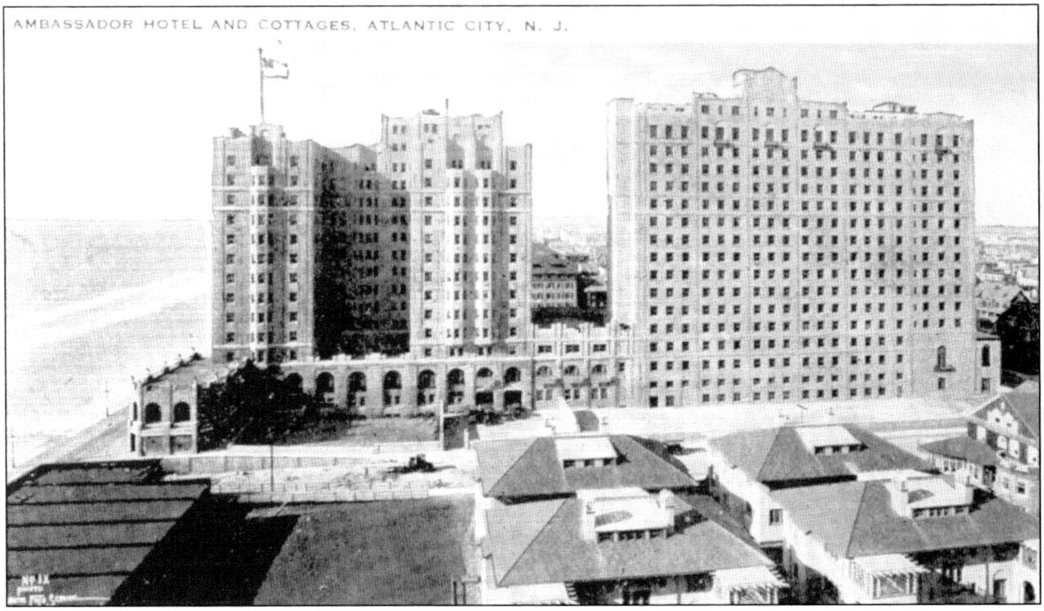

AMBASSADOR HOTEL AND COTTAGES. The Ambassador Hotel and its fashionable guest cottages stood on Brighton Avenue at the boardwalk. Opened in 1919, its clientele included such notable personalities as author Sir Arthur Conan Doyle, singers Enrico Caruso and Bing Crosby, bandleader Paul Whiteman, and Pres. Warren G. Harding. The hotel was torn down and became the site of the Tropicana Hotel Casino. (Sithens Post Card Company, *c.* 1924.)

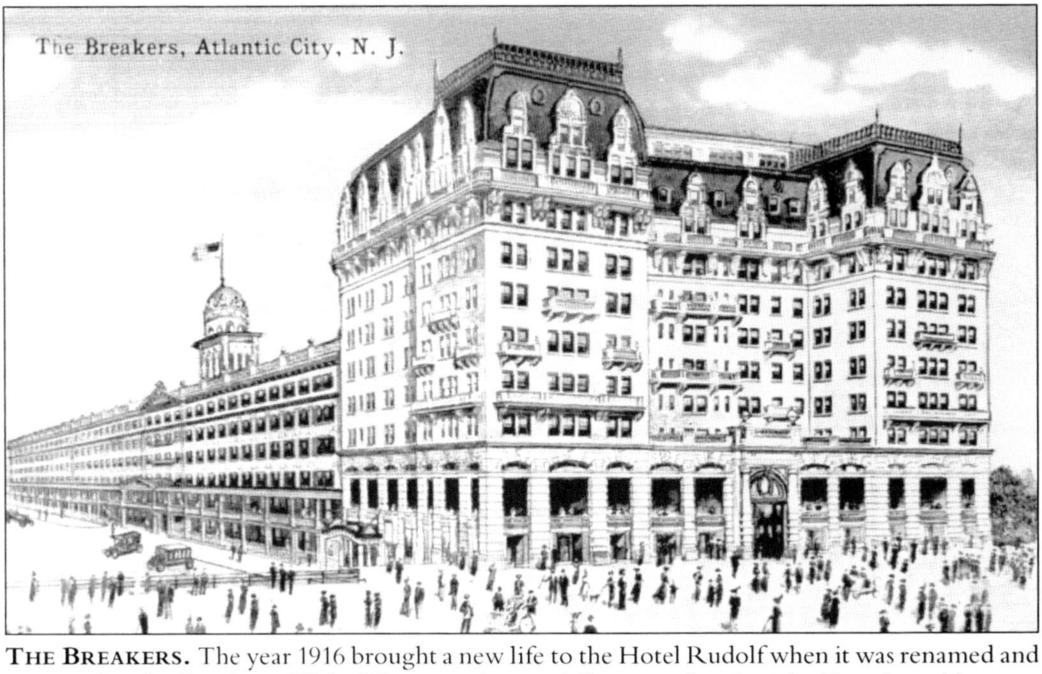

THE BREAKERS. The year 1916 brought a new life to the Hotel Rudolf when it was renamed and reopened as the Breakers. With 450 rooms, it especially catered to Jewish clientele and became known as the "aristocrat of Kosher hotels." Overlooking the boardwalk and ocean, the hotel continued as an Atlantic City landmark until it was ultimately demolished in 1974. (Virginia Avenue Post Card Company, *c.* 1918.)

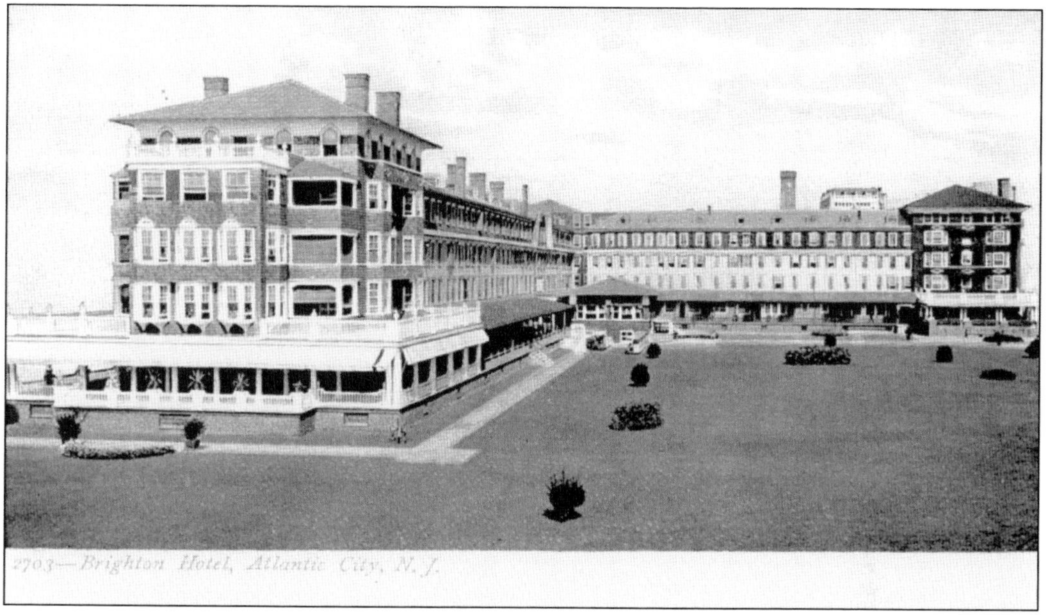

HOTEL BRIGHTON. Back in 1873, this hotel became the first in the city to offer year-round service. Situated on Indiana Avenue, the hotel catered to the "finest of clientele." At one time the hotel refused lodging to those who arrived by automobile, as it was deemed unfashionable. The hotel was famous for serving an alcoholic drink called the Brighton Punch. The building eventually fell to the wrecking ball in 1959. (Souvenir Post Card Company, *c.* 1906.)

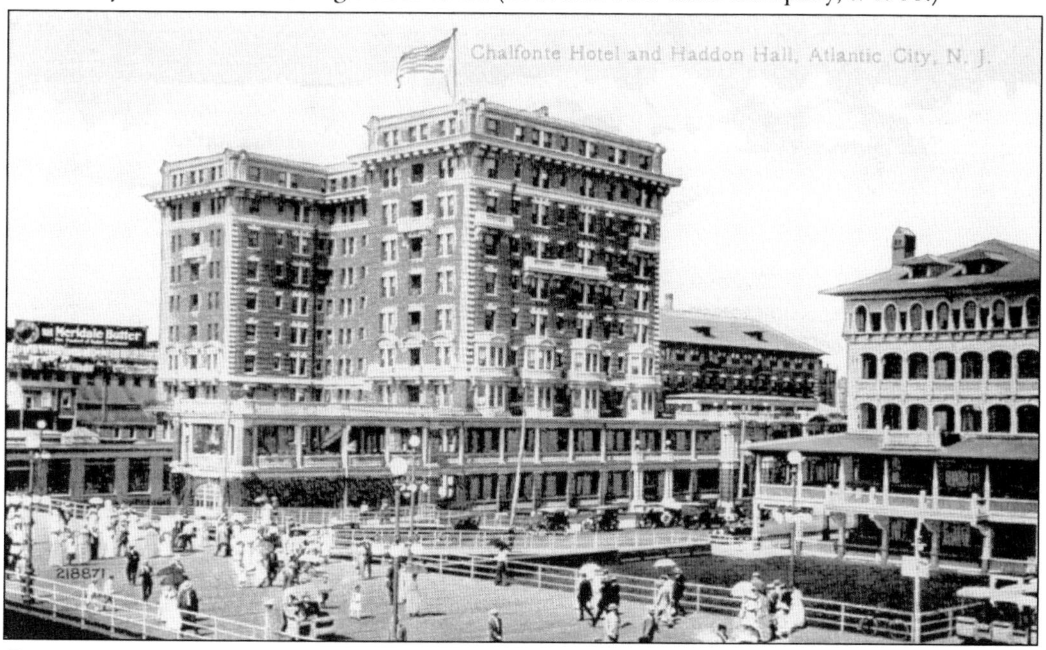

CHALFONTE HOTEL. On June 25, 1868, the Chalfonte Hotel opened on North Carolina Avenue. In 1904, it was moved closer to the ocean and enlarged to 10 stories. It was said to be the first fireproof hotel in the city. Four years earlier the hotel came under the same management as its neighbor Haddon Hall. The two would eventually merge to form the famous Chalfonte-Haddon Hall. (Post Card Distribution Company, *c.* 1914.)

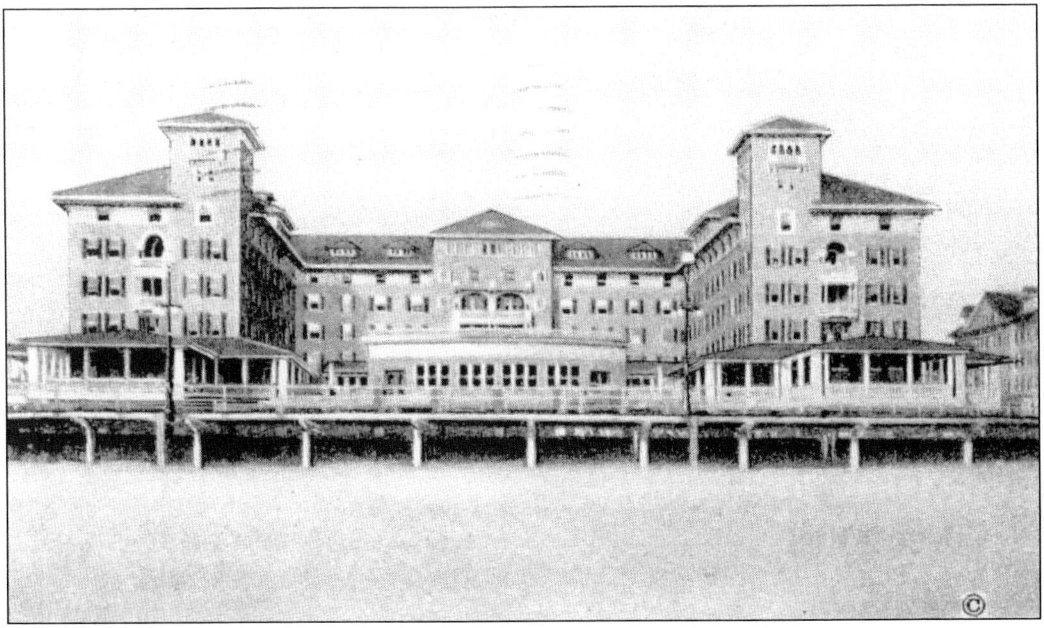

Hotel Chelsea. Dating back to 1899, the Hotel Chelsea, located at the lower end of the city, had many distinguished guests over the years. Presidents William Howard Taft, Woodrow Wilson, and Franklin Roosevelt all stayed here. A 12-story addition was built on to the original four-story 250-room structure in 1927. In 1942, the hotel was utilized to house army personnel. Later the hotel went on to become the Sheraton-Deauville. (H. B. Smith, *c.* 1916.)

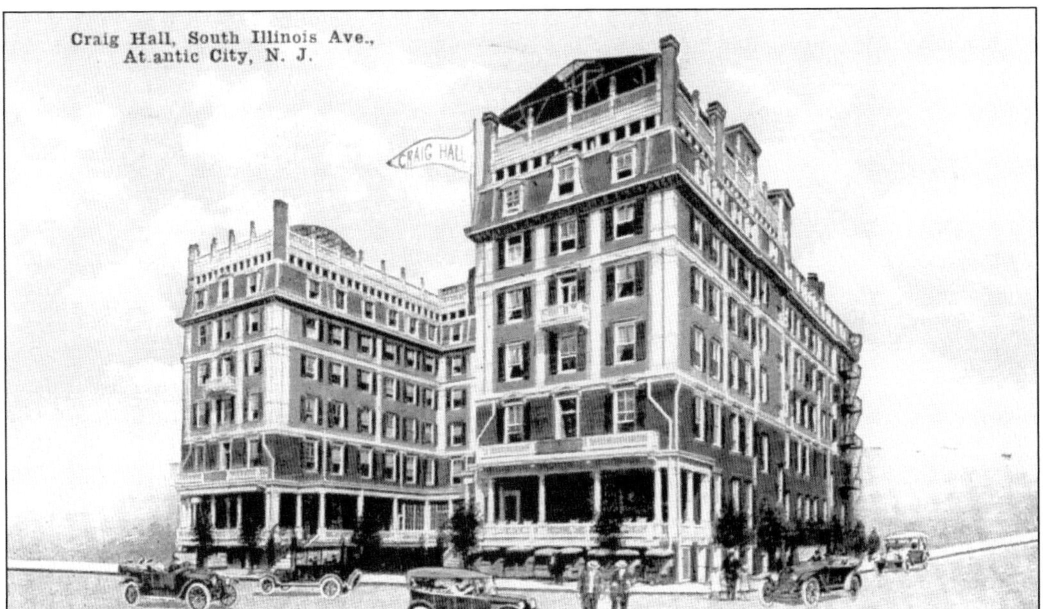

Craig Hall. Originally called the Garden Hotel, this seven-story, 166-room hotel was erected in 1897 at Illinois and Pacific Avenues. It was the first hotel in the city over 100 feet tall and was renowned for its rooftop garden. It was renamed when purchased in 1910 by Robert Craighead. The hotel was eventually torn down and replaced with a U.S. post office in 1937. (Virginia Post Card Company, *c.* 1920.)

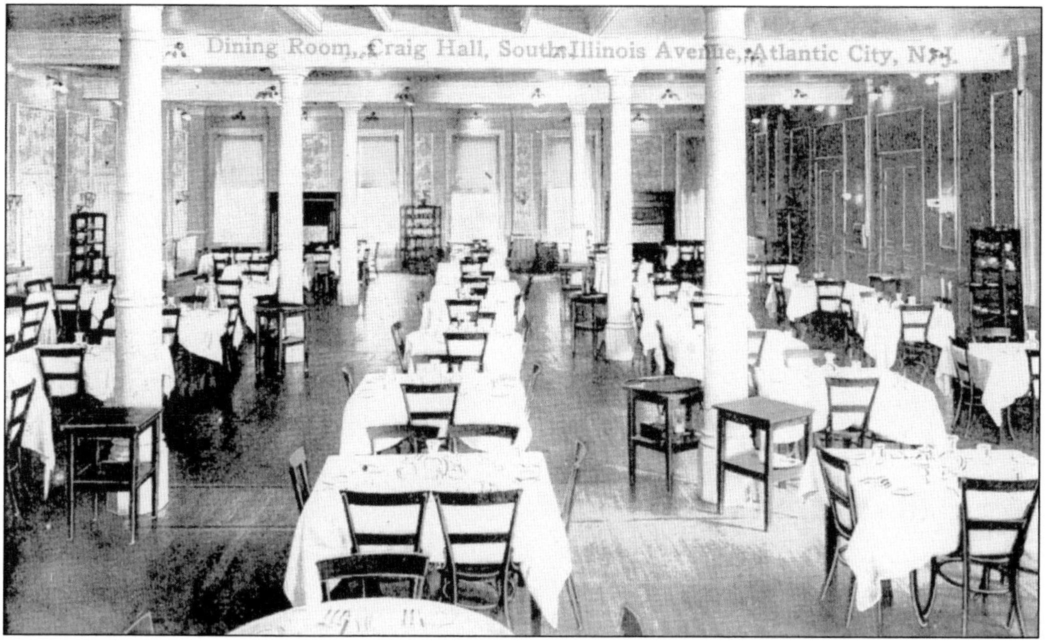

CRAIG HALL DINING ROOM. Elegantly set tables awaited the guests of this hotel. The wealthier clientele that tended to patronize Craig Hall expected such refinements. Fine meals served in this stylish atmosphere helped to make a stay here a memorable experience. (Publisher unknown, *c.* 1915.)

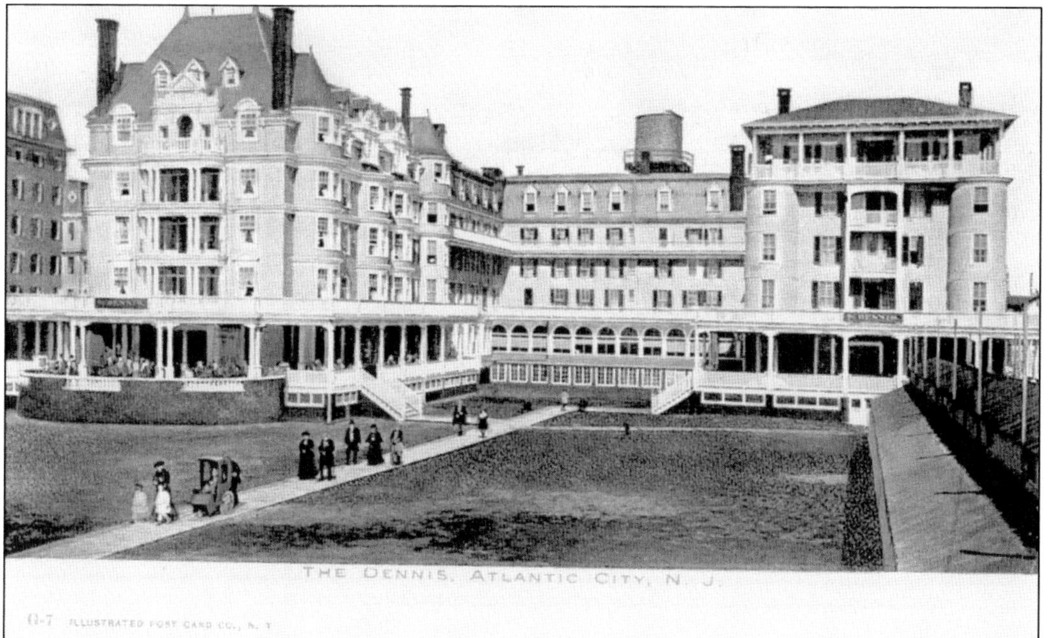

HOTEL DENNIS. Built as a summer cottage on Ohio Avenue in 1860 and expanded into a boardinghouse by 1892, this building was to evolve into a 250-room hotel. Rebuilt in stone in 1905, it was further enlarged to become a stately 550-room hotel. Today the Hotel Dennis lives on as part of the Bally's Park Place casino hotel. (Illustrated Post Card Company, *c.* 1906.)

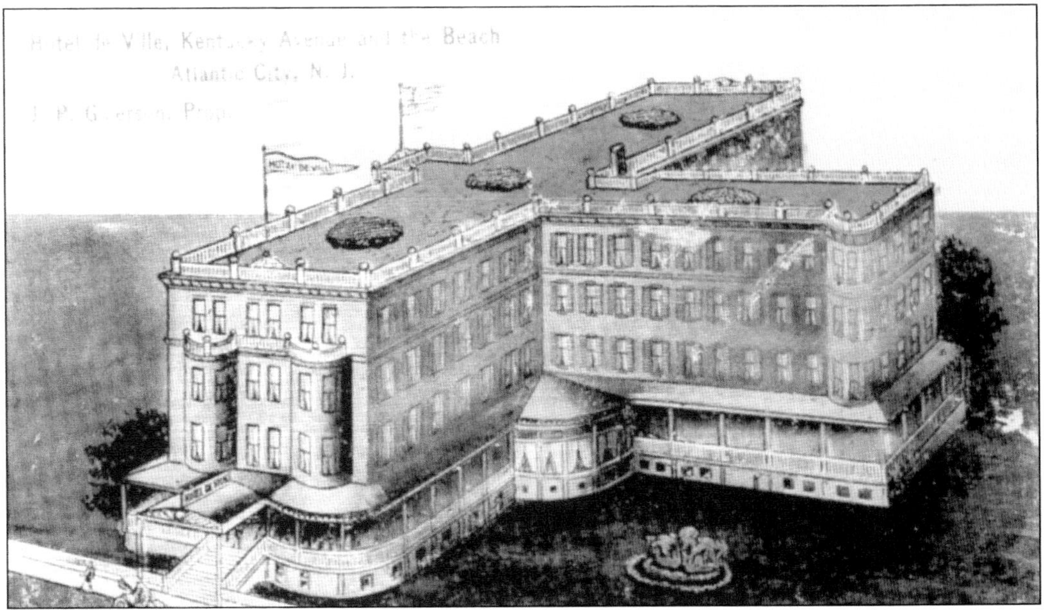

HOTEL DEVILLE. This four-story hotel was located at Kentucky Avenue and the beach. Its porches, which extended around most of the first floor, provided patrons a shaded place to sit and relax while enjoying the views. Open all year, the hotel's amenities included hot and cold running water in all rooms, electric lights, an elevator to the ground floor, and its own dance orchestra. (Chilton Company, *c.* 1910.)

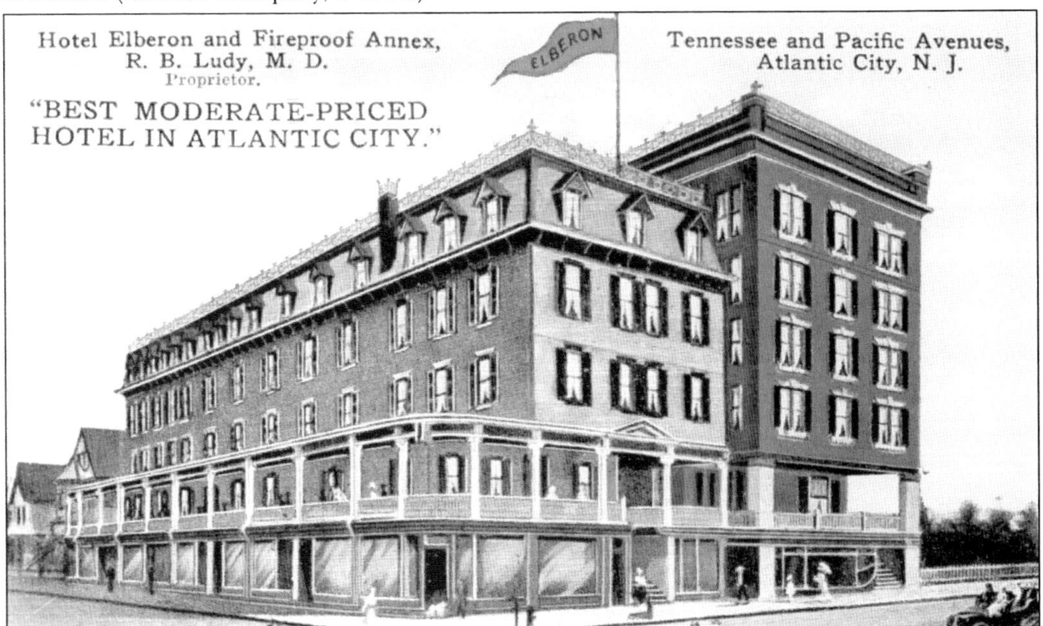

HOTEL ELBERON. Situated on the corner of Tennessee and Pacific Avenues, the Hotel Elberon advertised itself as the "best moderate priced hotel" in the city. With a capacity of 400, guests could expect rooms with screened windows, first-class mattresses, and running water. The price for such accommodations, depending on the time of season, ranged from $1 to $3.50 a day. (Publisher unknown, *c.* 1915.)

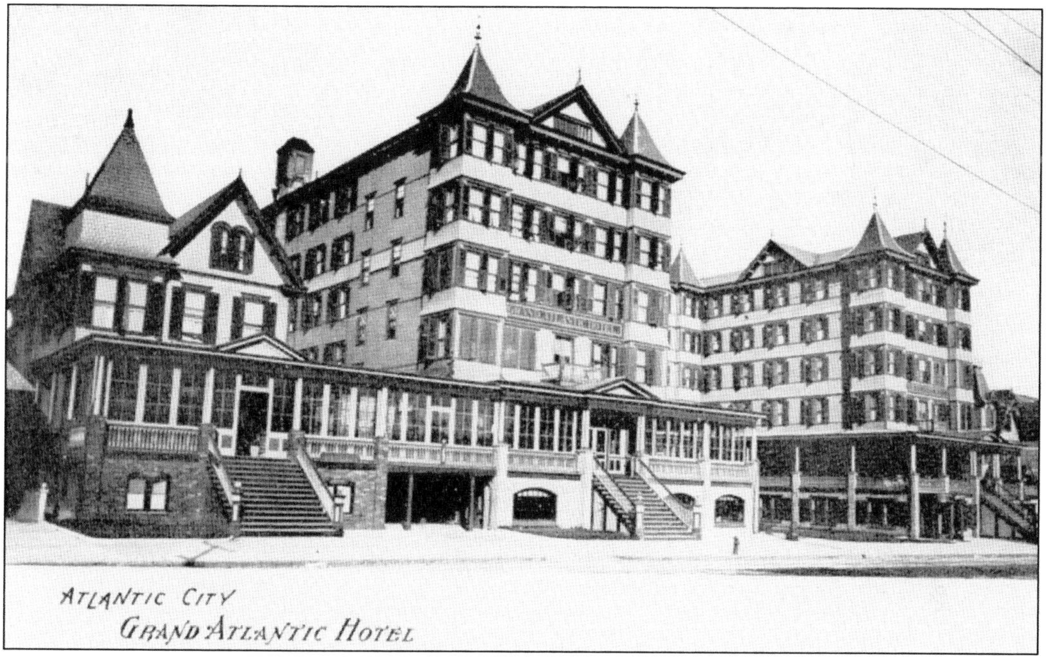

GRAND ATLANTIC HOTEL. Located on busy south Virginia Avenue, the Grand Atlantic was said to offer its clientele light and airy rooms. Some rooms had as many as four windows. Renovated around 1925, each room provided hot and cold running water and an electrical call service. The management claimed to take a personal interest in the wishes of every guest. Fire destroyed the building on April 5, 1937. (World Postcard Company, *c.* 1904.)

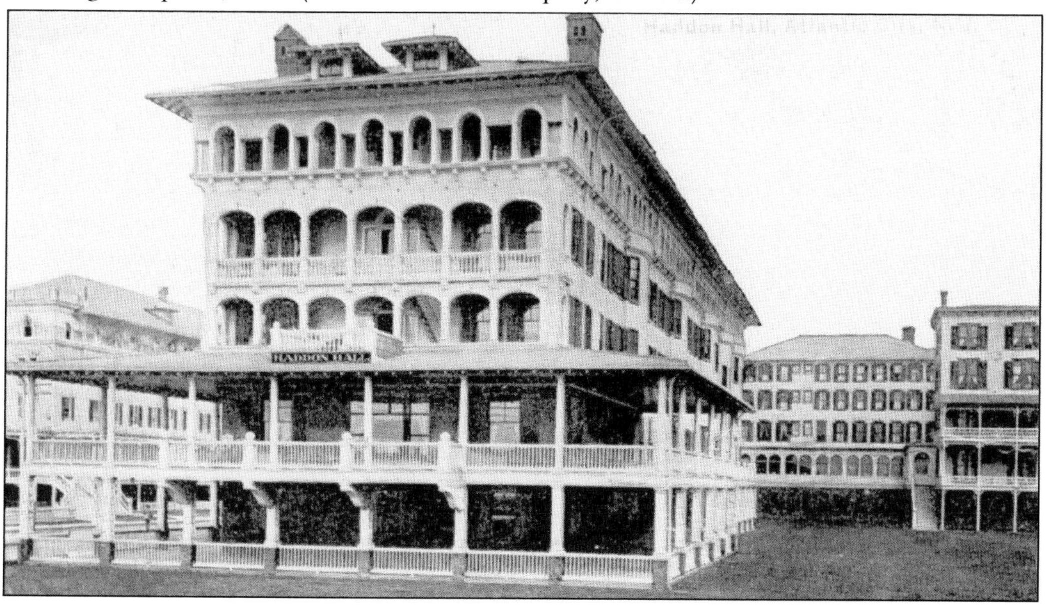

HADDON HALL. Built in 1869, this hotel would go on to see several major renovations over the years. By 1929 the hotel had expanded to a height of 11 stories and 680 rooms. During World War II it served as the Thomas M. England Hospital, one of the largest military hospitals in the nation. Ultimately the Chalfonte-Haddon Hall complex would become the famed Resorts International in 1978. (Publisher unknown, *c.* 1910)

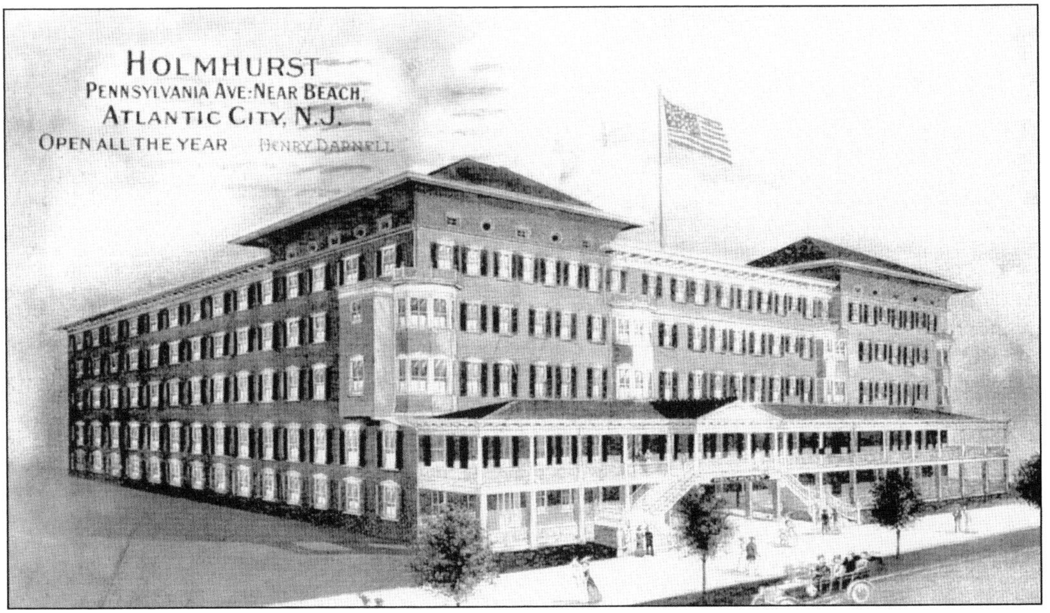

HOLMHURST. On Pennsylvania Avenue and close to the beach, many of this hotel's rooms had unobstructed views of the ocean. Having a capacity of 300, the hotel was equipped with steam heat, allowing it to remain open all year. Spacious porches, an elevator to the street, private baths, and running water in each room where among the amenities provided its guests. The hotel was demolished in 1985. (Americhrome Company, *c.* 1914.)

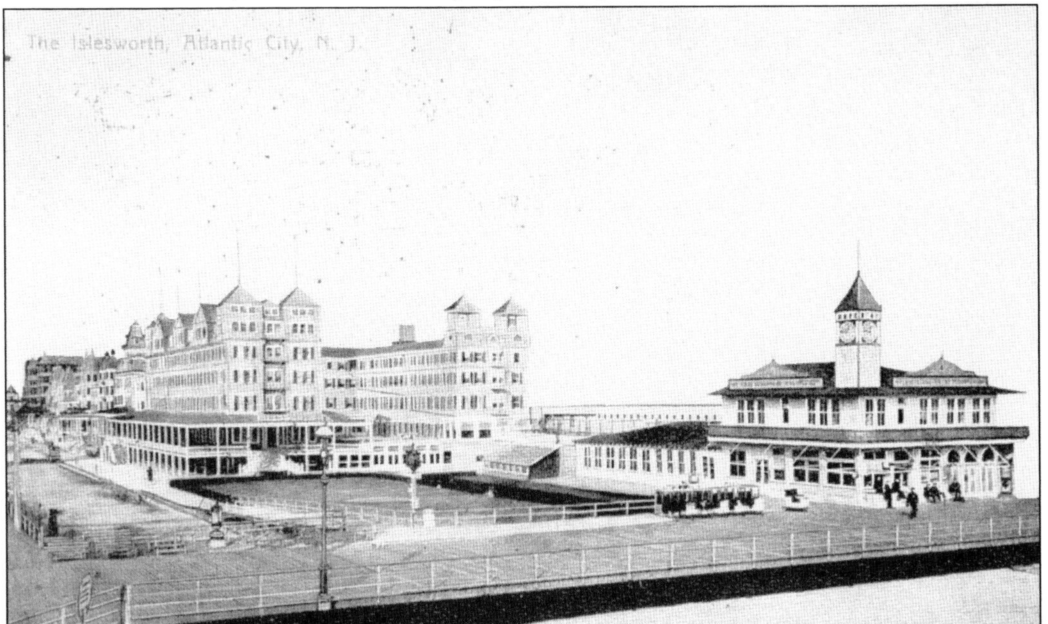

THE ISLESWORTH. Near the boardwalk, on Virginia Avenue, the Islesworth was popular with the theatrical crowd. The hotel had 230 rooms and in 1908 charged boarders between $18 and $35 a week for accommodations. It was noted for its first-class dining and superior service. Later it became the Blackstone Hotel and then the Jerome. (Metropolitan News Company, *c.* 1908.)

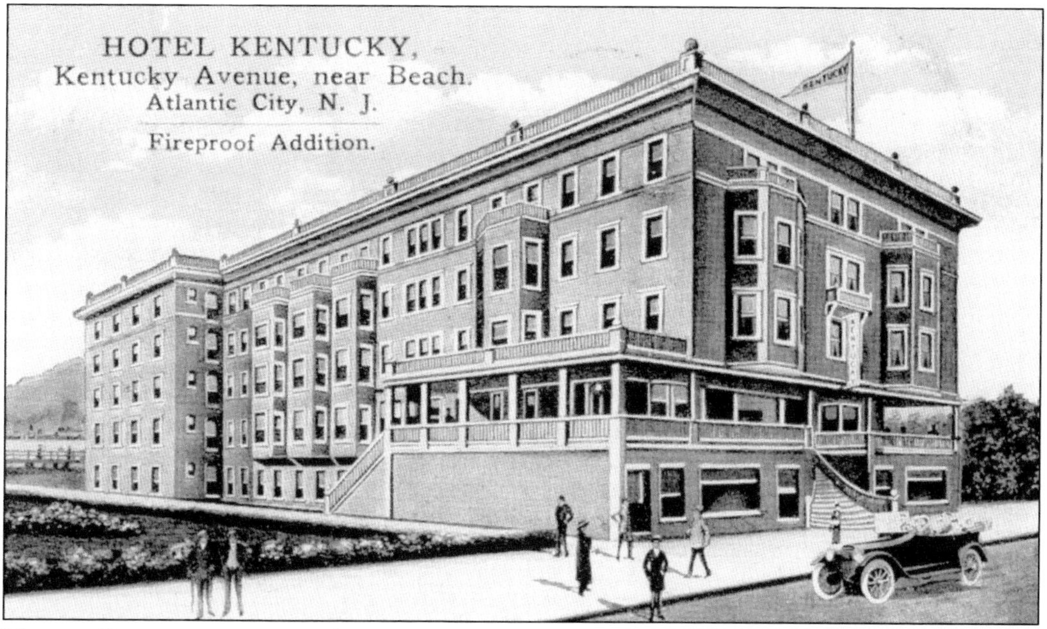

HOTEL KENTUCKY. Located on Kentucky Avenue near the beach, this establishment was appropriately named Hotel Kentucky. As early as 1905 it was promoting the fact that every room had electric lights and a telephone. Also advertised was the fact that 50 of its rooms had hot and cold running water, while 35 were equipped with private baths. These features were considered luxuries at the time. (Kropp, *c.* 1915.)

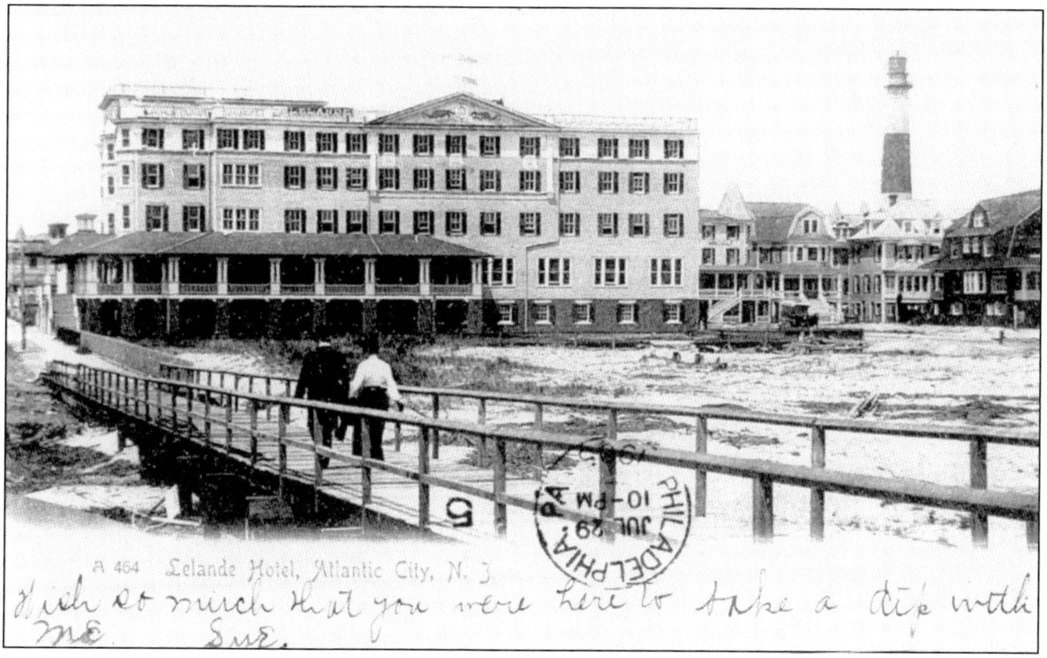

LELANDE HOTEL. The Lelande Hotel was located at the inlet end of the city between Massachusetts and Metropolitan Avenues near Oriental Avenue. As seen in this view, it was not far from the Absecon Lighthouse. This older grand hotel was ruined in the great hurricane of 1944. (Rotograph Company, *c.* 1905.)

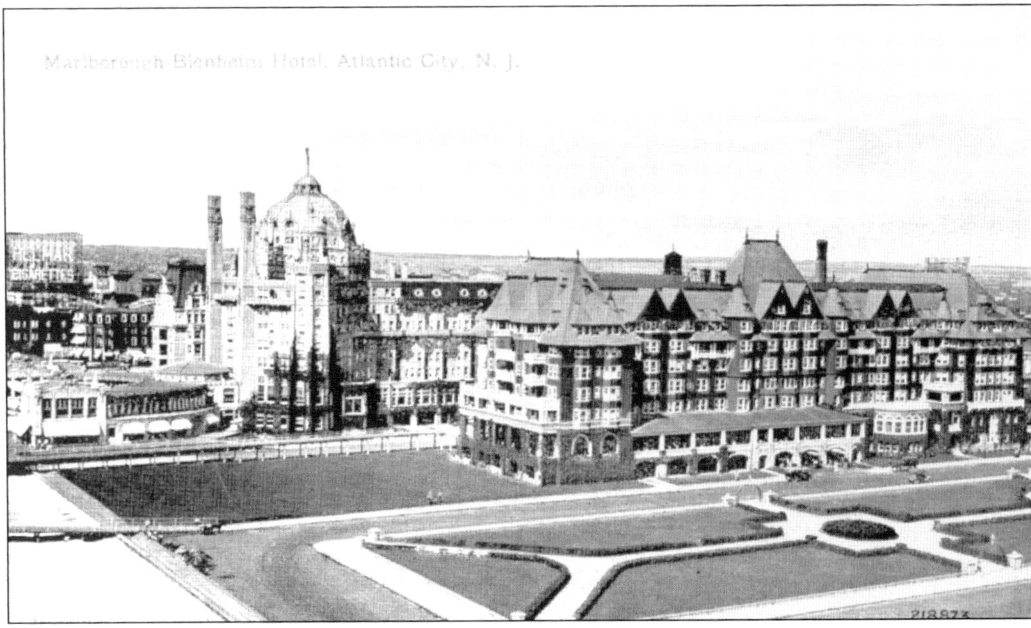

MARLBOROUGH-BLENHEIM HOTEL. This impressive hotel began with the Marlborough's construction in 1902. Using the same architect, William L. Price, the owners erected the Blenheim in 1906. It was the first hotel to have private baths for each room. The Blenheim was built with a type of cement invented by Thomas Edison, who personally oversaw construction. In 1978, the Marlborough was demolished, with the Blenheim suffering the same fate in 1979. (Post Card Distribution Company, *c.* 1916.)

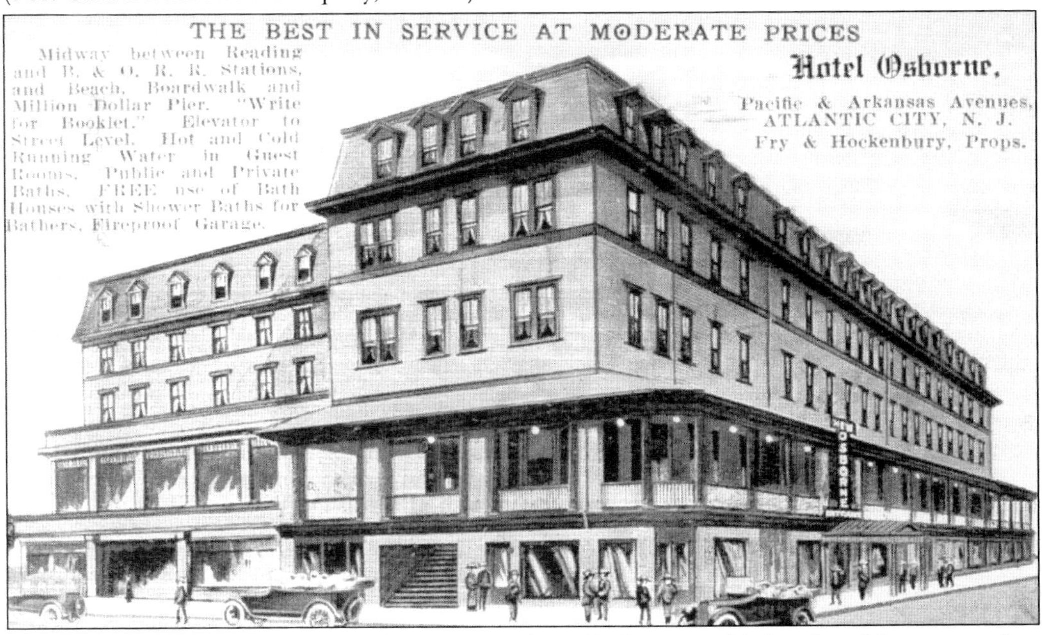

HOTEL OSBORNE. At the corner of Arkansas and Pacific Avenues, this hotel could accommodate 250 guests. Patrons were offered the choice of using the American or European plan. Guests had access to free use of bathhouses with showers, a fireproof garage, and an elevator to the street level. The hotel was even equipped with its own refrigeration and ice plant. (E. C. Kropp, *c.* 1920.)

THE PRESIDENT HOTEL. Opening on September 25, 1926, it was initially hoped that the President Hotel would serve as a summer White House for the nation's presidents. With 500 rooms and a special Presidential Suite on the top floor, it cost over $5 million to build. It even had its own indoor swimming pool, a rarity at the time. In 1968, it was converted into an apartment building. (E. C. Kropp, *c.* 1928.)

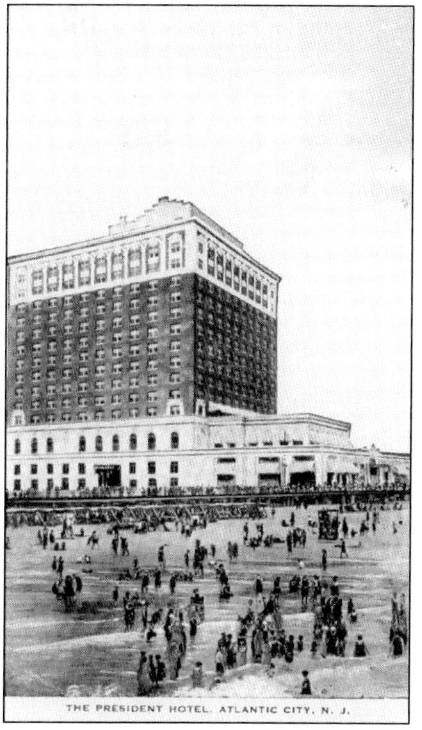

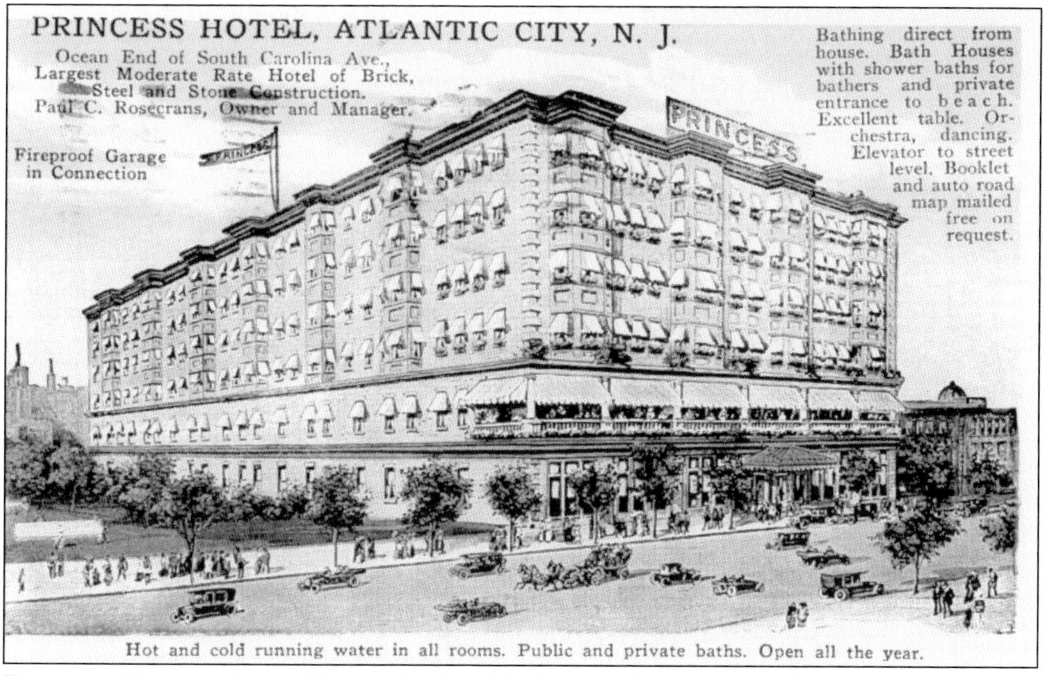

PRINCESS HOTEL. Open all year, this hotel had a rooming capacity of 500 people and stood at the ocean end of South Carolina Avenue. Constructed of brick, stone, and steel, the hotel had its own tennis court and fireproof garage. Other features included an elevator to the street level, a bathhouse, and a private beach entrance for the convenience of its guests. (E. C. Kropp, *c.* 1928.)

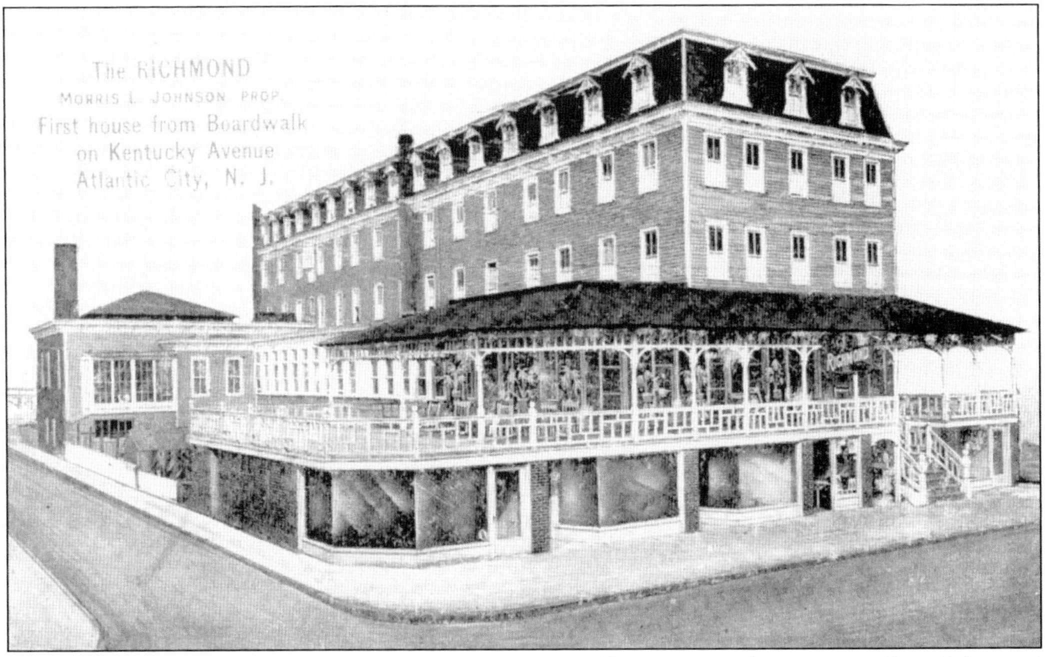

The Richmond. Occupying a site near the boardwalk on Kentucky Avenue, the Richmond was conveniently located. Patrons could easily access the boardwalk with all of its offerings. Or if they preferred, patrons could occupy a chair on the 4,000 square feet of deck and simply delight in being cooled by the ocean breezes. (Chilton Company, *c.* 1910.)

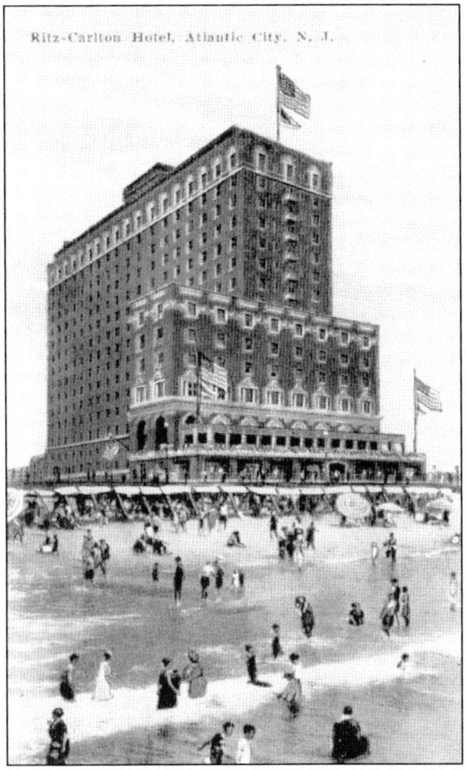

Ritz Carlton Hotel. From the day that it opened its doors on June 24, 1921, at Iowa Avenue and the boardwalk, the Ritz was considered to be one of the most lavish hotels in town. It was built at the cost of $6 million and had 475 rooms. One unique feature was its famous Merry-Go-Round bar. In 1969, it was converted to apartments. (Virginia Post Card Company, *c.* 1923.)

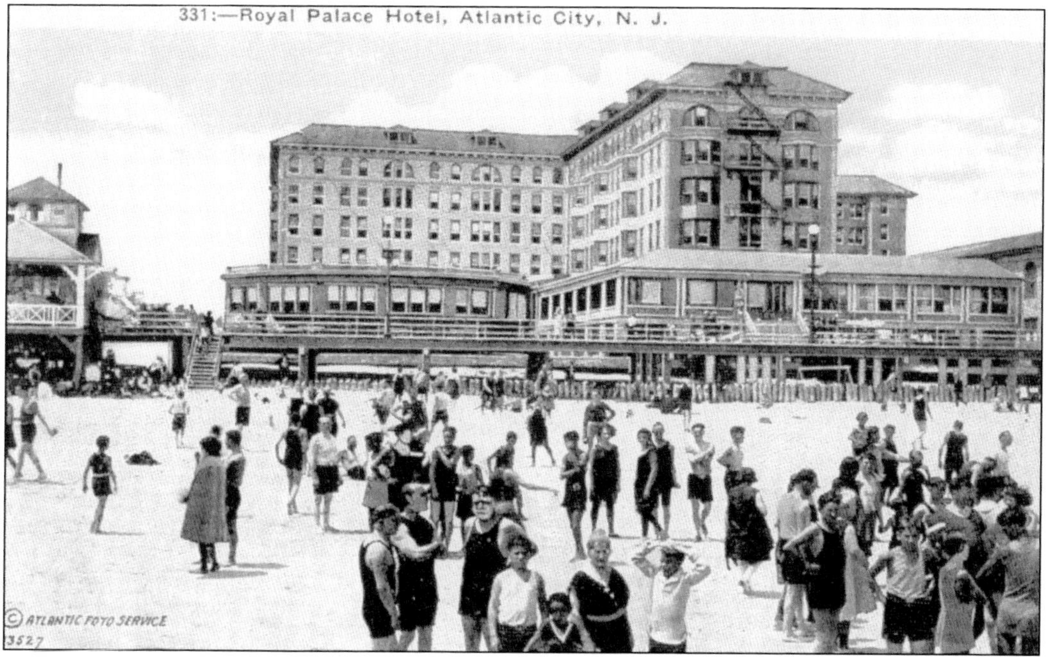

Royal Palace Hotel. This majestic hotel once stood at the very northern end of Pacific Avenue at the boardwalk. It offered guests ocean views from nearly all of its rooms. With one of the largest dining rooms in the city and a grill specializing in seafood at popular prices, it was a favorite eating place for many. Sadly, like so many other historic hotels in the city, it no longer exists. (P. Sander, *c.* 1920.)

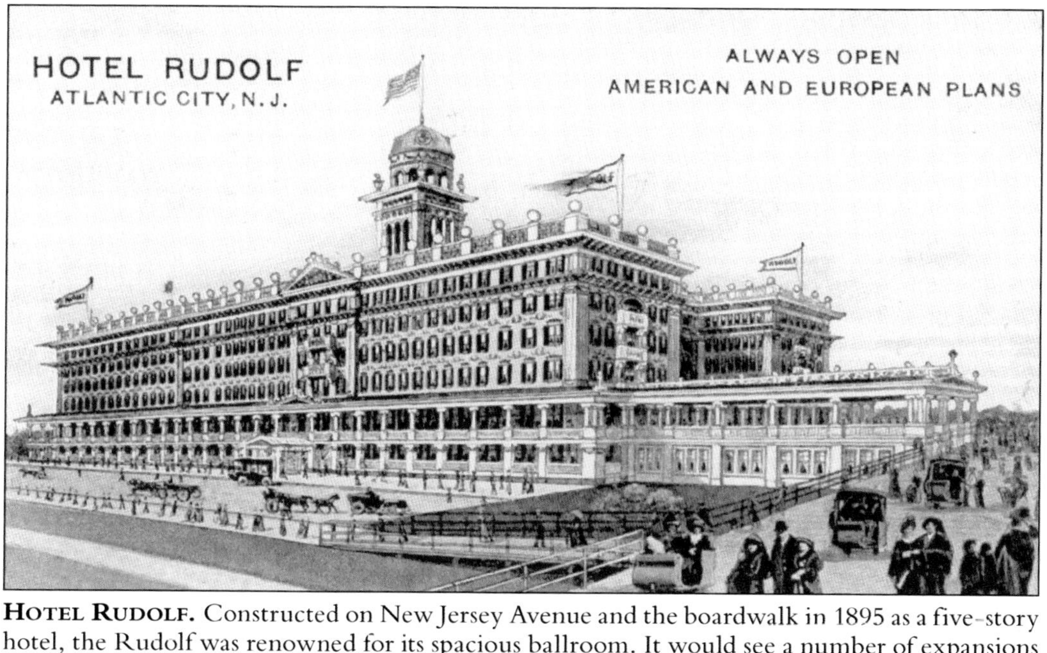

Hotel Rudolf. Constructed on New Jersey Avenue and the boardwalk in 1895 as a five-story hotel, the Rudolf was renowned for its spacious ballroom. It would see a number of expansions and numerous improvements over the years. The hotel even had its own artesian well to ensure an adequate water supply for its guests. In 1900, a night's stay here cost $5. (Charles Elliott, *c.* 1910.)

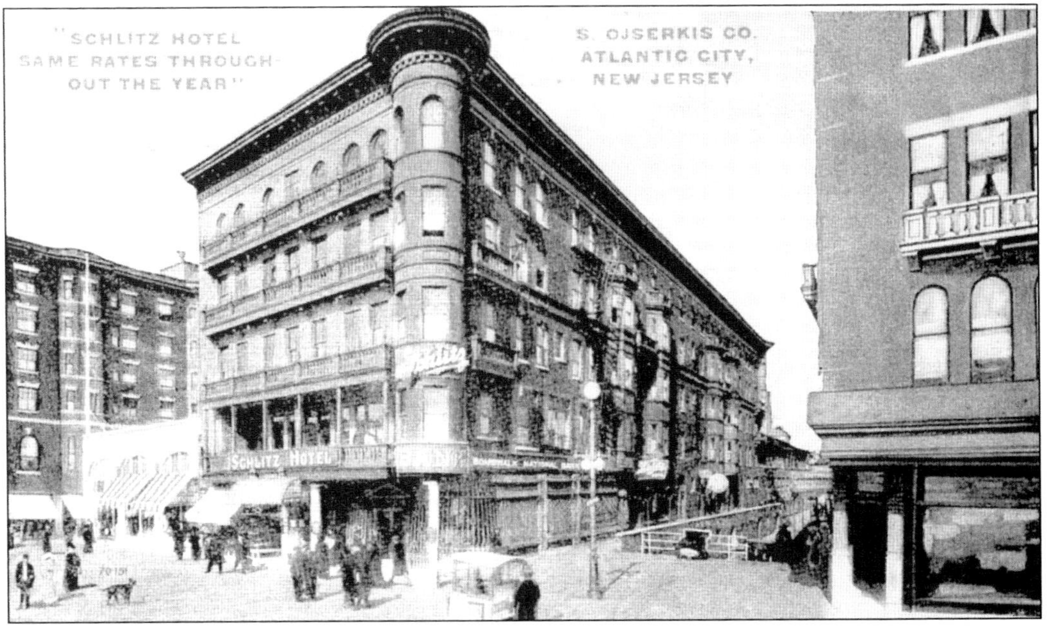

SCHLITZ HOTEL. Originally named the Waldorf-Astoria when it opened in 1898, the Schlitz Hotel sat right on the boardwalk at the corner of Ocean Avenue. Its 184 rooms offered modestly priced accommodations. The ground floor was occupied by the Boardwalk National Bank, which opened to the public in July 1907. It was the first and only bank on the boardwalk. (Publisher unknown, *c.* 1912.)

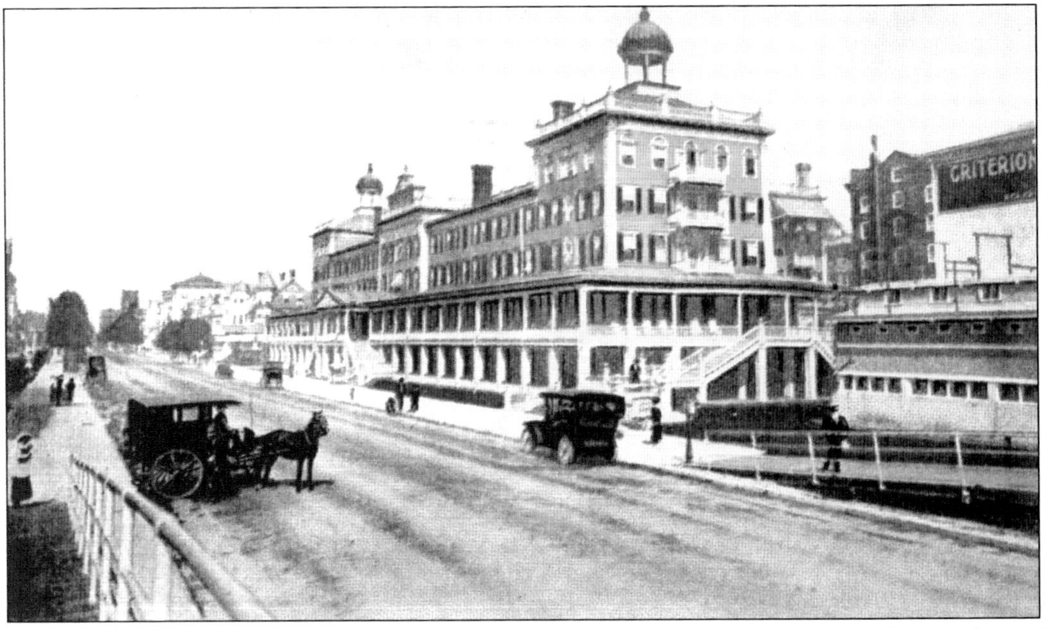

THE SEASIDE. Built in 1862 on Pennsylvania Avenue, this hotel was expanded a number of times over the years. In 1923, the hotel was home to Atlantic City's first radio station, WHAR. During the Great Depression it was the first to offer guests a package deal weekend. The $12 cost included the room, tickets to movies and Steel Pier, and a midnight dinner dance. This grand hotel was razed in 1984. (Post Card Distribution Company, *c.* 1912.)

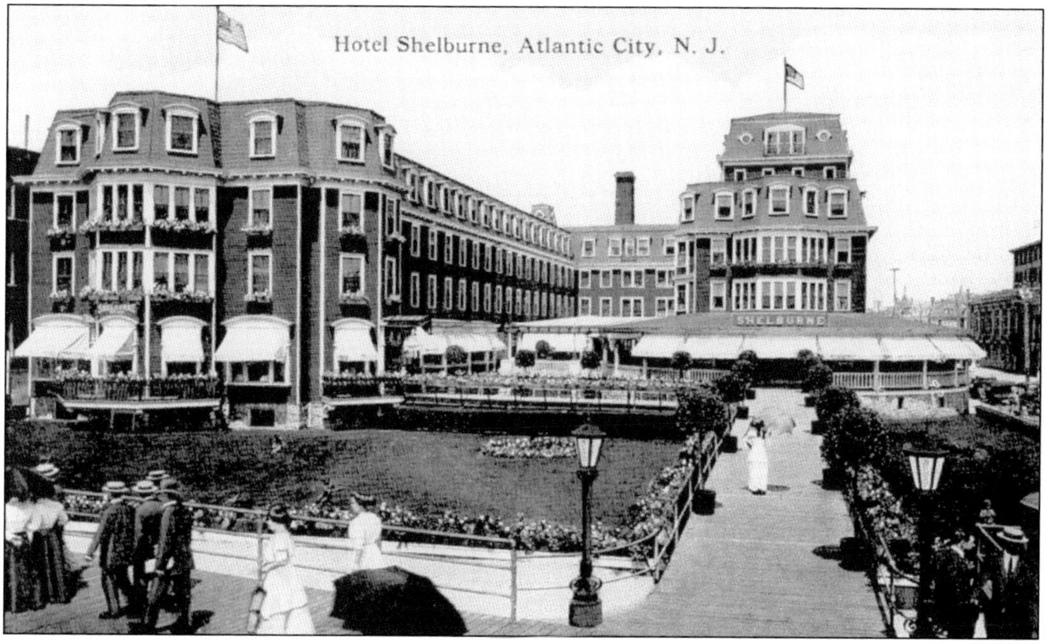

SHELBURNE HOTEL. Opened in 1869 as a wooden-frame building, the Shelburne at Michigan Avenue and the boardwalk evolved into a multistory brick hotel by the early 1900s. Entertainers and celebrities often roomed here. Included among them were "Diamond Jim" Brady, Lillian Russell, George M. Cohan, Victor Herbert, John Philip Sousa, and Al Jolson. Like many other grand hotels, it was eventually demolished. (Post Card Distribution Company, *c.* 1918.)

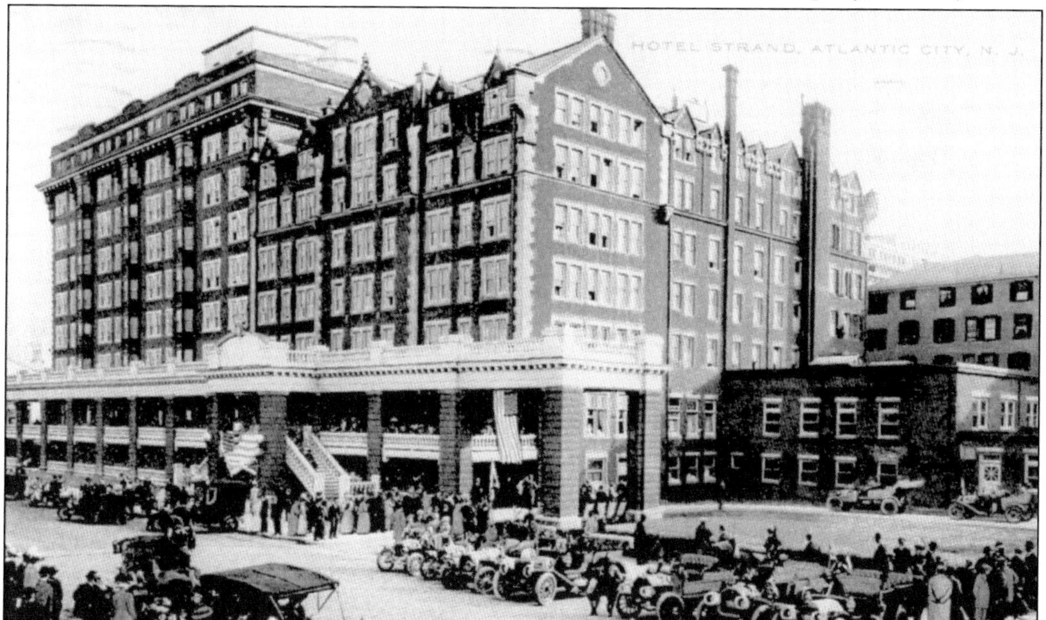

HOTEL STRAND. Occupying a prime location across the boardwalk from Steel Pier, at Pennsylvania Avenue, this multistory brick hotel was noted for its homelike atmosphere. In its advertisements in 1926, the hotel stated that it had a capacity of 600 persons and boasted of having a fireproof garage and baths supplied with running saltwater. (L. Beard, *c.* 1910.)

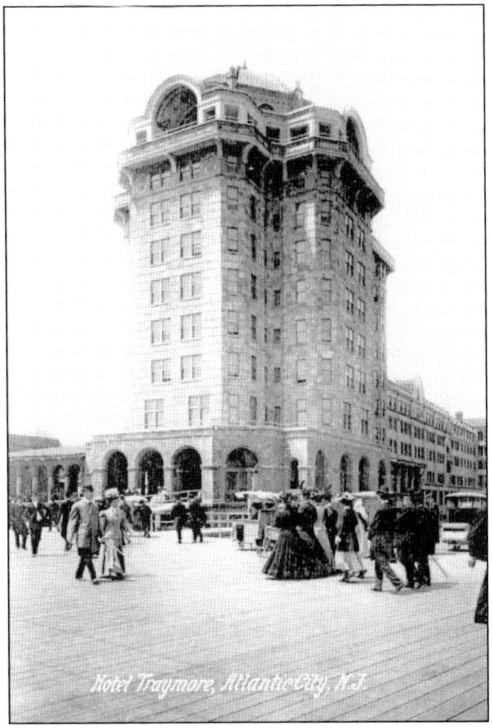

THE TRAYMORE HOTEL. What began as a 10-room cottage in 1879 later evolved into a 14-story concrete hotel designed by architect William L. Price. Located at Illinois Avenue and the boardwalk, it could accommodate 1,500 guests. It once advertised itself as being the world's largest resort hotel. The grand ballroom was capable of holding 4,000. This magnificent landmark hotel was demolished on April 27, 1972. (Rotograph Company, *c.* 1908.)

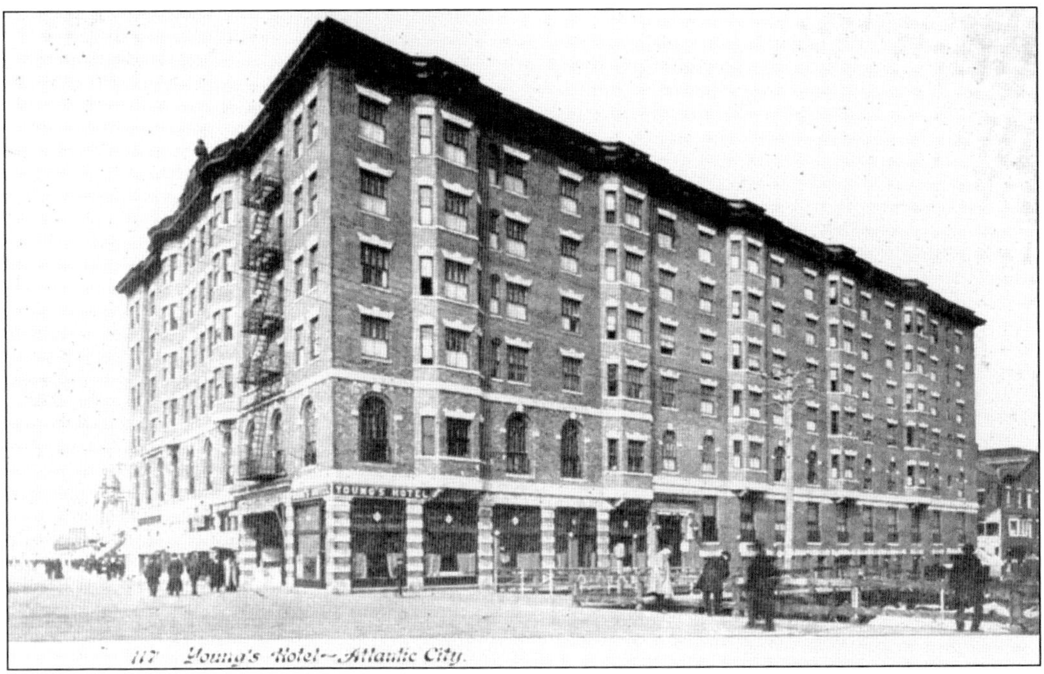

YOUNG'S HOTEL. This building was erected by Capt. John L. Young on Tennessee Avenue in 1901. It was initially a seven-story apartment house with 112 units and eight stores on the first floor. Soon Young turned it into a hotel. The first brick hotel on the boardwalk, it changed ownership many times and later operated under such names as the Alamac, Knickerbocker, and Mayflower. (J. Murray Jordan, 1906.)

Three

The Boardwalk

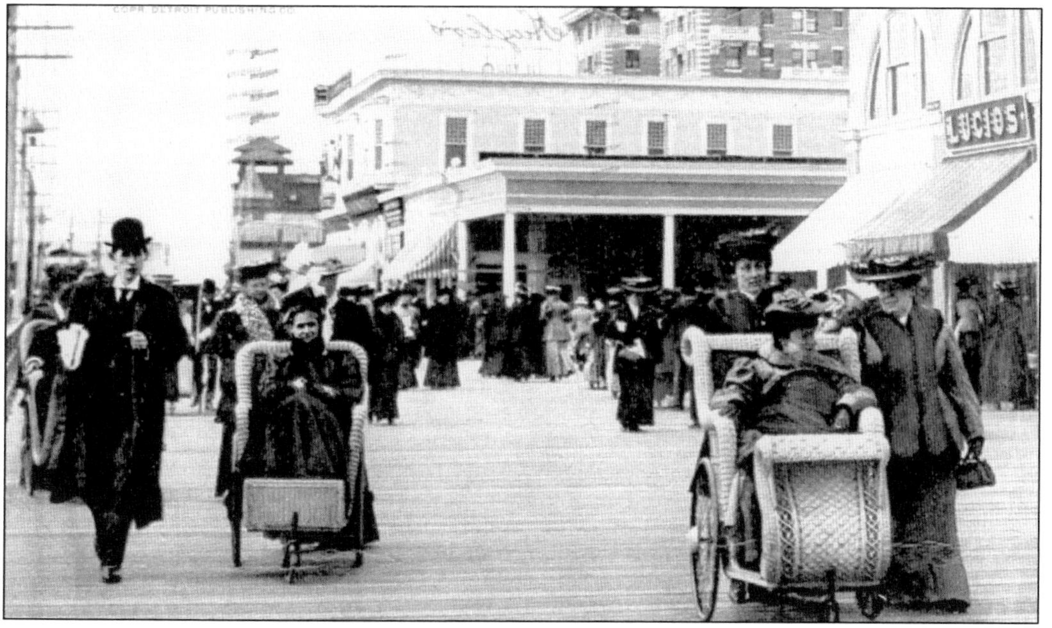

THE BOARDWALK. A true hallmark of Atlantic City, the boardwalk began as a simple wooden planked walkway designed by Alexander Boardman to keep sand from entering hotels and railroad cars. Officially declared a street in 1896, the boardwalk has a tradition of offering just about anything a person could desire. This great wooden way has become indispensable to Atlantic City and an important part of the nation's cultural heritage. (Detroit Publishing, 1903.)

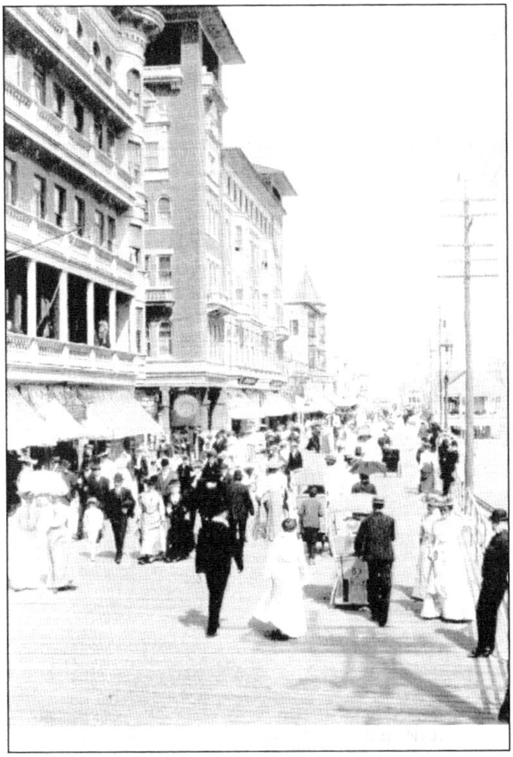

A Popular Part of the Boardwalk. A typical daytime boardwalk scene during the early 1900s is captured in this view looking northward. The boardwalk was often promoted as the "eighth wonder of the world." During this era it was considered proper etiquette to stroll the boards in one's best clothing. Casual attire for such activity was not yet the custom of the day. (S. Langford, *c.* 1905.)

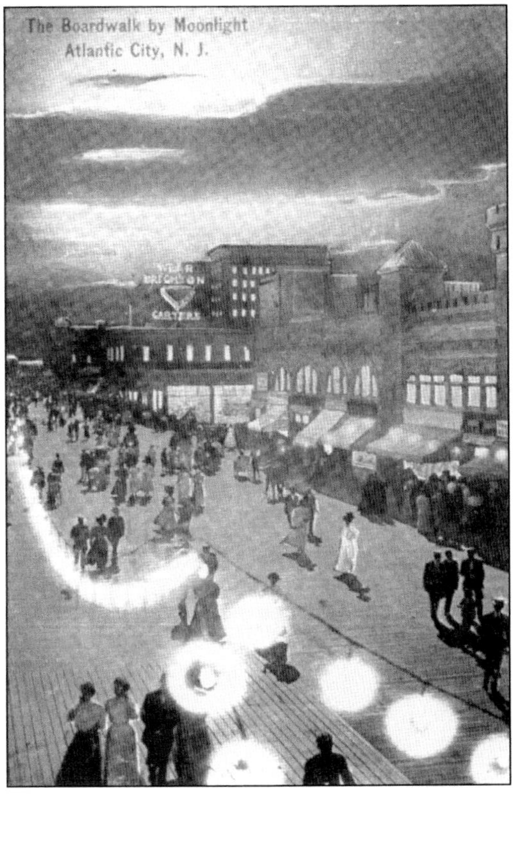

Boardwalk by Moonlight. The first electric lights appeared in 1883 as strings of lightbulbs running down the center of the boardwalk, as seen in this postcard view looking south from Steel Pier. In 1912, a total of 299 ornamental light poles were installed to replace them. In later years these lighting fixtures would be moved to the sides of the wooden promenade. (Chilton Company, *c.* 1910.)

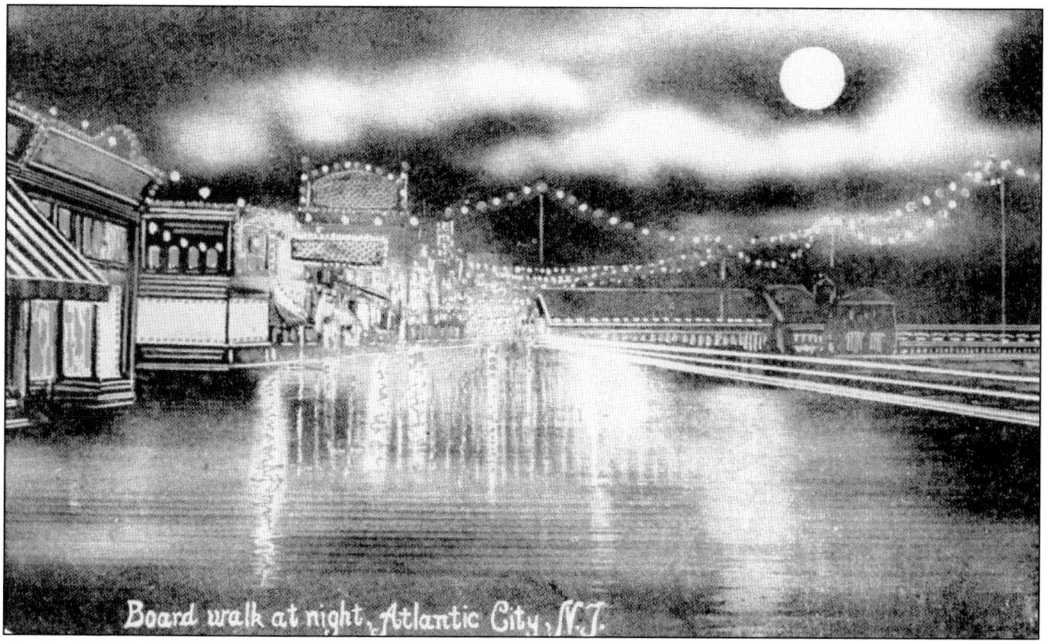

BOARDWALK AT NIGHT. As the sun went down and night fell, the boardwalk took on an entirely different ambiance as multitudes of colorful electric lights lit up the thoroughfare. The glitter and illumination ensured that excitement and entertainment would last long into the evening hours. (Beard, *c.* 1910.)

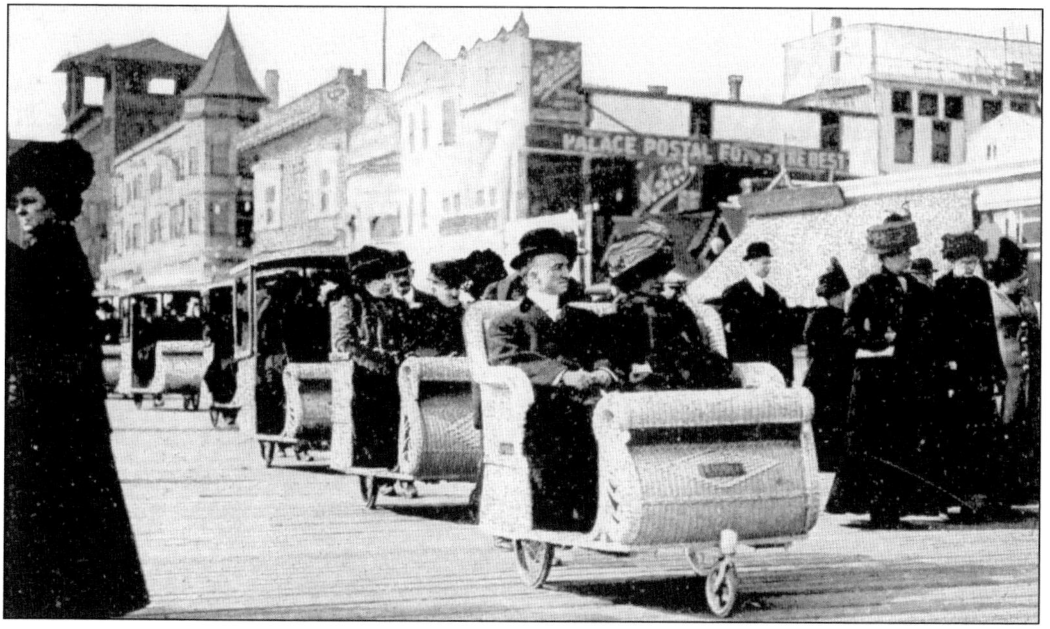

ROLLING CHAIRS. A distinctive means of transport, the rolling chair was developed by William Hayday in the late 1880s. Having rented wheelchairs to invalids for years, he came to the realization that visitors might enjoy being rolled along the boardwalk for a small fee. Chairs, manufactured by Harry Shill of Philadelphia, were then redesigned to hold two patrons and the traditional vehicle was born. (Post Card Distribution Company, *c.* 1912)

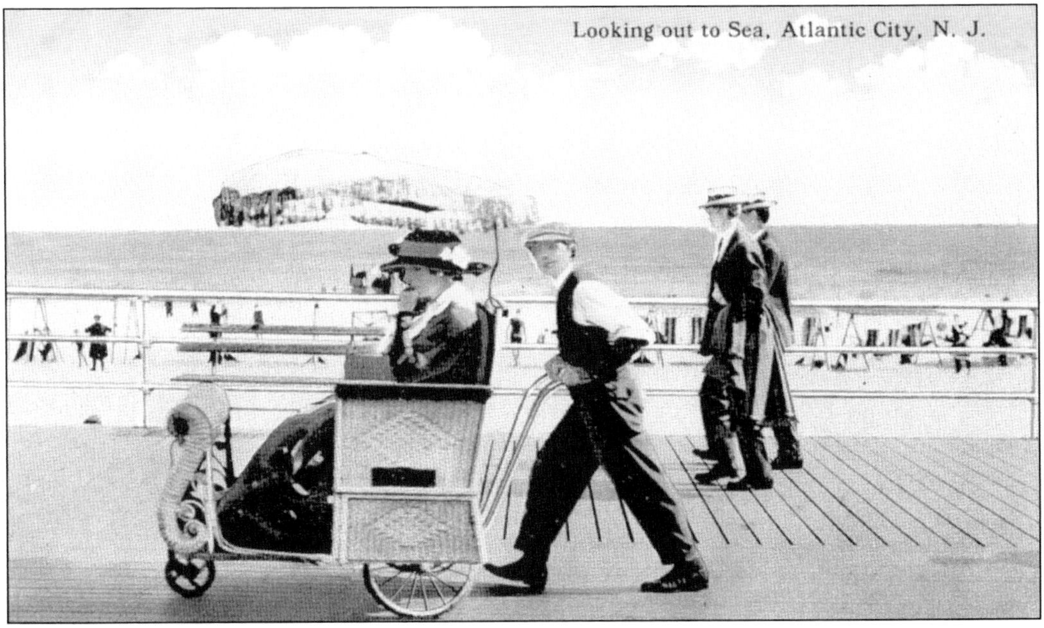

RIDING A ROLLING CHAIR. Being pushed comfortably along in a wicker cart became a fashionable means of traversing the boardwalk. In 1904, a city ordinance legalized the use of the two-passenger rolling chair and required operators to obtain a $15 license. Later, in 1914, the city redesigned sections of the boardwalk with longitudinal planking to make the ride smoother for patrons. (Post Card Distribution Company, *c.* 1914.)

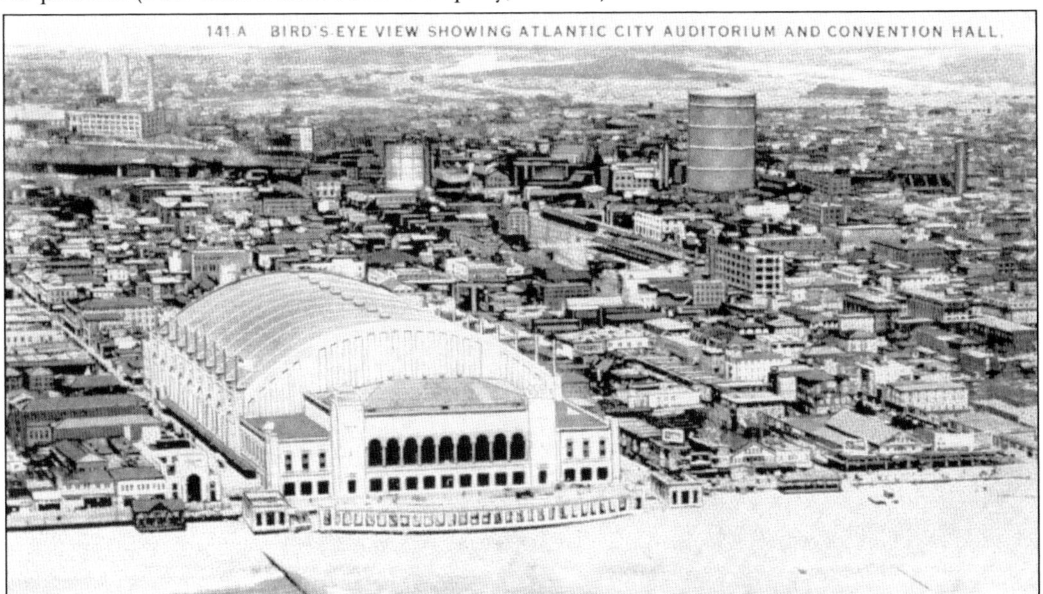

AUDITORIUM AND CONVENTION HALL. When it was dedicated on May 31, 1929, the Atlantic City Convention Hall was the largest structure of its kind in the world. Occupying the land between Mississippi and Georgia Avenues at the boardwalk, it was erected at a cost of $15 million. Vice president of the United States Charles Curtis spoke at its opening, and off shore, the battleship USS *Wyoming* fired a celebratory salute. (Saltzburg, *c.* 1930.)

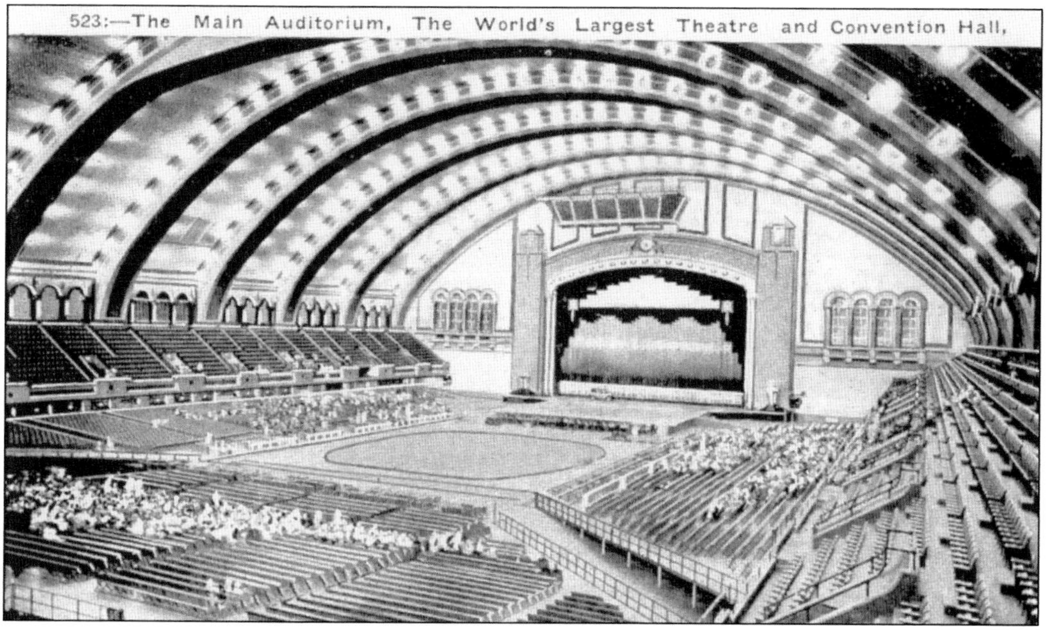

MAIN AUDITORIUM OF CONVENTION HALL. This immense auditorium, covering three and one-half acres, contained what was and still is the world's largest pipe organ. Events held there have included football and ice hockey games, concerts, exhibitions, and conventions, and during World War II it served as a training facility for the Army Air Corps. The building has been restored and continues to operate as the Boardwalk Convention Hall. (P. Sander, *c.* 1930.)

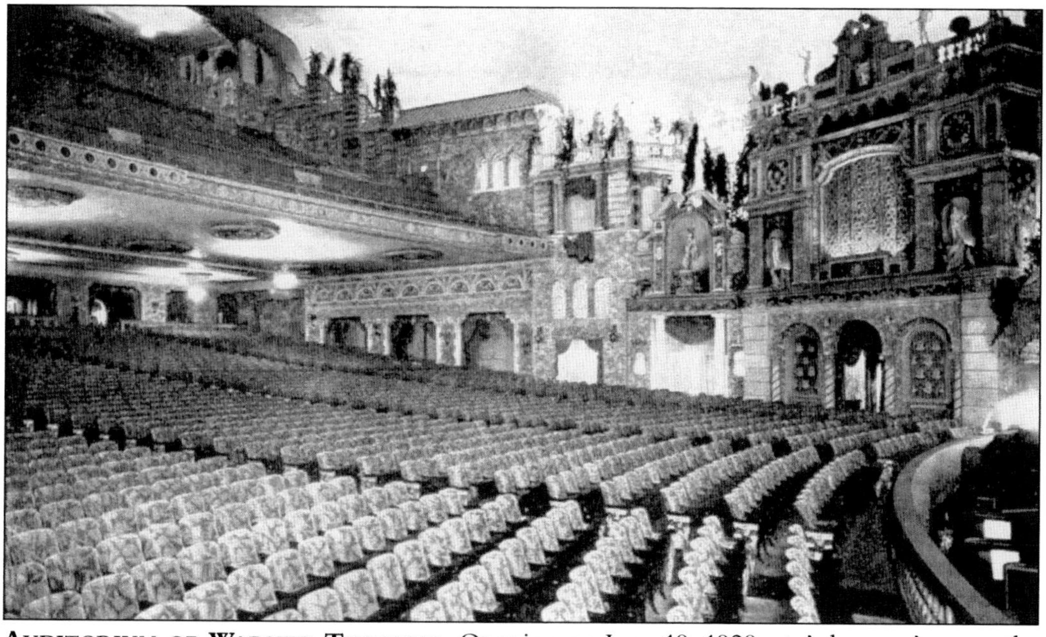

AUDITORIUM OF WARNER THEATRE. Opening on June 19, 1929, at Arkansas Avenue, the Warner Theatre advertised itself as the world's most beautiful theater. Constructed in the Spanish Mediterranean style at a cost of $2.7 million, its ceiling was filled with twinkling lights representing the stars and constellations. It later became the Warren Theater and finished its days as a bowling alley. Today only the front facade remains. (Kropp, *c.* 1930.)

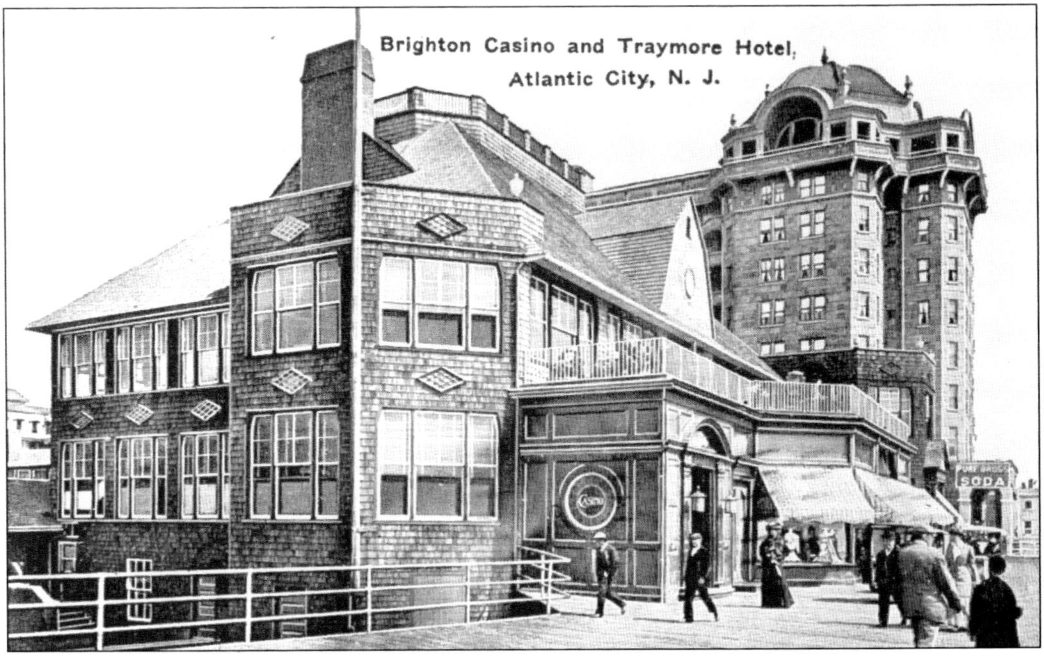

BRIGHTON CASINO. The Brighton Casino was part of the Brighton Hotel on Indiana Avenue. Opened in 1892, the casino had an entrance on the boardwalk. Not a gambling establishment, the casino instead had a dance floor, an orchestra, and even a swimming pool. Its sun deck was a favorite spot for many to sit and watch strollers on the boardwalk below. The building was razed in 1959. (Koffman, *c.* 1908.)

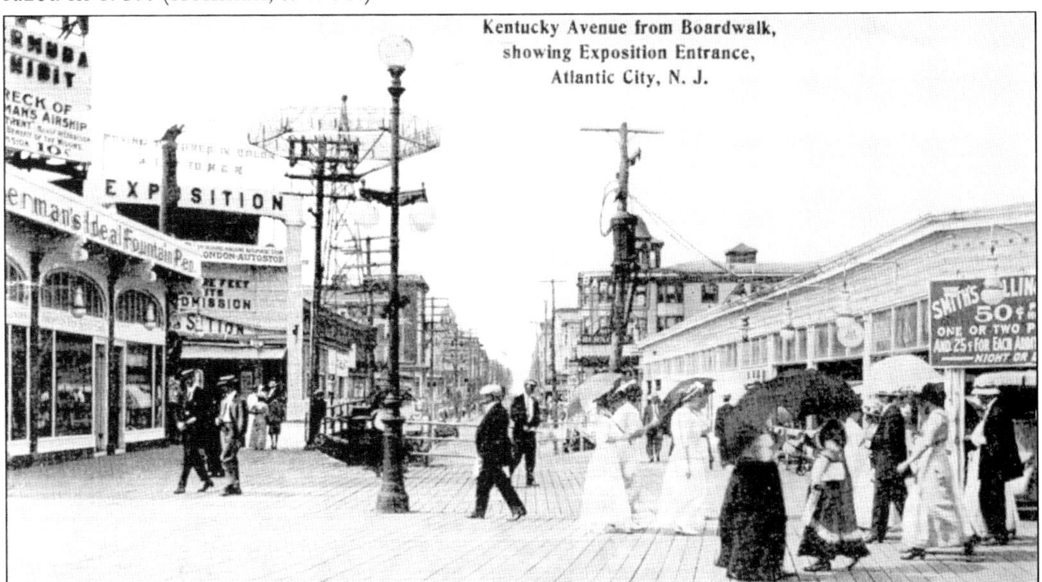

EXPOSITION HALL. Sitting behind the Waterman's Fountain Pen Store, at the corner of Kentucky Avenue, was Exposition Hall. A sign on its roof advertises an exhibit related to the wreck of the airship *America,* which occurred in 1910. The dirigible, which left from Atlantic City under command of explorer Walter Wellman, was attempting to cross the Atlantic Ocean. It crashed into the sea, and its crew was rescued. (Postcard Distribution Company, *c.* 1910)

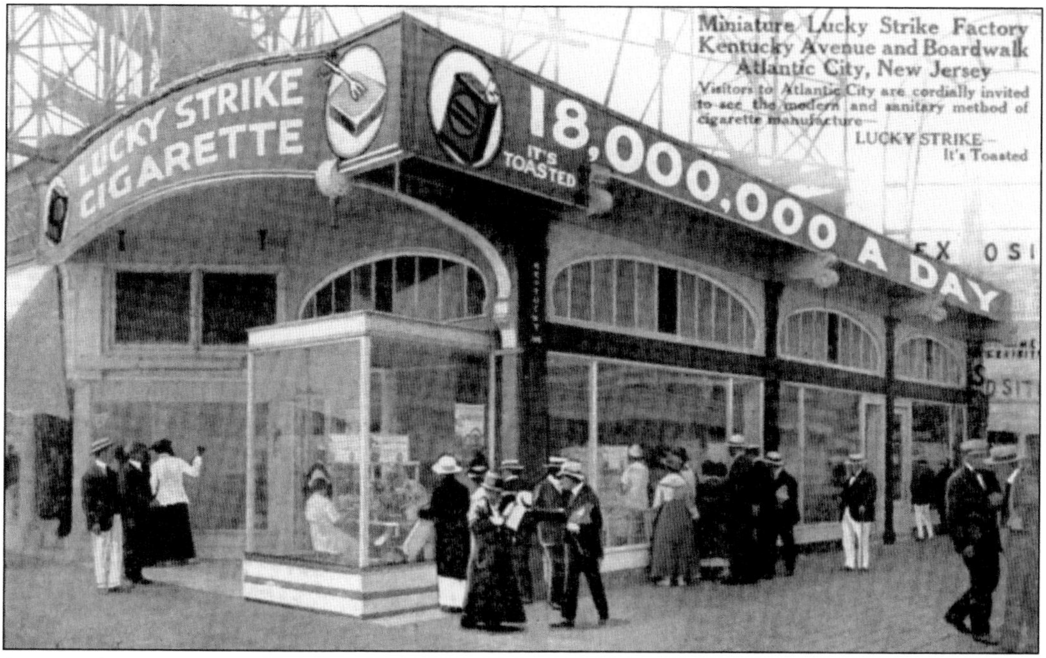

LUCKY STRIKE FACTORY. The site of the Waterman's Fountain Pen store later became the Lucky Strike cigarette factory. Here visitors were invited to observe the production of cigarettes by the "modern and sanitary method." This was a novel way of helping to promote and sell the product. The sign above the store advertises sales as being 18 million per day nationwide. The slogan "It's Toasted" was introduced in 1917. (Publisher unknown, *c.* 1920.)

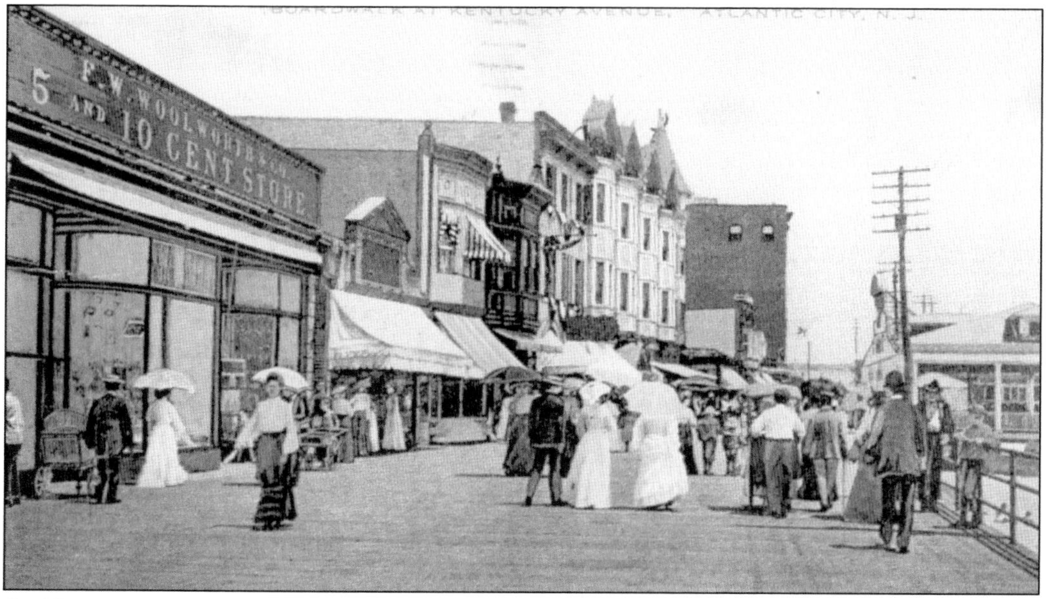

AT KENTUCKY AVENUE. Near Kentucky Avenue stood a F. W. Woolworth's store. Woolworth opened his first store in Camden in 1879. By the time this postcard was published there were over 1,000 stores throughout the country. Like its competitor, J. G. McCrorey, Woolworth's sold a variety of merchandise at fixed prices, usually 5¢ or 10¢. By 1979 Woolworth's was the largest department store chain in the world. (L. Beard, *c.* 1912.)

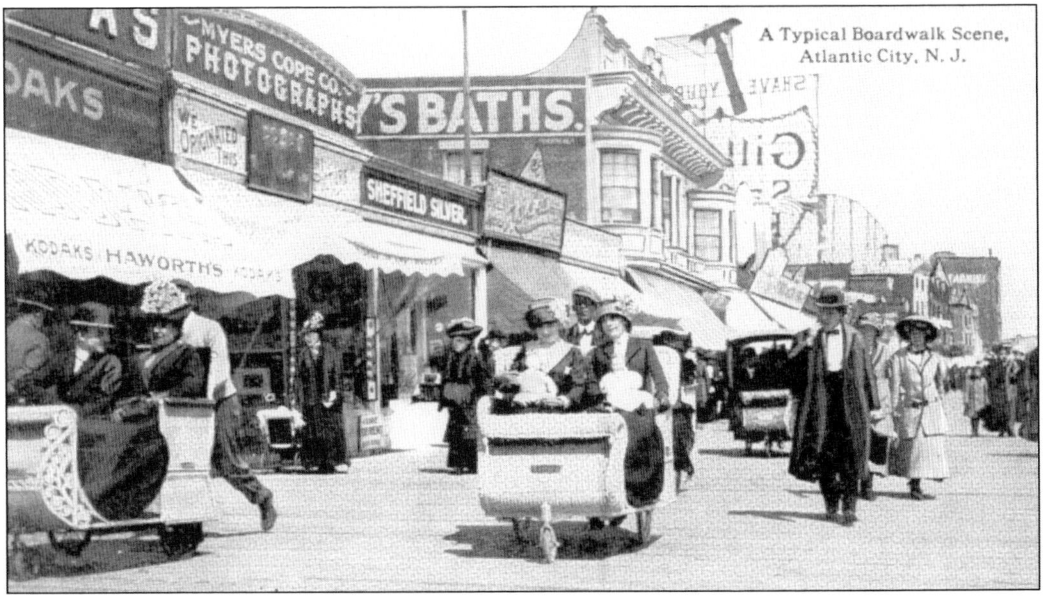

A Typical Boardwalk Scene. As rolling chairs transport customers down the boardwalk, below New York Avenue, they travel past such diverse businesses as a bathhouse, jewelry store, and photographic studio. Visible atop a building in the distance is a large electrical sign advertising Gillette Safety Razors. Erected in 1905, it was the first of its kind on the boardwalk. Such electrified promotional signs would soon become commonplace. (Post Card Distribution Company, *c.* 1914.)

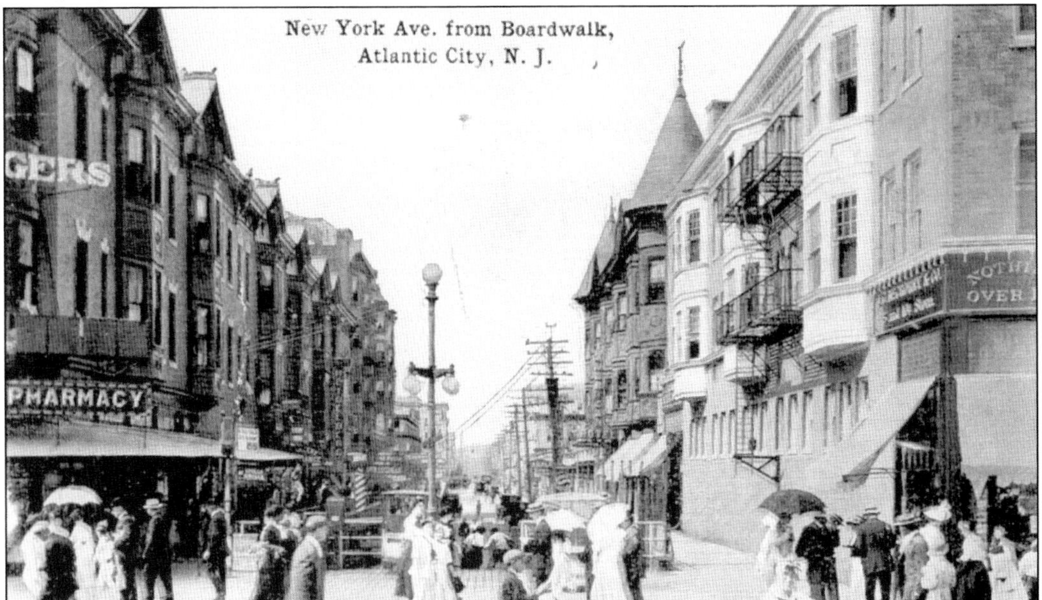

New York Avenue. People stroll by the New York Avenue entrance to the boardwalk. Here two important businesses are found occupying opposite corners. On the left-hand side stands Fralinger's Pharmacy, home of the famous saltwater taffy. The other corner is the site of a J. G. McCrorey store. (Post Card Distribution Company, *c.* 1914.)

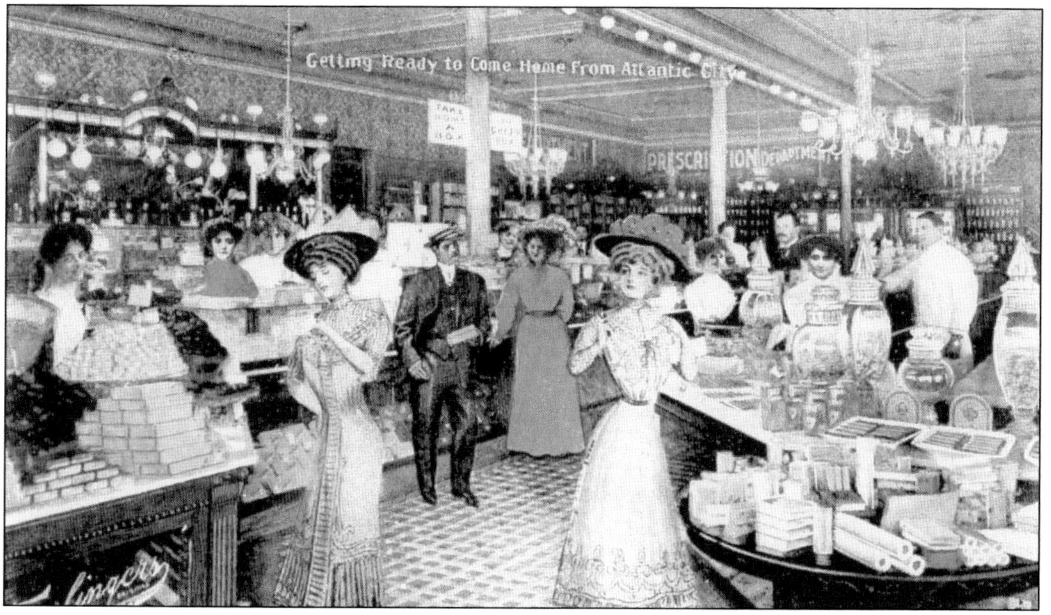

Fralinger's Pharmacy. A bountiful display of sweet treats greeted shoppers at Fralinger's Pharmacy, which was known as the home of saltwater taffy. Joseph Fralinger began his business in 1889 and became recognized as the saltwater taffy king. Much of his success was attributed to his idea of selling his product in boxes suitable for mailing. Available in over 20 flavors, his famous confection was shipped around the world. (Chilton, *c.* 1906.)

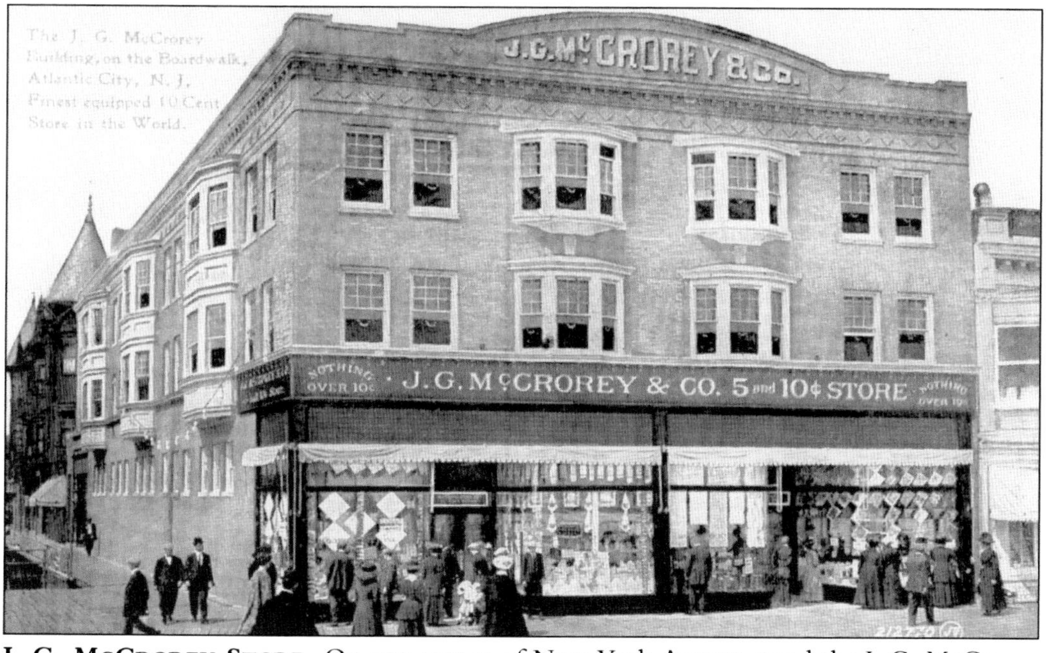

J. G. McCrorey Store. On one corner of New York Avenue stood the J. G. McCrorey 5 and 10 Cent Store. Here all items cost 10¢ or less. John Graham McCrorey opened his first store in Pennsylvania in 1882 and by 1917 had 143 stores nationwide. By the 1960s the company was the fourth-largest retailer in the country. It finally went out of business in 2001. (Valentine and Sons, *c.* 1910.)

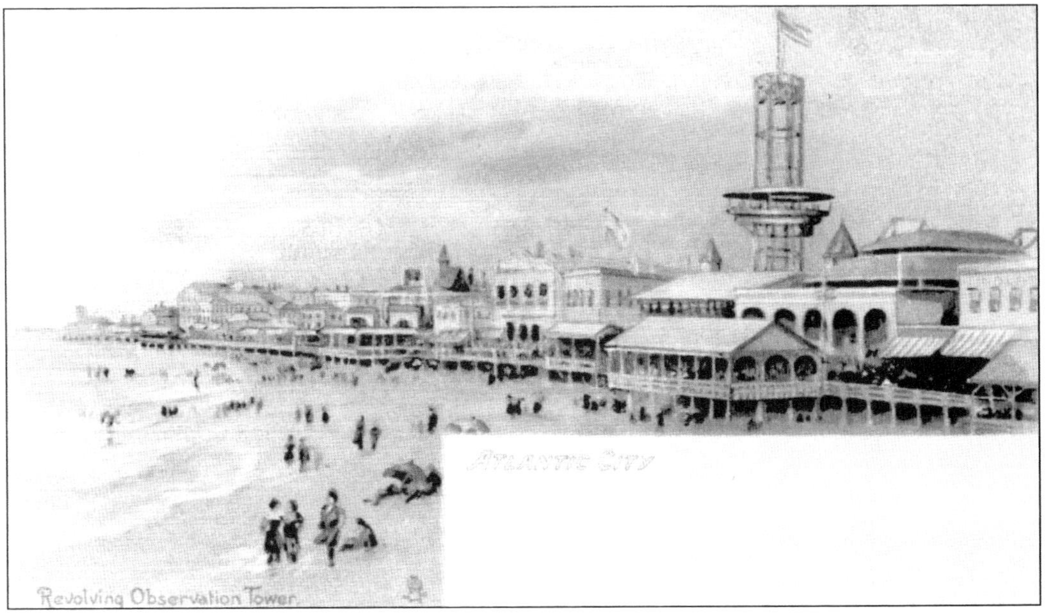

REVOLVING OBSERVATION TOWER. In 1895, a popular ride called the Revolving Observation Tower was installed at Massachusetts Avenue and another at New York Avenue. Customers paid 10¢ to stand on a rotating circular platform, 60 feet in diameter, which would slowly rise from the ground to a height of 103 feet. This provided the rider a breathtaking view of the city, beaches, boardwalk, and ocean. (Raphael Tuck and Sons, *c.* 1900.)

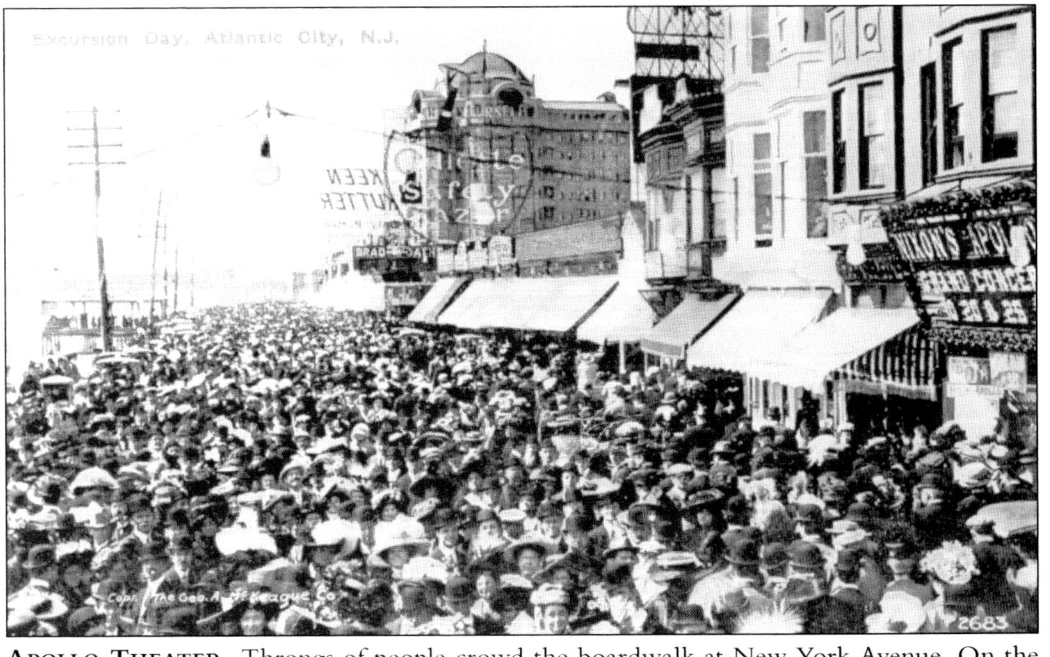

APOLLO THEATER. Throngs of people crowd the boardwalk at New York Avenue. On the right is the entrance to Nixon's Apollo Theater. Opening for theatrical productions in 1908, this building was originally the Academy of Music. It was here, at the Apollo, that shows would try out before heading to Broadway. It was converted to a movie theater in 1924 and lasted into the 1970s. (Post Card Distribution Company, *c.* 1912.)

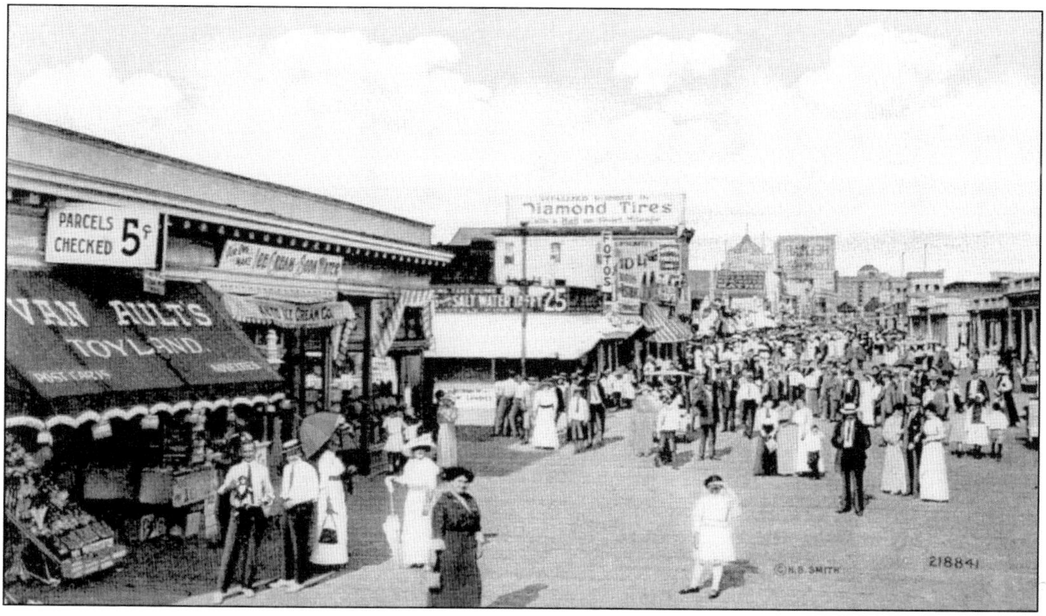

BOARDWALK SCENE. In this view south of Tennessee Avenue, a number of shops can be seen lining the boardwalk. Prominent among them is Van Aults Toyland. Van Aults was one of many stores that sold postcards, novelties, souvenirs, and similar products to its customers. Next door is an ice-cream parlor where people could refresh themselves with some homemade ice cream and soda water. (Post Card Distribution Company, *c.* 1914.)

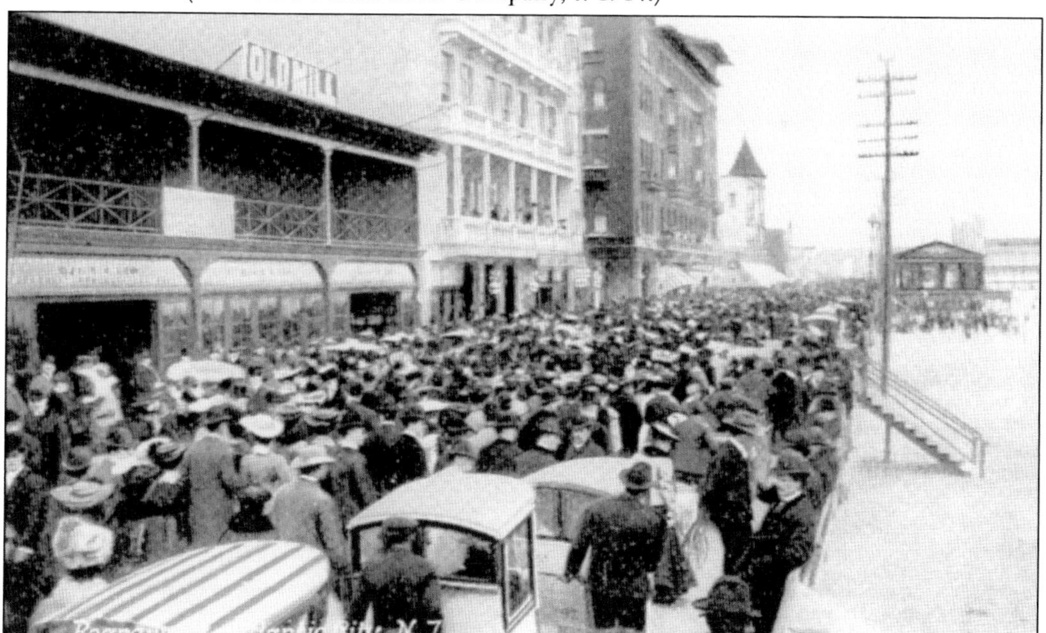

TENNESSEE AVENUE AND BOARDWALK. The northeast corner of Tennessee Avenue was once the site of the Old Mill ride. This attraction was a slow, tunnel of love–style boat ride where a young man might enjoy some time cuddled up with his sweetheart. Eventually the building changed ownership, and it became the location of Atlantic City's first Childs Restaurant. (Illustrated Postal Card Company, *c.* 1907.)

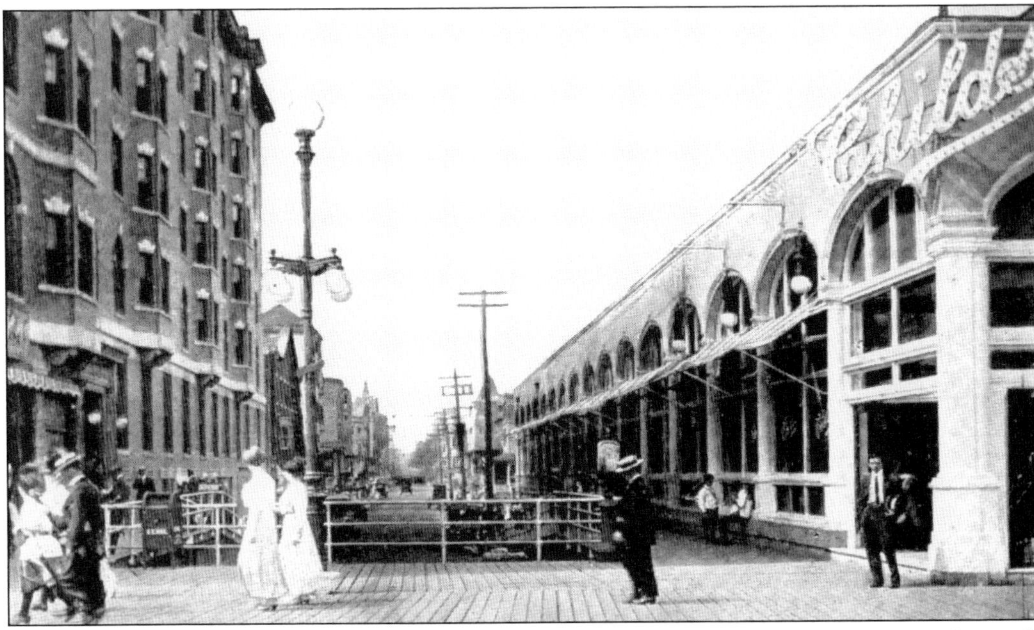

TENNESSEE AVENUE. The site of the former Old Mill, across from the Hotel Alamac (formerly Young's Hotel), became a Childs Restaurant. Founded in 1889 by William and Samuel Childs, the Childs Restaurants went on to become, for a time, the largest chain of restaurants in the nation. One of its most famous locations was at Coney Island in New York. (National Post Card Company, *c.* 1920.)

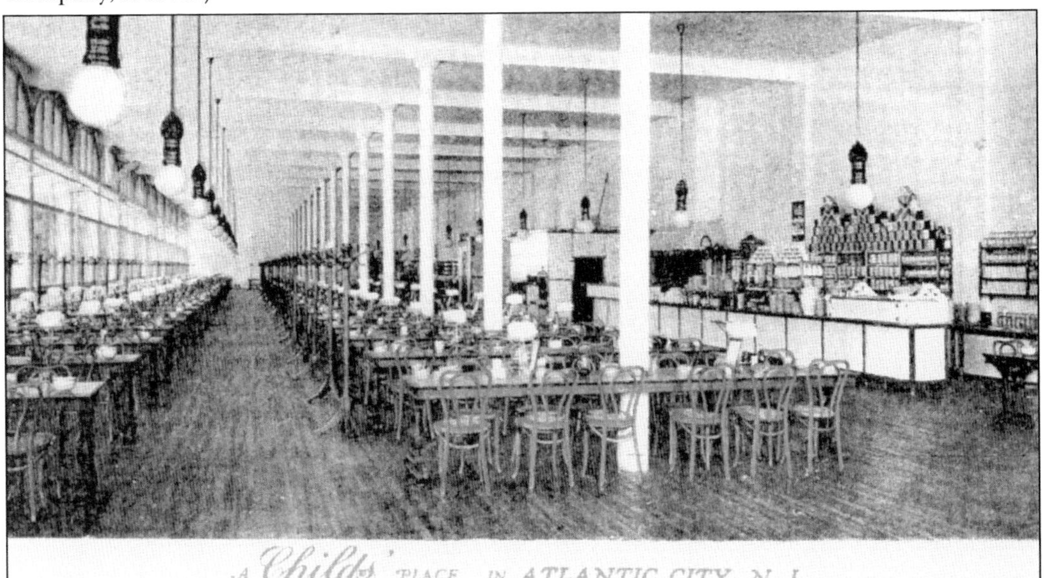

A CHILDS' PLACE. This Childs Restaurant, at Tennessee Avenue, was said to seat 1,000 customers. In 1927, the establishment moved to a different site just up the boardwalk at South Carolina Avenue. The Childs Restaurant chain is said to have initiated the self-serve cafeteria and owed much of its success to offering its clientele quality food at reasonable prices. (Plantinachrome Company, *c.* 1906.)

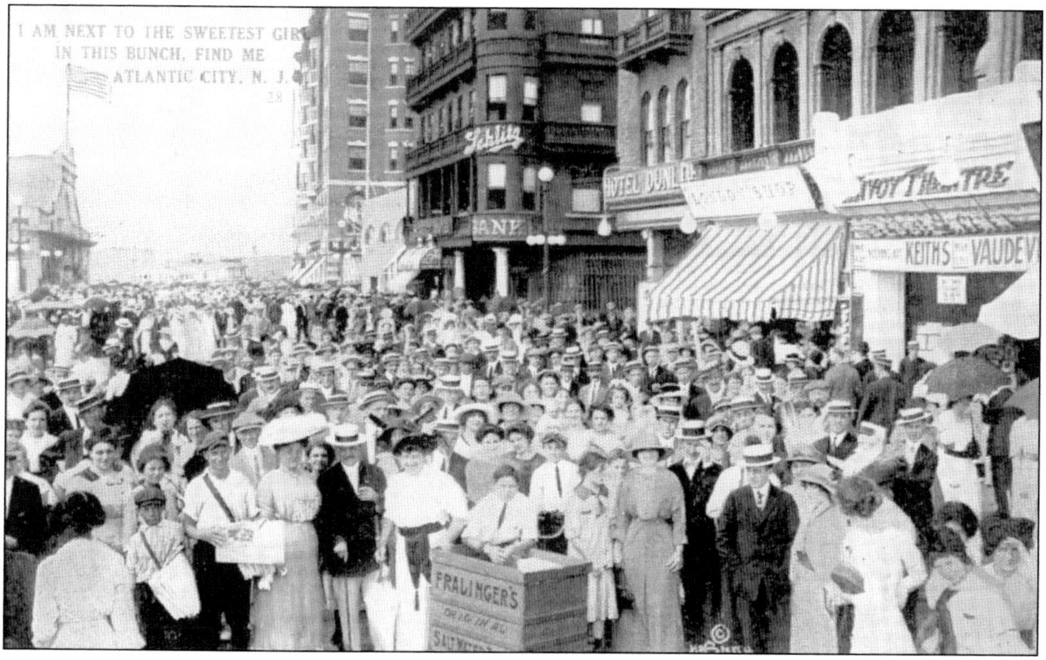

NEXT TO THE SWEETEST GIRL. A summer crowd stretches far into the distance. A vender in the center of the boardwalk sells Fralinger's salt-water taffy. To the right is the Savoy Theater, which is advertising the appearance of B. F. Keith's vaudeville acts. While down the block, on the corner of Ocean Avenue, sits the Schlitz Hotel and Boardwalk Bank. (Atlantic Postcard Company, *c.* 1912.)

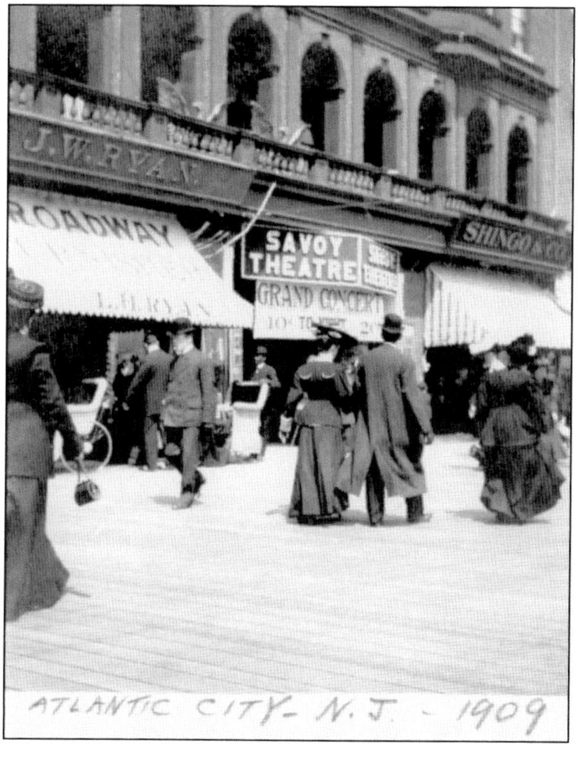

SAVOY THEATRE. One of several theaters located on the boardwalk, the Savoy was found just north of Ocean Avenue. Originally a legitimate stage theater when it opened in 1903, it was converted into a movie house in 1917. Having a seating capacity of 1,500, it had the distinction of being the first boardwalk theater to have two balconies. (Publisher unknown, 1909.)

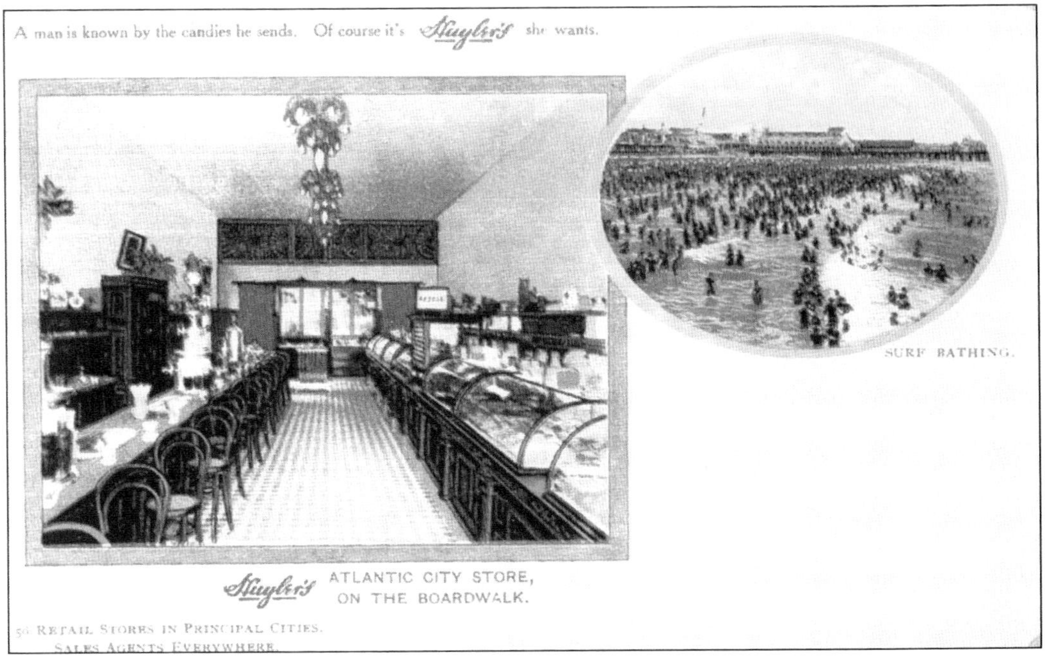

HUYLER'S CANDY. Started in 1874 by John S. Huyler in New York City, this company went on to become a leading brand of candy by 1923. Here is the interior of its boardwalk store at Pennsylvania Avenue near Haddon Hall. It not only sold candy that was "A Token of Good Taste," but also ice cream. The family business was bought out in 1926. (Publisher unknown, *c.* 1908.)

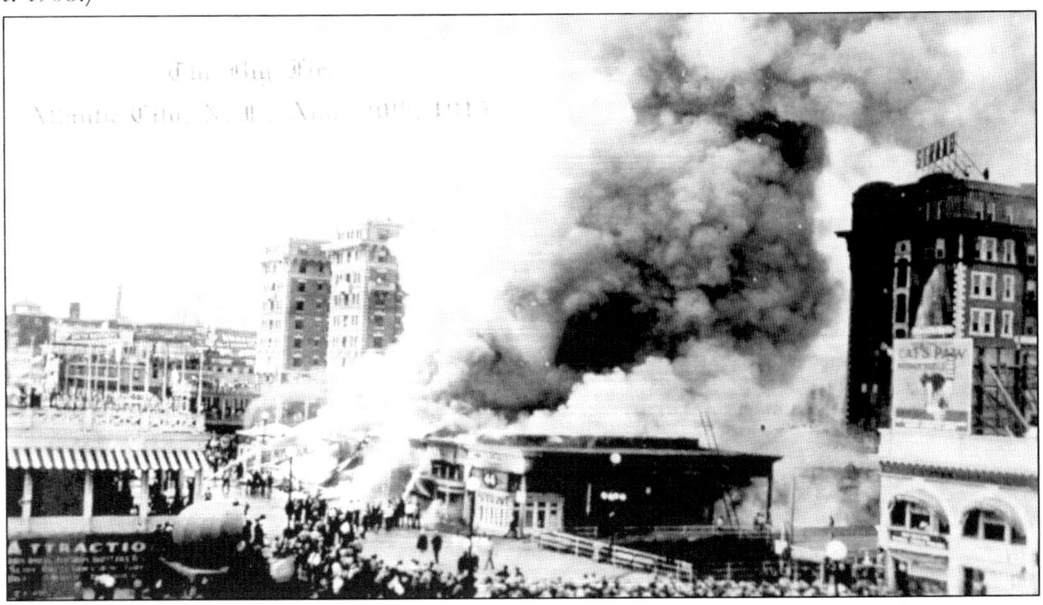

THE BIG FIRE. Numerous fires have consumed portions of the boardwalk and amusement piers over the years. August 20, 1915, saw a large fire strike near Pennsylvania Avenue. Twelve businesses, including Huyler's candy store and an art studio, were burned. Nearby Steeplechase Pier and the Strand Hotel were only slightly damaged in the conflagration. (Hubin's Big Post Card Store, 1915.)

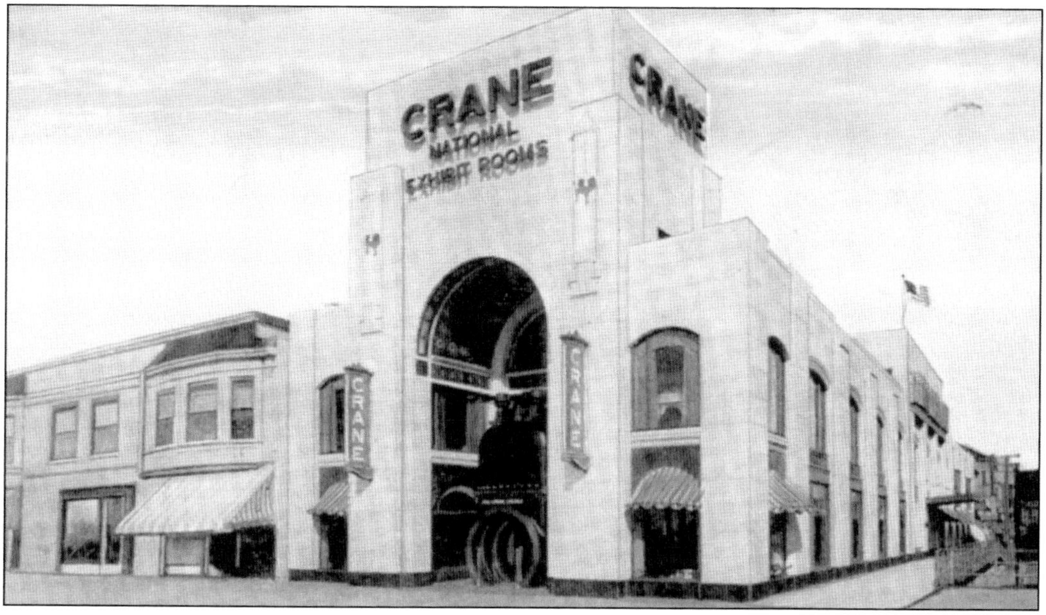

CRANE NATIONAL EXHIBIT. Starting in the 1920s, the Crane Company displayed its products in what it called its National Exhibit Rooms. These were located at Pennsylvania Avenue. Visitors were invited to view elaborate displays of the company's heating equipment and plumbing fixtures in modern bathroom settings. It advertised that this was all done in "unmistakable good taste." By 1925 the Crane Company moved to a site near Georgia Avenue. (E. C. Kropp, *c.* 1923.)

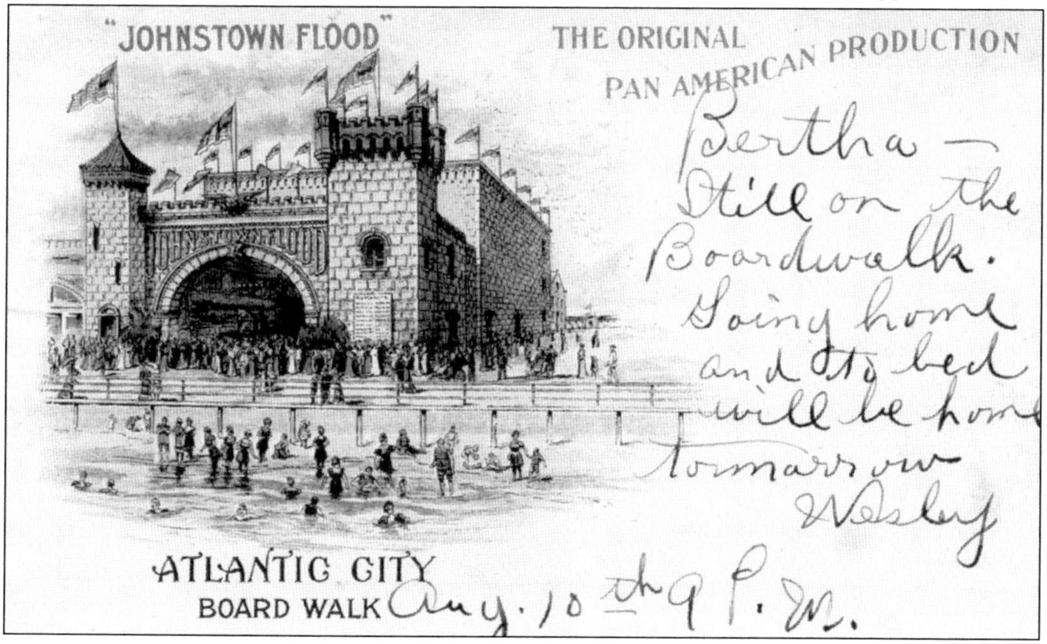

JOHNSTOWN FLOOD. Located across from the entrance to Steel Pier was the unique Johnstown Flood exhibit. Customers experienced a cyclorama display that graphically re-created the devastation of the famous Pennsylvania flood of May 31, 1889. To add to the realism, live actors played the role of victims of the tragedy. Seen earlier at the Pan American Exposition of 1901, this display was duplicated here and at Coney Island. (Publisher unknown, *c.* 1904.)

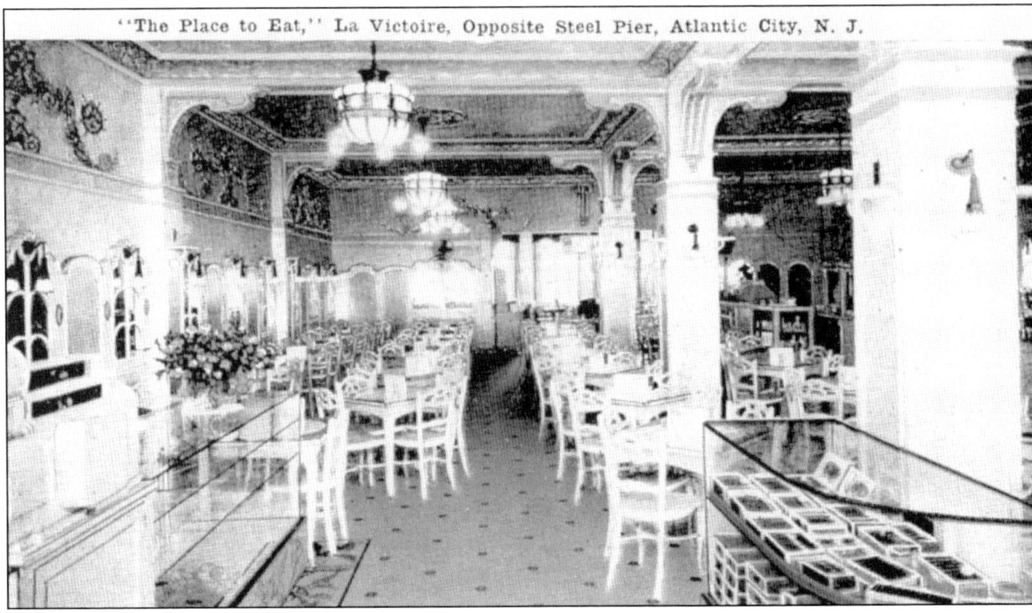

LA VICTOIRE RESTAURANT. During the late 1920s, the La Victoire Restaurant was situated opposite Steel Pier at 1003 Boardwalk. The owner, Harry L. Katz, offered a special blue-plate platter with a variety of seafood items along with a half lobster for $1.50. Such low prices helped to make this a popular eating establishment. Late-dining patrons were entertained with music performed by Warner MacFarlane's La Victoire Melody Maids. (E. C. Kropp, *c.* 1926.)

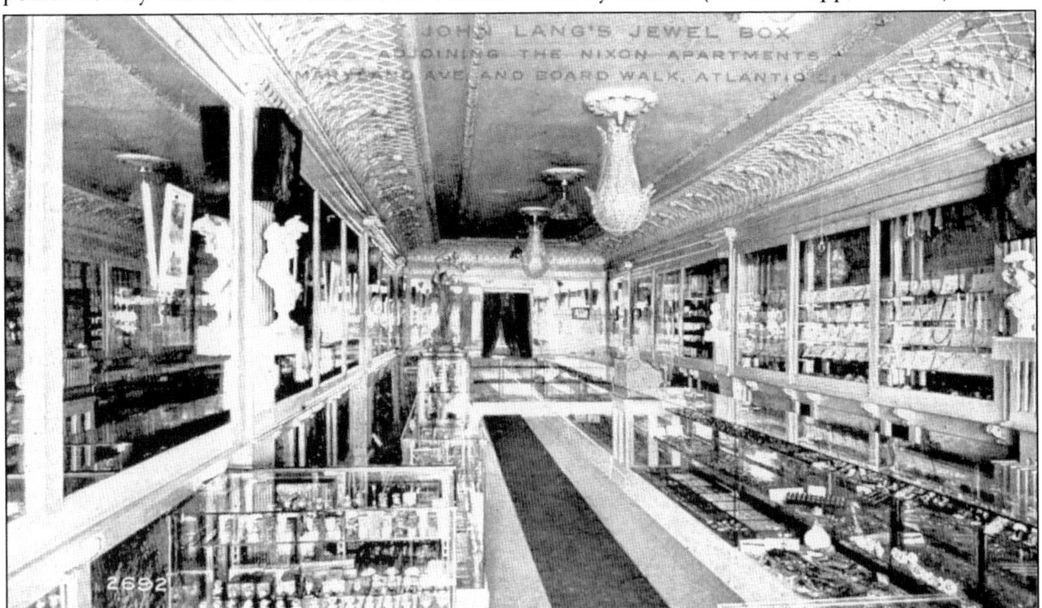

LANG'S JEWEL BOX. It was said that just about anything and everything could be purchased on the boardwalk. From the cheapest of trinkets and souvenirs to very expensive luxury items, all could be found in the stores that lined the wooden walkway. Shown here is the lavish interior of one of the more elegant emporiums, John Lang's Jewel Box, which was located at Maryland Avenue. (Publisher unknown, *c.* 1910.)

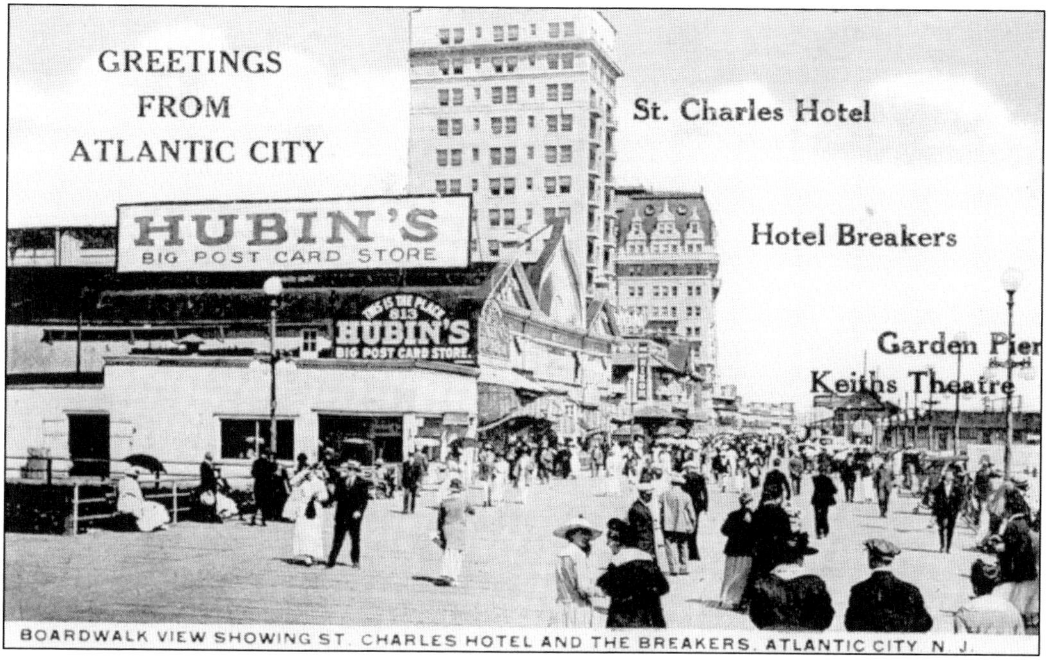

HUBIN'S. Perhaps the largest retailer of postcards on the boardwalk was Hubin's Big Post Card Store, located just above States Avenue. Dating back to at least 1907, the store not only sold postcards but published some of its own views as well. It remained in business at this site until around 1921. Nearby are the St. Charles and Breakers Hotels. (Sithens Post Card Company, *c.* 1918.)

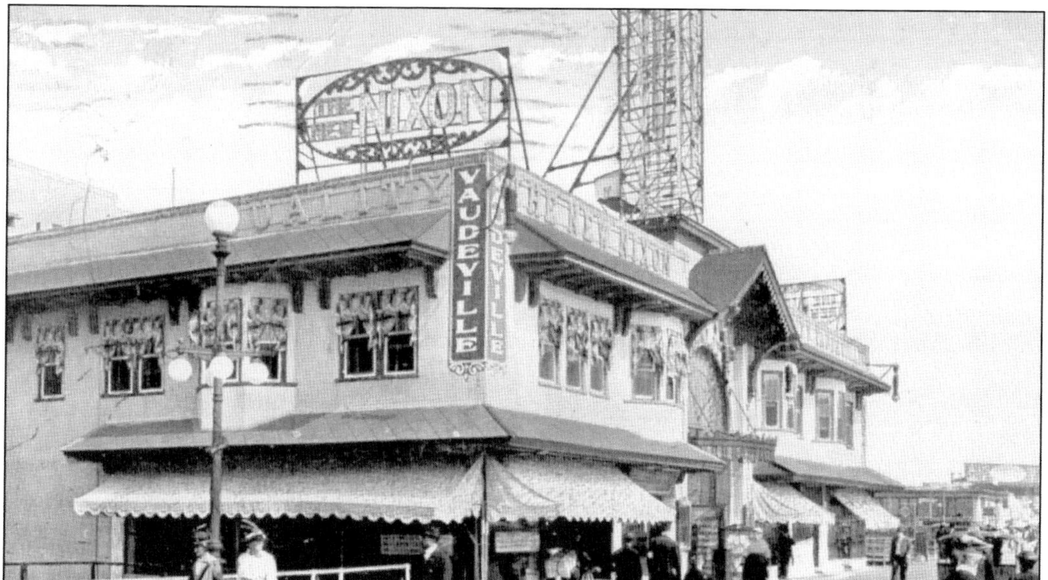

NEW NIXON THEATRE. At the corner of Delaware Avenue stood the New Nixon Theatre. To compete with the other theatrical houses in the city, this theater offered the public a wide range of entertainment. Vaudeville, musical and Broadway revues, movies, and Sunday concerts brought in customers over the years. (Publisher unknown, *c.* 1918.)

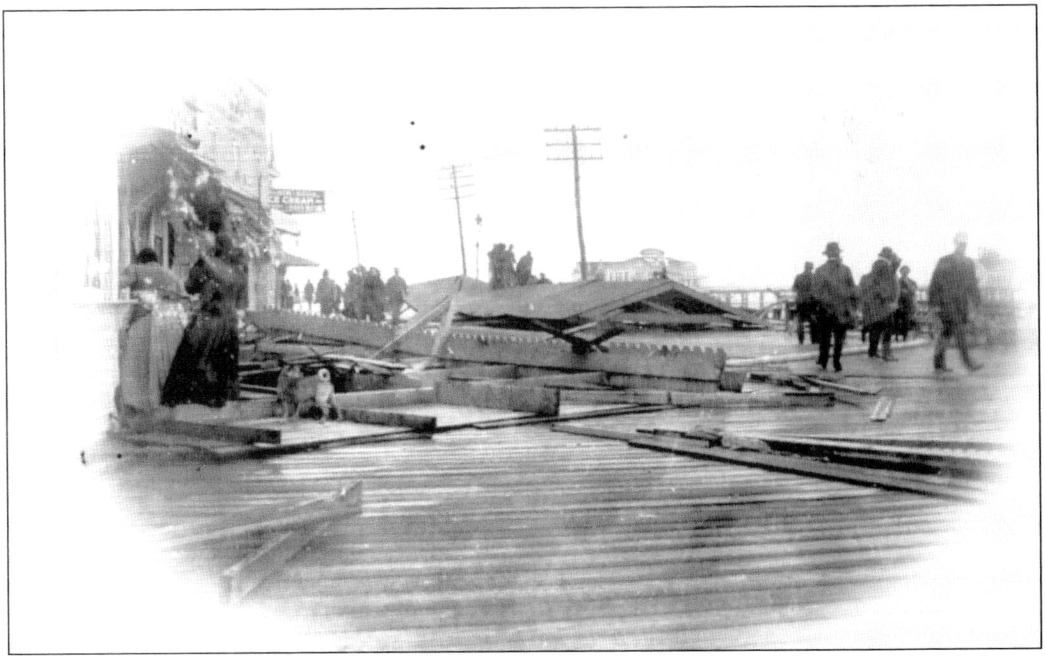

STORM DAMAGE. Not only has fire been a threat to the boardwalk but nature's storms were also. Here damage from the "vagabond" hurricane of 1903 is visible between Connecticut and Massachusetts Avenues. The storm with 75-mile-per-hour winds struck on September 16. A number of boardwalk businesses, as well as some hotels, reported damages. Tens of thousands of people later came to see the destruction, which early reports had highly exaggerated. (Publisher unknown, 1903.)

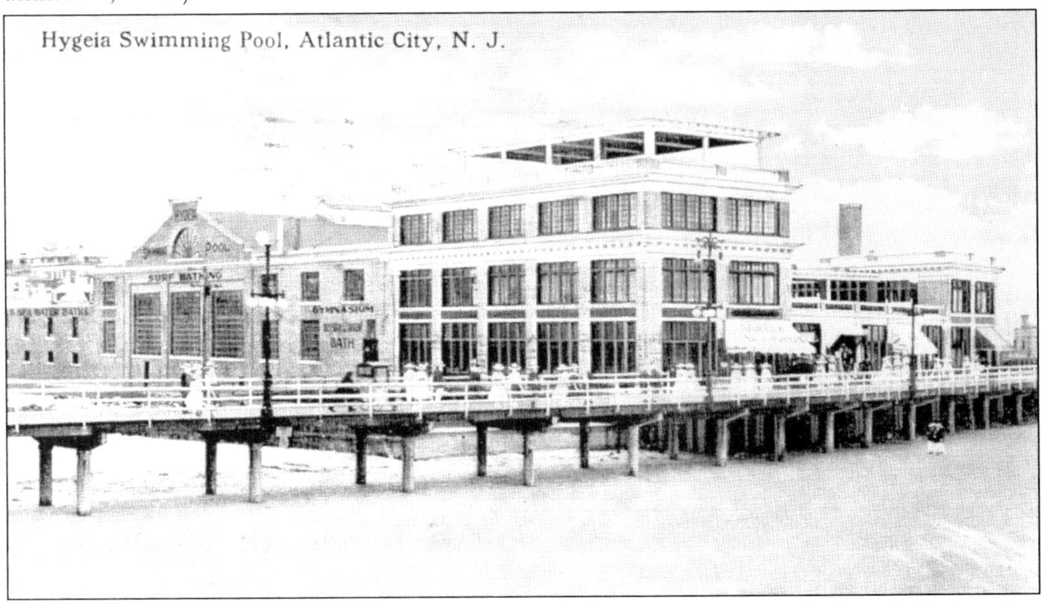

HYGEIA POOL. A very popular site on the boardwalk for many years was the Hygeia Swimming Pool. The indoor pool facility advertised that it was open 24 hours a day and provided both hot and cold waters in which to swim. Built in 1910 at Rhode Island Avenue and the boardwalk, it was eventually demolished in 1947. (Post Card Distribution Company, *c.* 1918.)

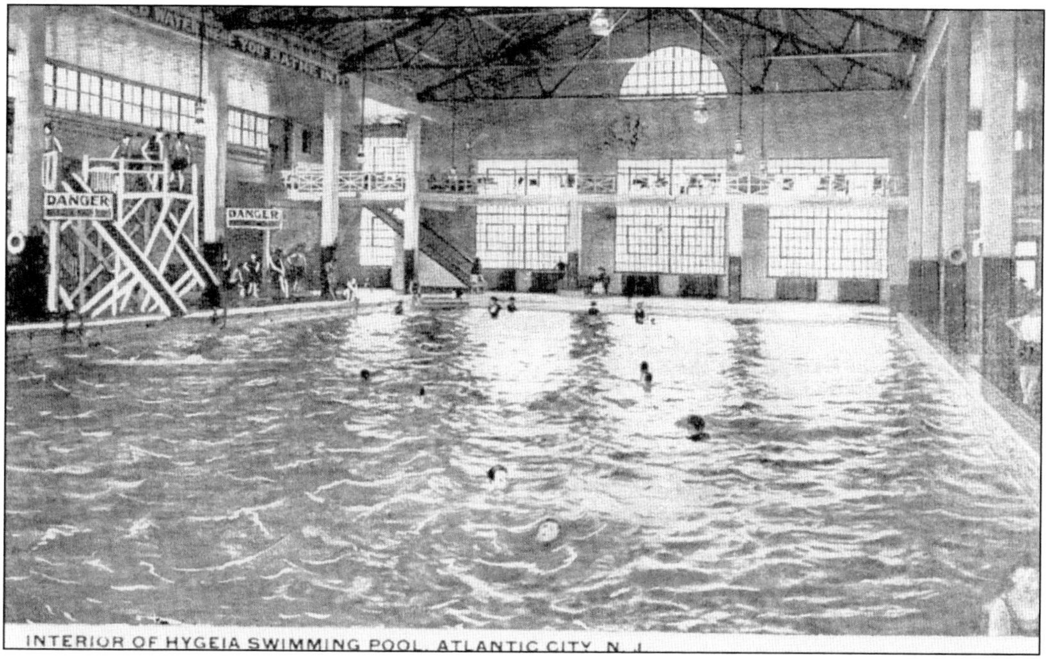

INTERIOR OF HYGEIA POOL. The large indoor pool at the Hygeia provided people an alternative to ocean bathing. Here patrons could even receive swimming instruction if they desired. The Hygeia was also known for its sponsorship of swimming teams that competed nationally. In 1927, it sponsored a local 15-mile open ocean swimming event. (Sithens, *c.* 1920.)

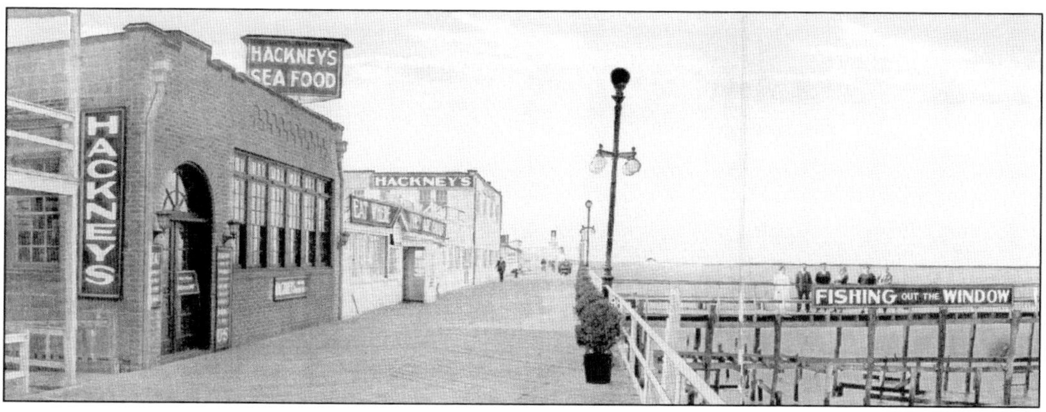

HACKNEY'S. Near the inlet end of the boardwalk once stood an Atlantic City landmark known as Hackney's Seafood Restaurant. Starting with a small lunch wagon in 1912, Harry Hackney went on to build a restaurant that by 1929 could seat 3,200. Directly across from its boardwalk entrance was a fishing pier for those who wished to fish. The restaurant, whose slogan was "Eat Them Where They're Caught," was destroyed by fire in 1963. (E. C. Kropp, *c.* 1925.)

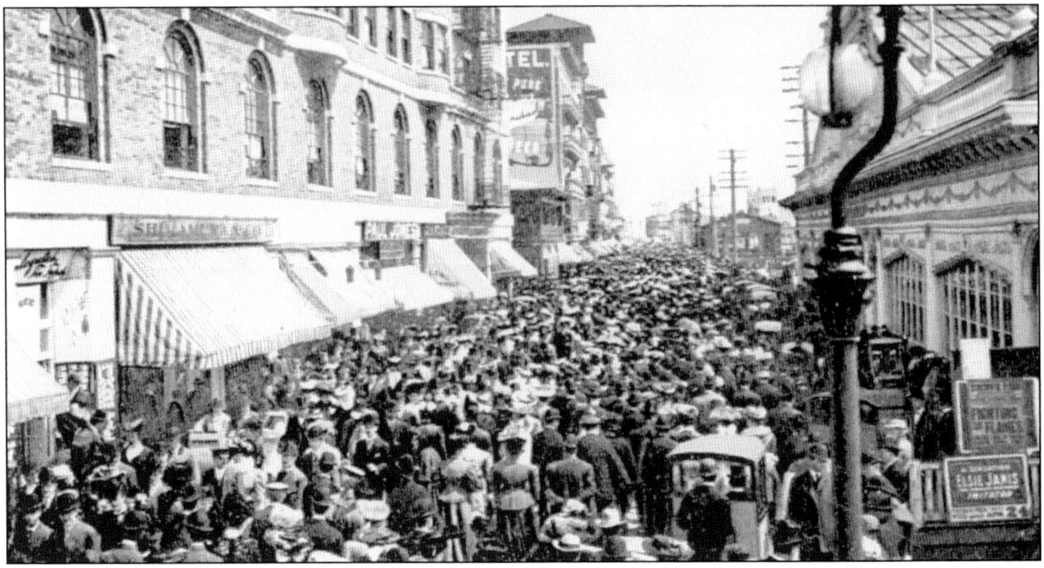

EASTER PARADE. The tradition of the annual boardwalk Easter parade began on April 16, 1876. It was a way of attracting large crowds to the resort prior to the official summer season. And draw large crowds it did. Hundreds of thousands of people, wearing their finest fashions, could be found packed tightly together, walking the boards on Easter Sunday. (Detroit Publishing, 1905.)

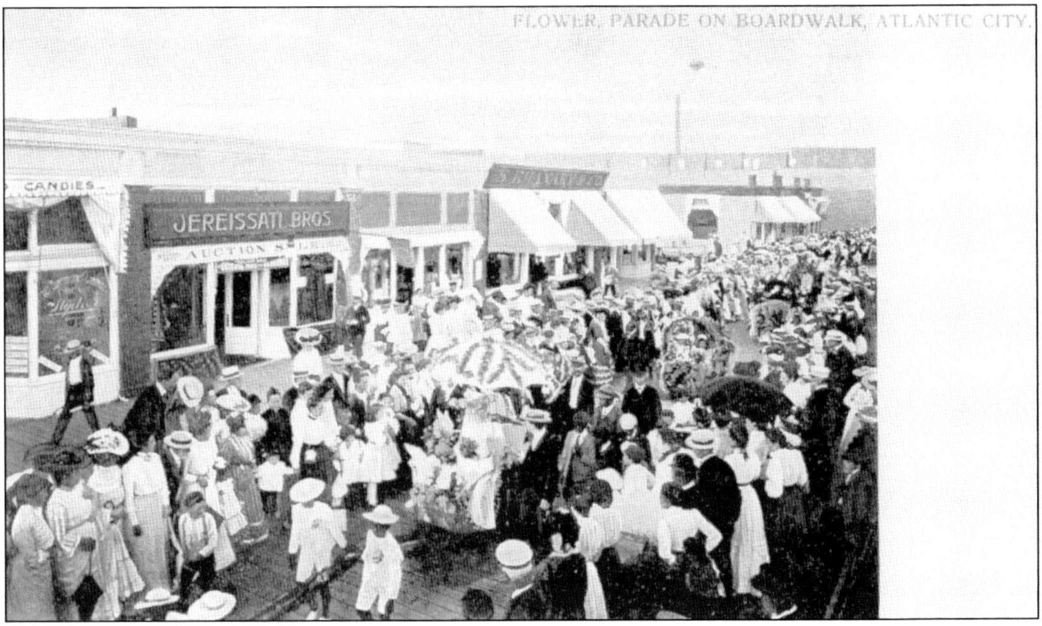

FLOWER PARADE. Another parade was the floral parade, where contestants traveled down the boardwalk in rolling chairs festively embellished with flowers. This tradition, which began on August 1, 1902, eventually led to the Miss America Pageant that started in 1921. Winners of the floral parade were judged on the attractiveness of the decorated chair and not its occupant. (Philadelphia Postal Card Company, *c.* 1904.)

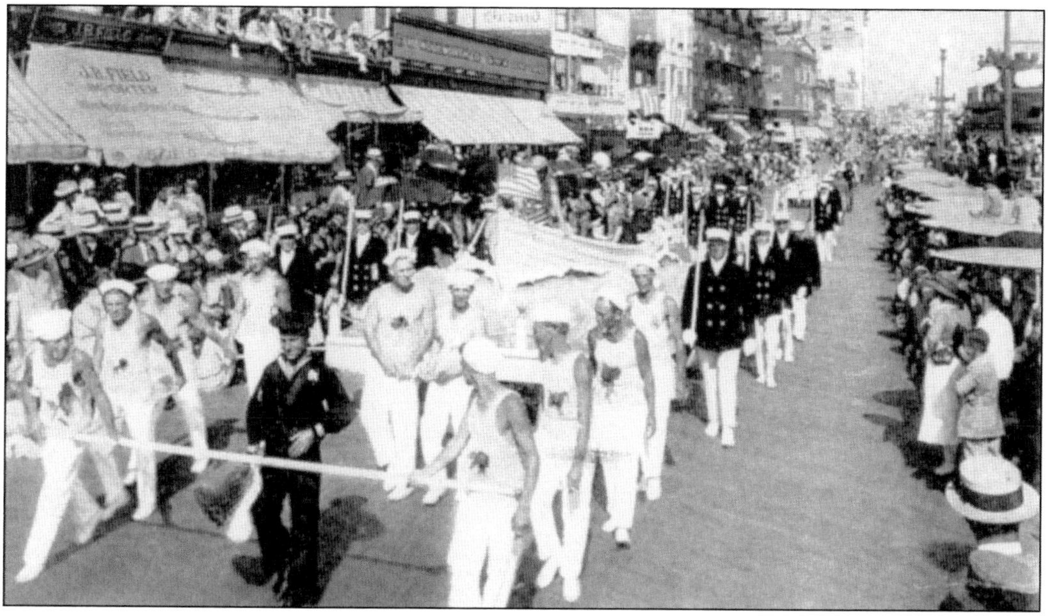

LIFE GUARDS ON PARADE. Crowds lining both sides of the boardwalk look on as members of the Atlantic City Beach Patrol proudly march by. This postcard image is probably from one of the annual Miss America Pageant parades, which were held as part of the weeklong festivities for that renowned event. (I. Robbins and Sons, *c.* 1923.)

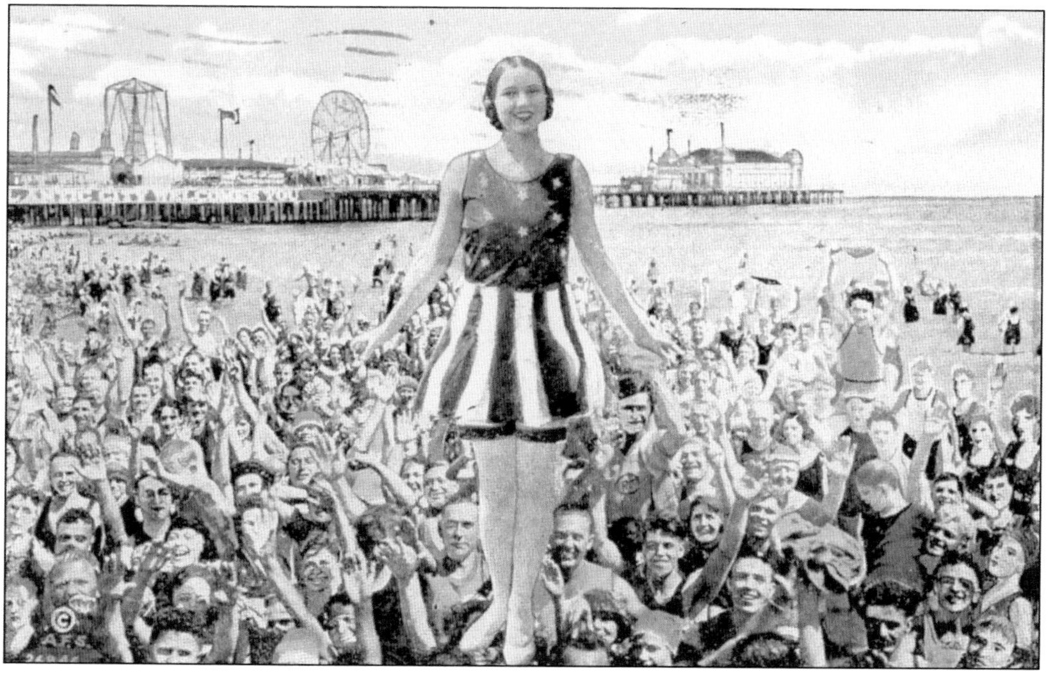

MISS AMERICA. In 1921, Atlantic City hosted what was called the Inter-City Beauty Contest, featuring eight contestants. This post Labor Day event evolved into the Miss America Pageant, the nation's most famous beauty contest. During the early years, the ceremonies were held on the various amusement piers before moving to the convention hall in 1940. Seen here is Miss America of 1926, Norma Smallwood from Tulsa, Oklahoma. (P. Sander, *c.* 1927.)

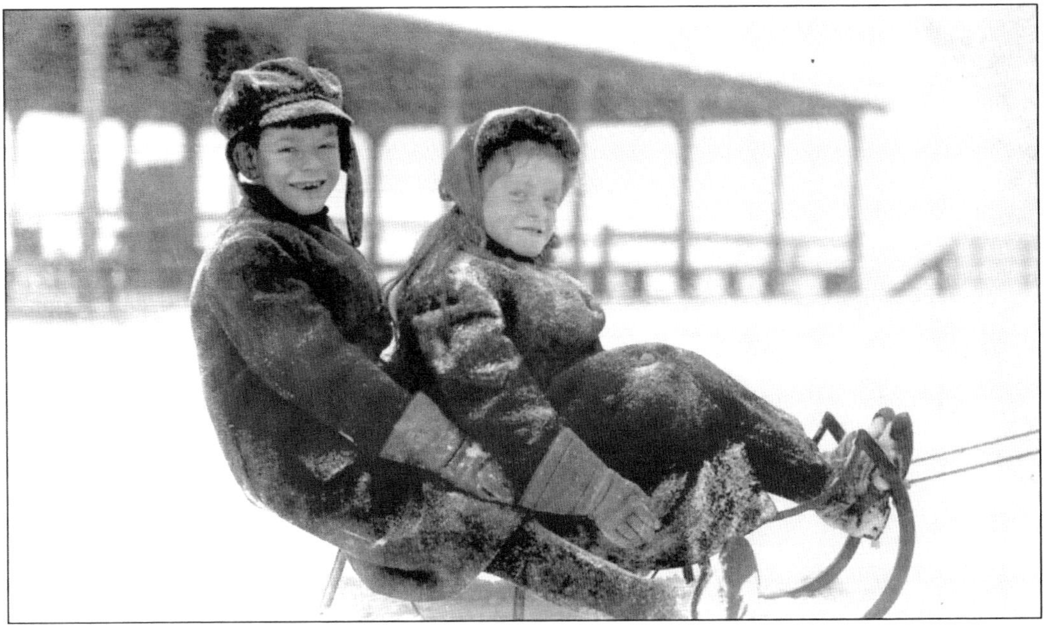

WINTER FUN. Most people would rarely associate the boardwalk with snow, but this form of winter precipitation does occasionally blanket the area. Two children, possibly brother and sister, seem to be enjoying such an event while being pulled along the snow-covered boardwalk in 1907. (Publisher unknown, 1907.)

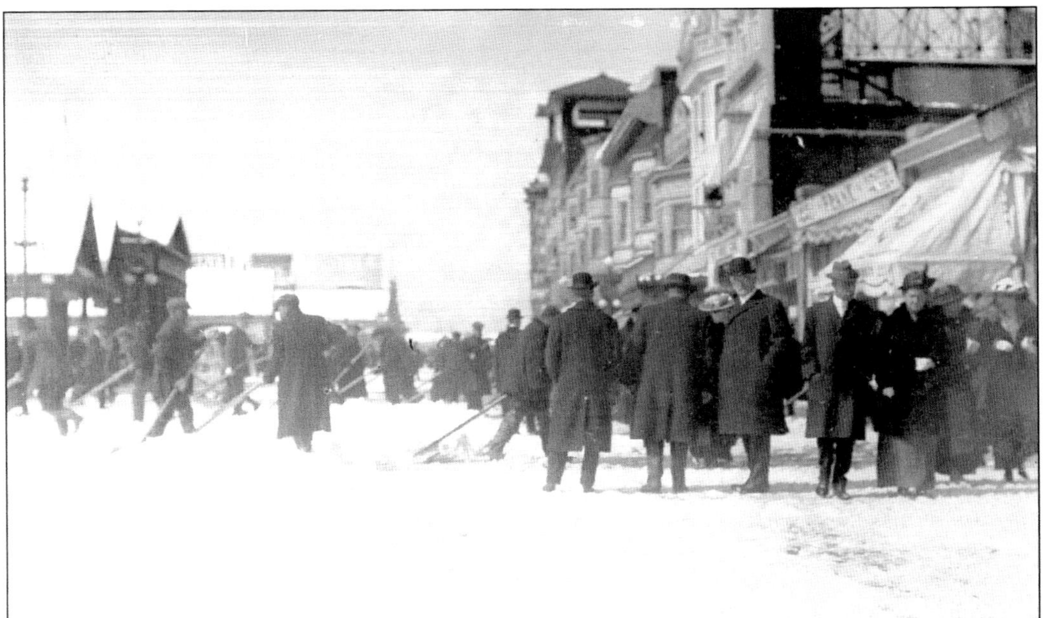

BOARDWALK SNOW. A major snowstorm hit the Atlantic City area on Saturday, April 3, 1915, dumping six inches of snow and larger amounts inland. Here workers shovel the snow from the boardwalk in preparation for the Easter parade to be held the next day. The local newspaper reported that the weather reduced the number of participants to about 100,000. (Albert Studio, 1915.)

Four

The Great Amusement Piers

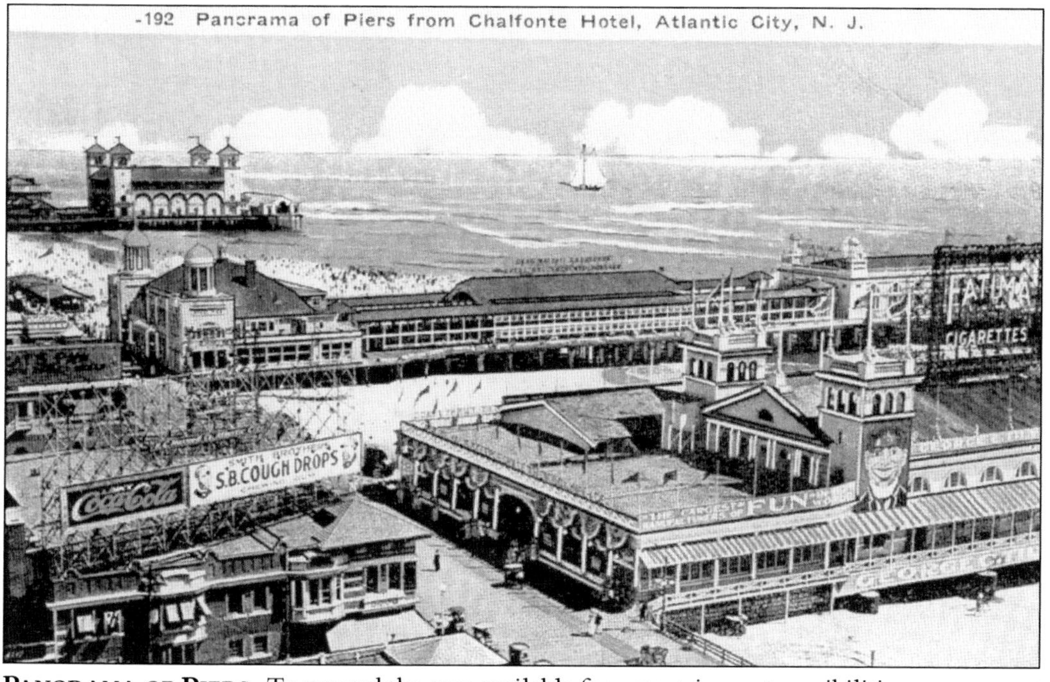

Panorama of Piers. To expand the area available for entertainment possibilities, amusement piers were built extending out from the boardwalk into the ocean. The first pier was constructed as early as 1881, and by 1907 there were "five great ocean piers—in all the world the greatest piers devoted exclusively to recreation." By 1913 a sixth pier would be added to this list. (Sander, *c.* 1916.)

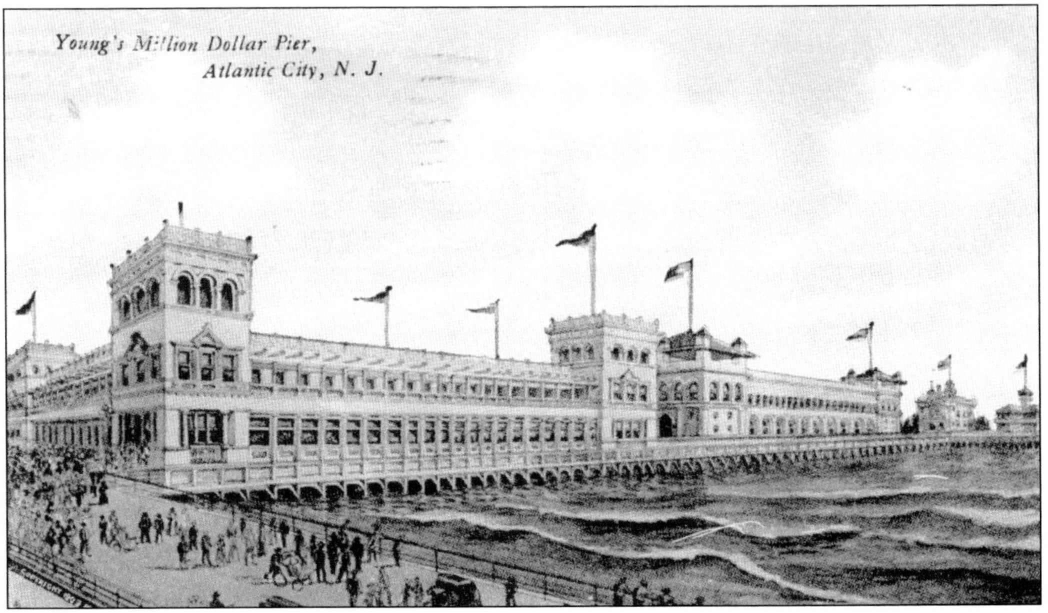

YOUNG'S MILLION DOLLAR PIER. On July 26, 1906, Capt. John L. Young opened a pier at Arkansas Avenue. Claiming the project cost $1 million, he named it accordingly. The 1,600-foot-long pier boasted of having the world's largest ballroom as well as a hippodrome, skating rink, exhibit hall, and even an aquarium. It soon became one of the most popular spots on the boardwalk. (Taylor Art Company, *c.* 1910.)

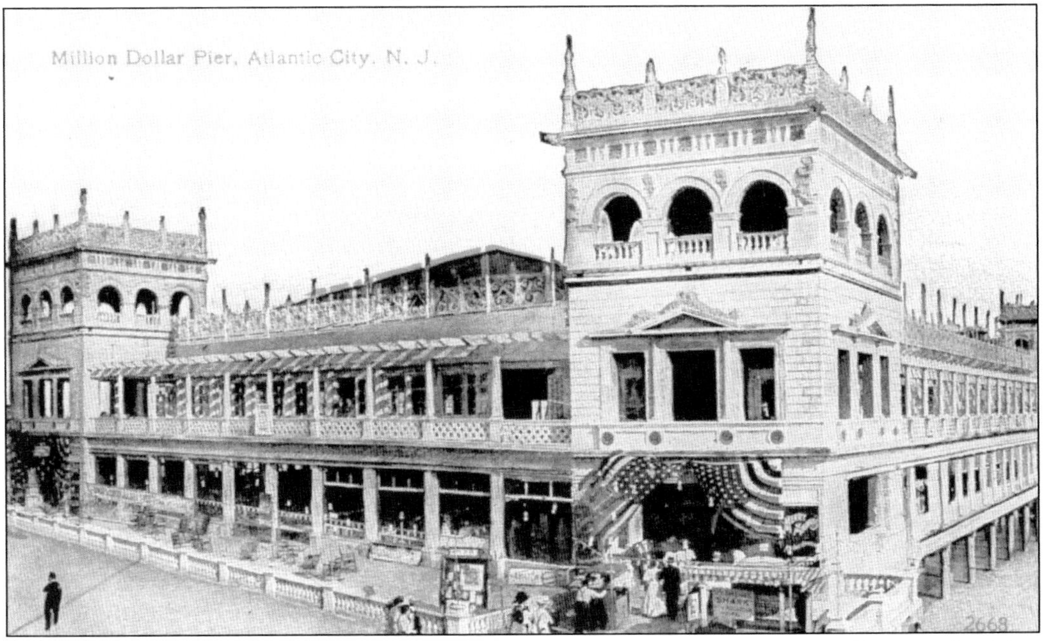

MILLION DOLLAR PIER. People walk through a flag-draped entrance to Million Dollar Pier. Once on the pier, a wide variety of entertainment choices were available. During the life of the pier, vaudeville acts, movies, exhibits, dance marathons, and much, much more would provide hours of enjoyment to its customers. Every summer people would return to see what new wonders were in store for them. (Post Card Distribution Company, *c.* 1914.)

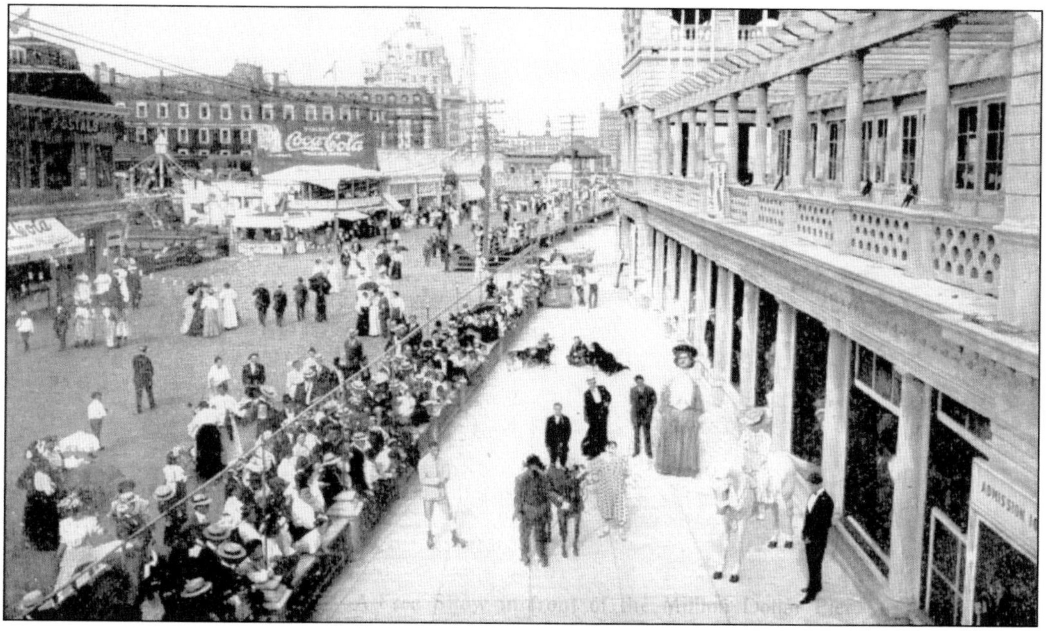

A Free Show. A small crowd gathers to watch a group of performers put on a free show in front of the Million Dollar Pier. Such ploys were used to help attract attention and hopefully entice people to pay the price of admission to the pier. (Publisher unknown, *c.* 1910.)

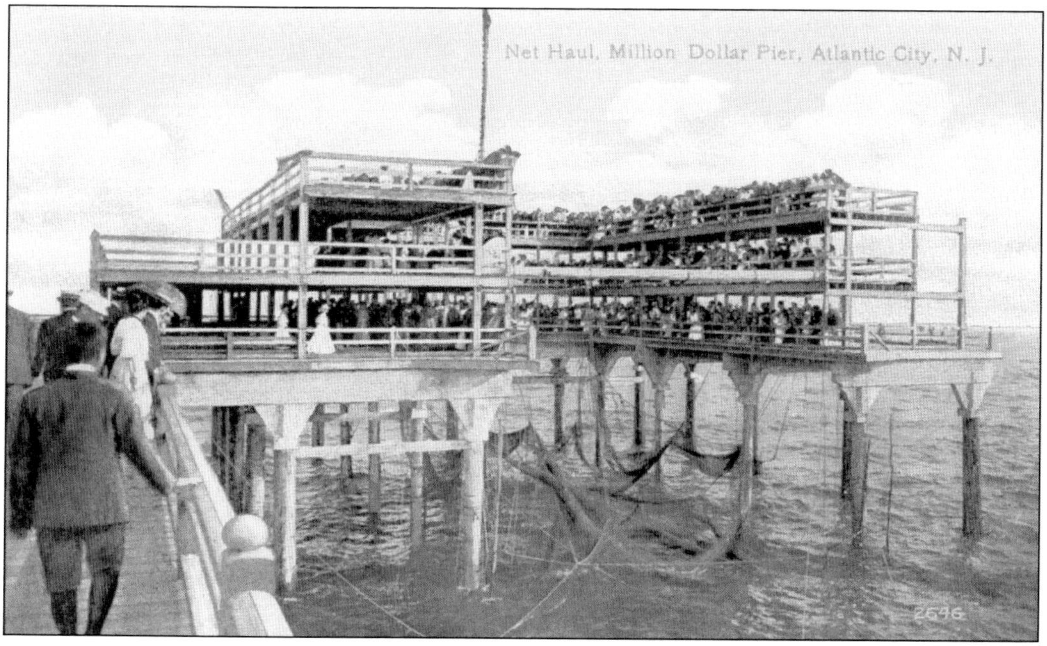

Net Haul. Having been such a great success on his original pier, Young moved his net haul operation over to his newer Million Dollar Pier in 1907. Twice a day the nets, containing all manner of marine life, would be lifted from the sea. Onlookers were amazed and delighted with what they witnessed. This fascinating demonstration would bring back patrons again and again. (Post Card Distribution Company, *c.* 1916.)

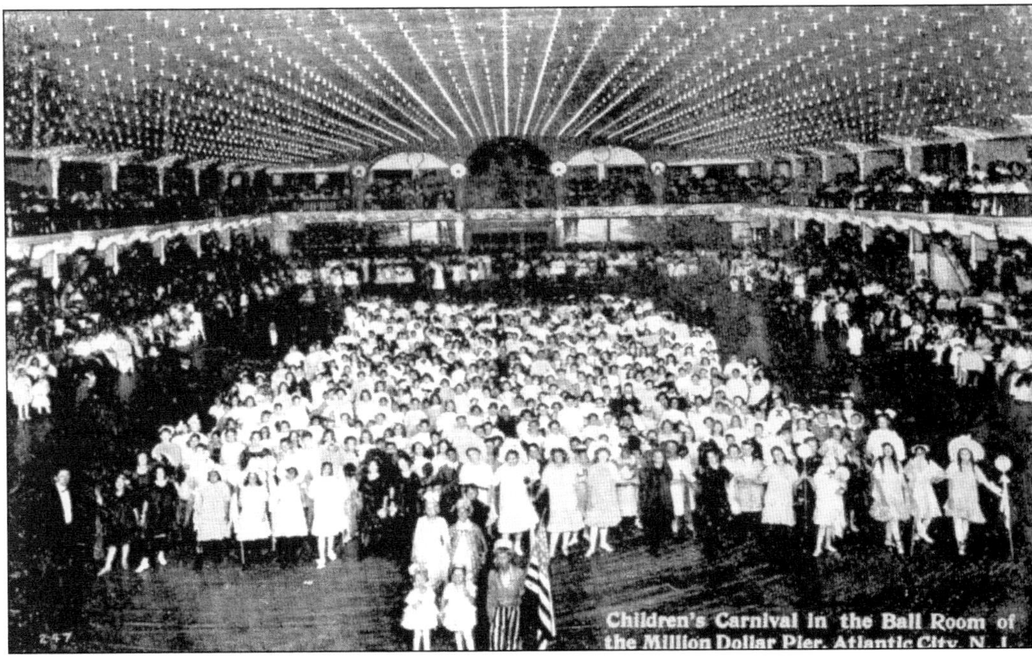

CHILDREN'S CARNIVAL. The amusement piers offered enticements for patrons both young and old. A major attraction that brought in large numbers of youngsters was the children's carnival, which took place in the spacious ballroom of the Million Dollar Pier. Every Monday, Wednesday, and Friday evening a grand march was held at 8:00. Each participating child received a "beautiful souvenir." (Chilton Company, *c.* 1910.)

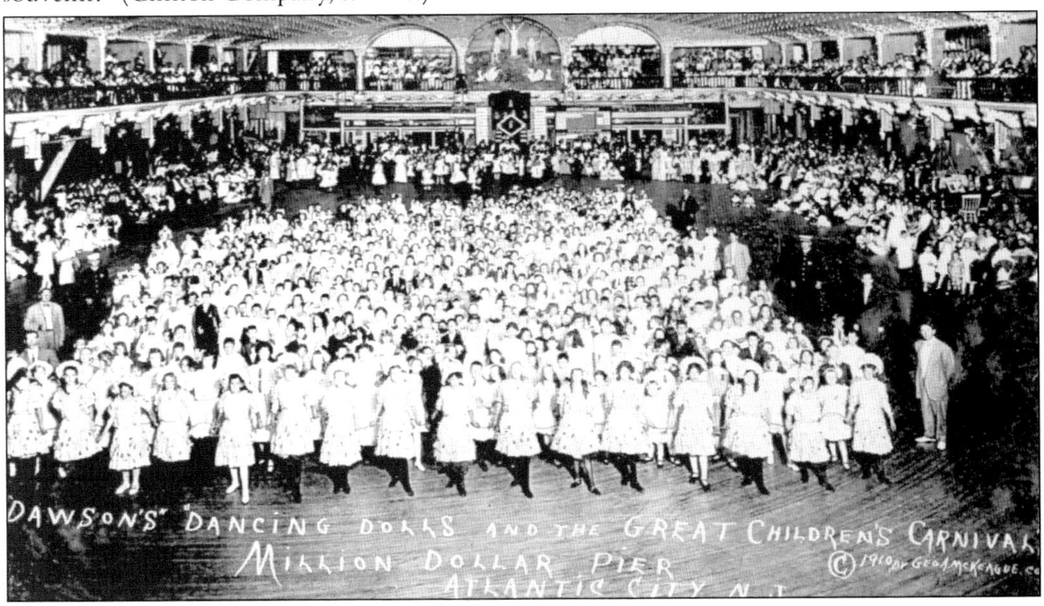

DAWSON'S DANCING DOLLS. Prof. Joseph Dawson, the dancing master at the pier, organized a group known as Dawson's Dancing Dolls. These 100 youngsters, dressed in gorgeous gowns, performed beautifully choreographed dance numbers for the audience. Here members of the Dancing Dolls pose with other children who participated in the "Great Children's Carnival." (George A. McKeague, 1910.)

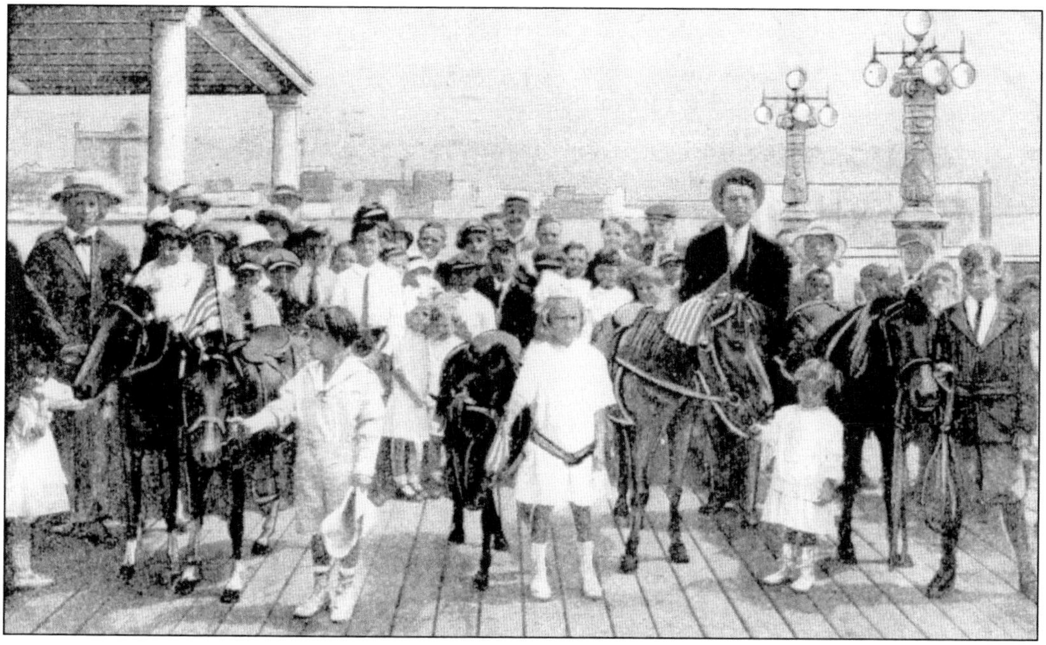

LUCKY CHILDREN. Five lucky children are presented with ponies on the Million Dollar Pier. These happy youngsters were probably winners of a promotional contest of some sort. Pier owners were always coming up with new and different ideas to draw in customers. (Publisher unknown, *c.* 1915.)

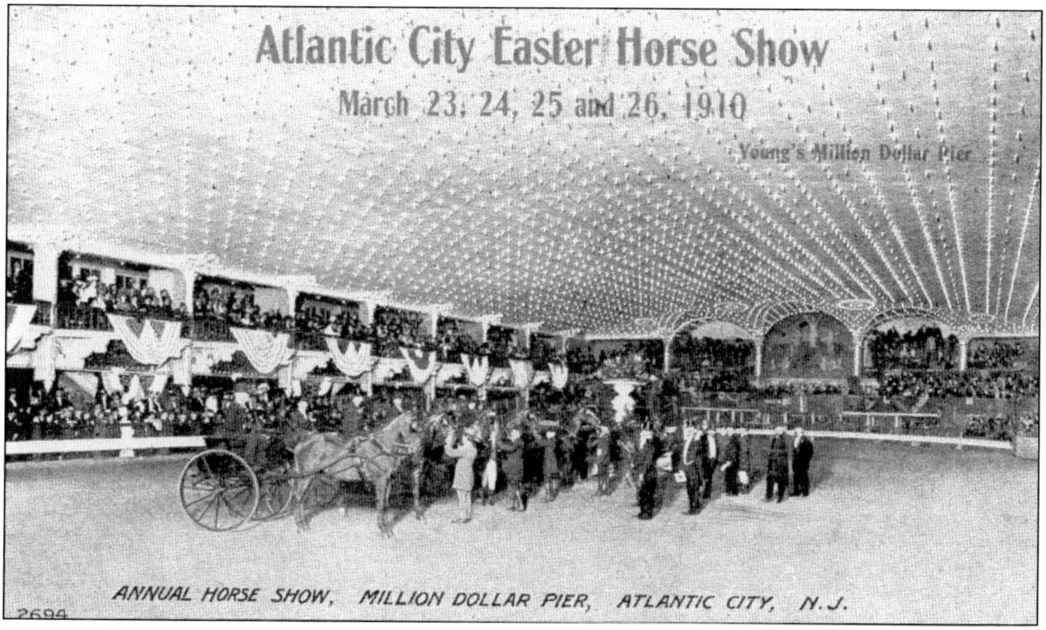

EASTER HORSE SHOW. One of the more unusual attractions to be held on the pier, for several years, was the annual Atlantic City Horse Show. The horse show featured numerous equestrian events and displays that were judged over a four-day period. This competition drew leading horse owners and aficionados from many states. (Publisher unknown, 1910.)

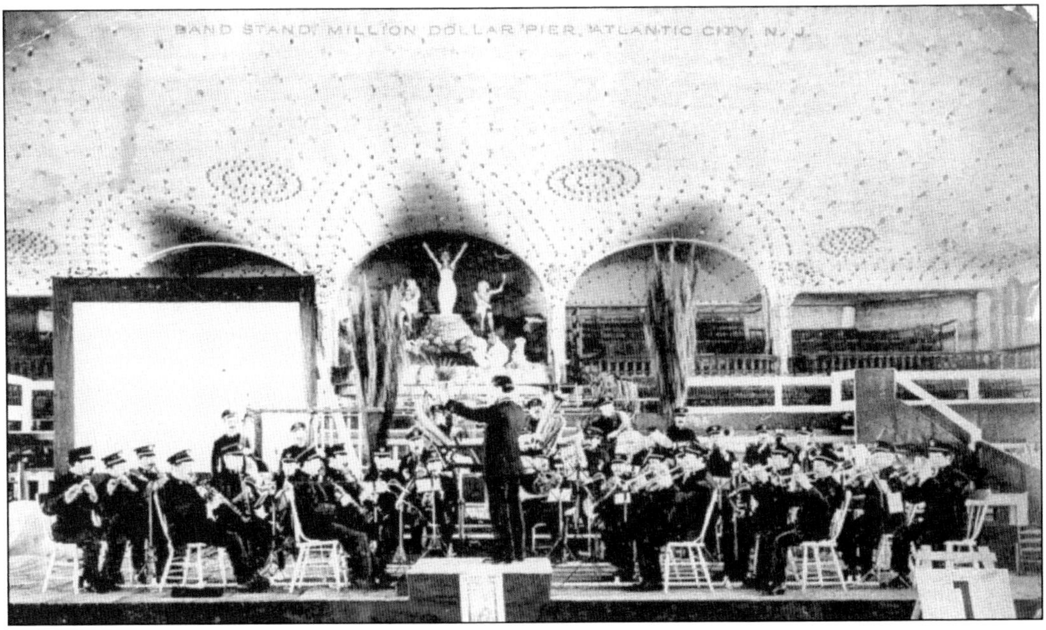

BANDSTAND. A conductor raises his baton to lead an unidentified band in a concert in the Million Dollar Pier's ballroom. Musical performances were an integral part of the entertainment scene on the boardwalk for decades. Numerous bands, including the Royal Philippine Band, performed here at the Million Dollar Pier over the years. (Post Card Distribution Company, *c.* 1912.)

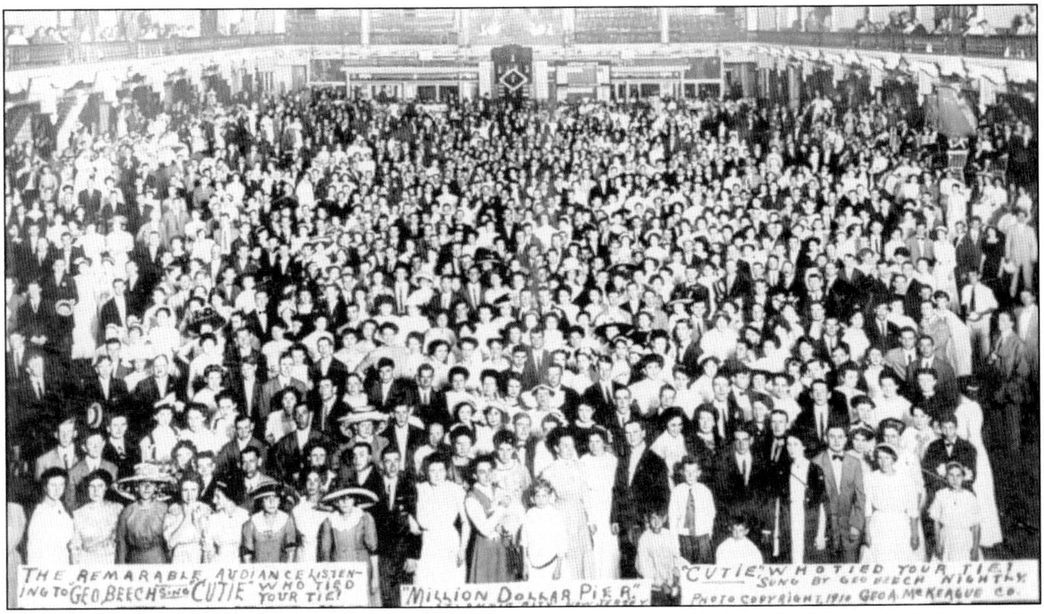

A REMARKABLE AUDIENCE. Live entertainment was provided both day and night on the Million Dollar Pier. This postcard shows an enormous audience gathered to hear singer George Beech sing "Cutie Who Tied Your Tie?" during the summer of 1910. Beech performed his act nightly for admiring crowds. (George A. McKeague, 1910.)

PHILIPPINE CONSTABULARY BAND. On May 2, 1909, the Philippine Constabulary Band received a contract from Captain Young to perform on his pier. Composed of native Filipinos, this musical group was conducted by an African American named Walter Loving. The band had been created with help from Nellie Taft, the wife of Pres. William Howard Taft, when he had been governor-general of the Philippines. (Albert Studios, 1909.)

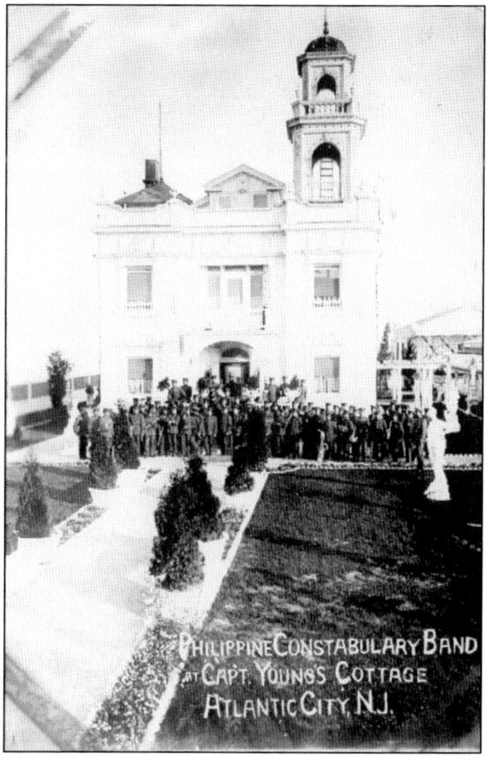

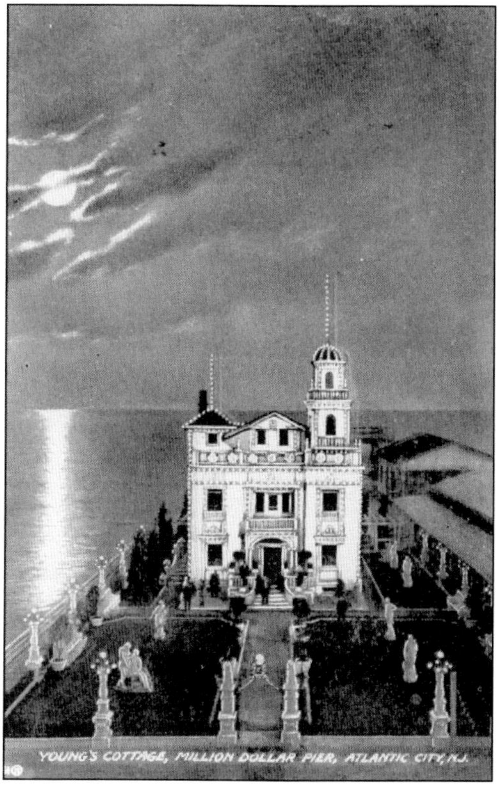

CAPTAIN YOUNG'S RESIDENCE. In 1908, Capt. John L. Young built a luxurious home for himself at the end of the pier. His miniature mansion cost him $70,000 to construct. An Italian-style garden with numerous marble statues, referred to as the "Garden of Eden," sat in front of the home. The exterior of the building was illuminated at night by over 3,000 electric bulbs, a system designed by his friend Thomas Edison. (Publisher unknown, *c.* 1914.)

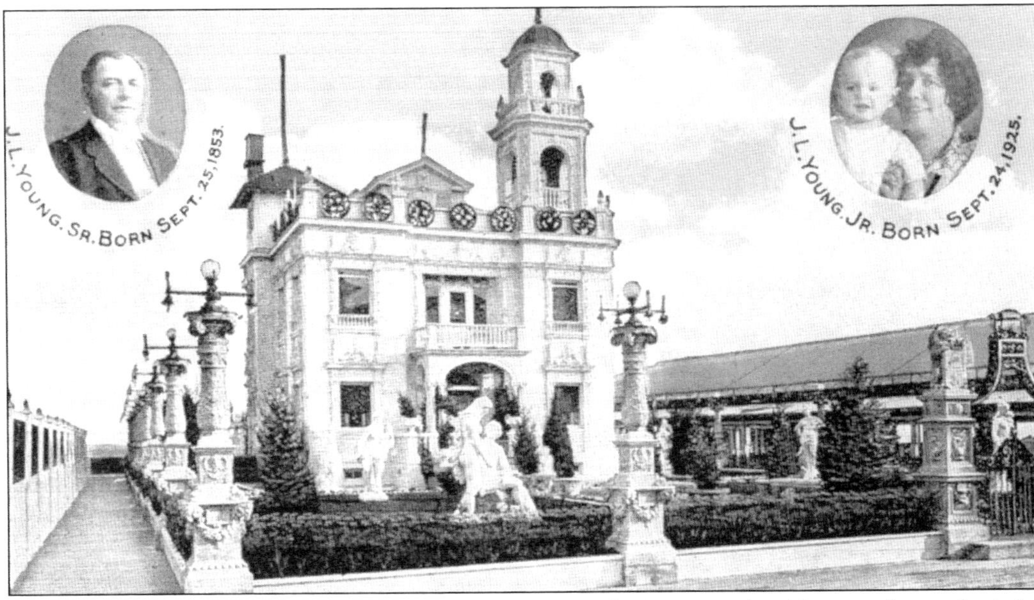

Captain Young's Cottage. Referred to as Young's Cottage, the 12-room home had the postal address 1 Atlantic Ocean. It was filled with many extravagant and ornate decorations, including a $10,000 chandelier that once graced the royal palace in Vienna, Austria. This very unique and magnificent residence was eventually torn down in March 1953. Shown on the postcard are images of Capt. John L. Young, his wife, and his young son. (Sander, *c.* 1926.)

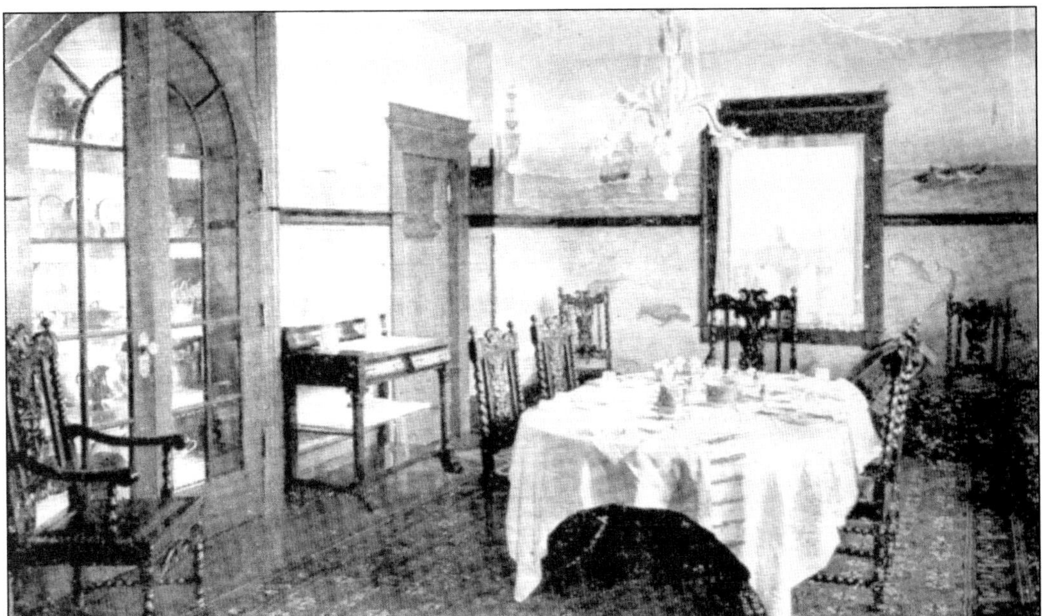

Captain Young's Dining Room. One of the mansion's 12 rooms was this lavish dining room. The walls were decorated with murals depicting sailing vessels and below that images of marine life. A fancy chandelier hung over the elaborately set table where the captain hosted a dinner in 1911 for Pres. William Howard Taft. The menu for that affair included fresh fish caught off Million Dollar Pier. (Taylor Art Company, 1909.)

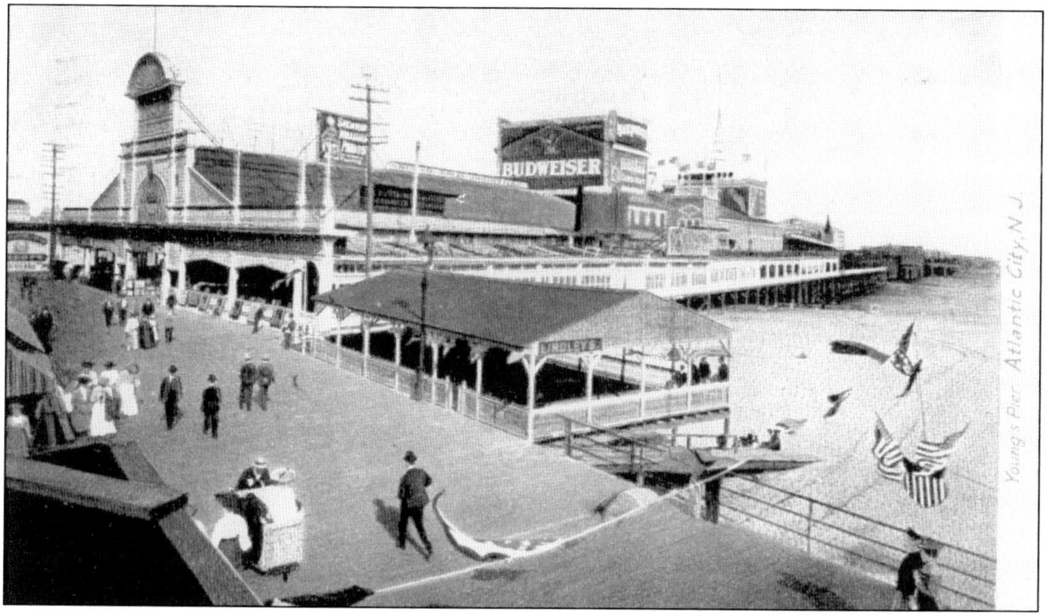

YOUNG'S PIER. In 1891, Capt. John L. Young and his partner, Stewart McShay, purchased the old Applegate Pier at Tennessee Avenue for $56,000. It was lengthened to 2,000 feet and eventually renamed Young's Pier. The expansion allowed plenty of space to offer vaudeville and theatrical productions as well as other forms of amusement, including rides and midway games. Soon it was one of the leading attractions on the boardwalk. (Hugh C. Leighton, *c.* 1907.)

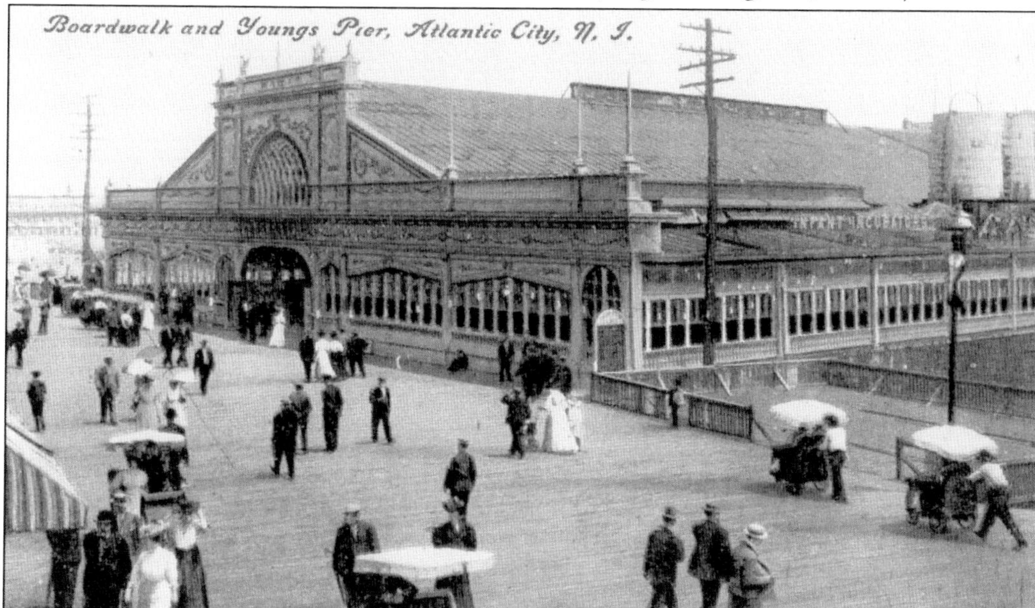

YOUNG'S OLD PIER. This view shows the entranceway onto Young's Pier. The playhouse on the pier was famous for its stage productions. Young was even able to get the famed French actress Sarah Bernhardt to come perform at his theater. After the opening of his newer Million Dollar Pier nearby, this pier became commonly referred to as "Young's Old Pier." (Illustrated Post Card Company, *c.* 1910.)

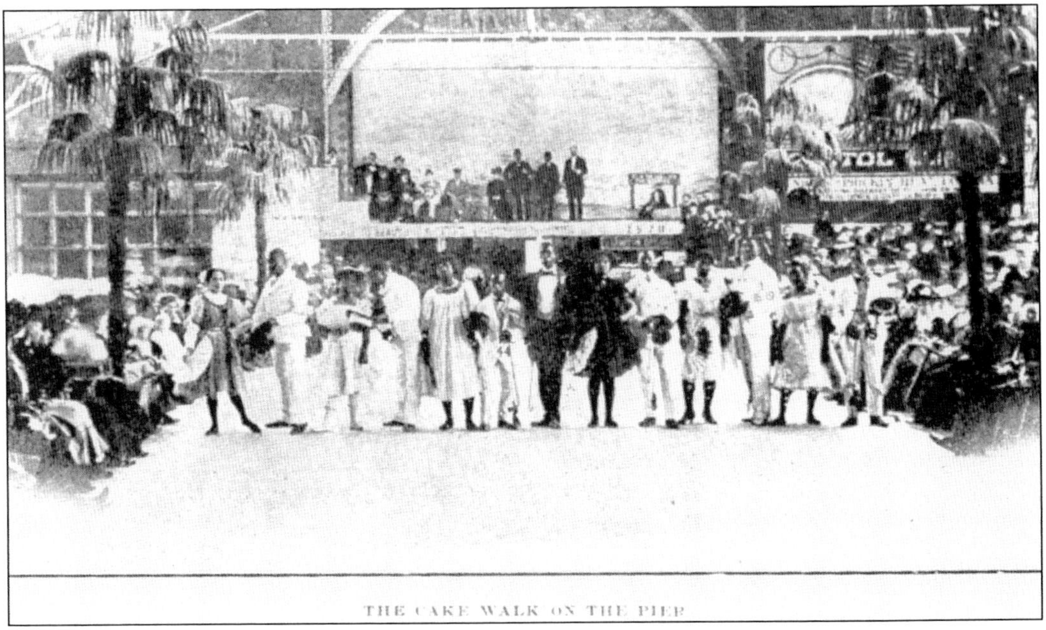

CAKEWALK ON THE PIER. Young's Pier became known as the "Home of the Cakewalk" when dancer Dora Johnson introduced the dance here on the boardwalk. Dora and her husband, Charles Johnson, were the most famous cakewalk performers of the day. This very popular dance of the era had its origins in slaves parodying the ballroom dances done by southern plantation owners in the 1860s. (Independent Photo-Card Company, *c.* 1902.)

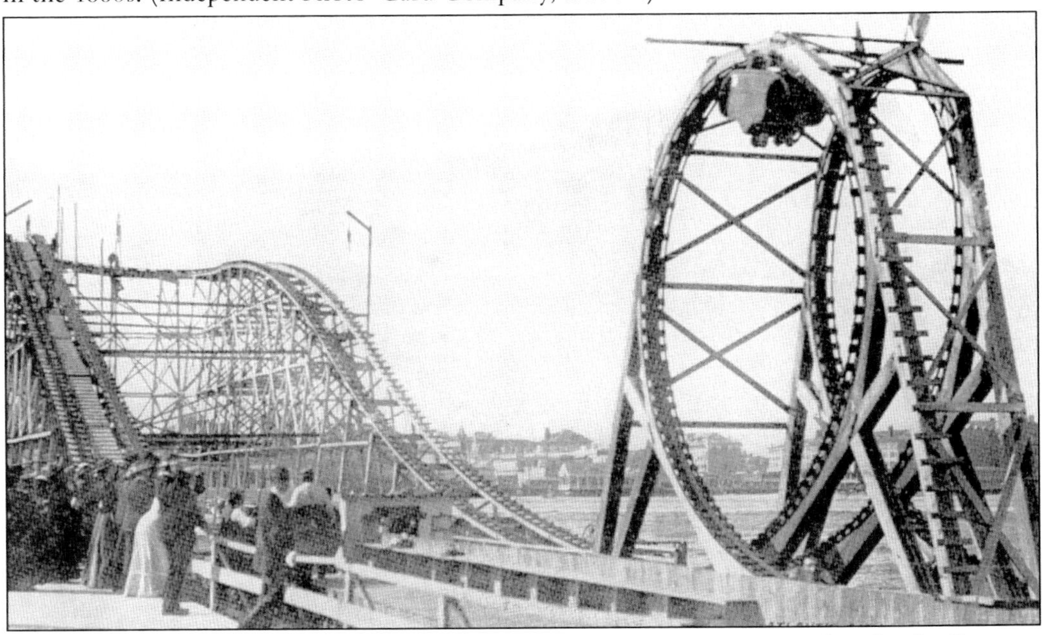

LOOP THE LOOP. Developed by Edward Prescott, the Loop the Loop or Flip Flap Railway on Young's Pier was one of the forerunners of today's roller coaster. Similar to the one at Coney Island, this thrill ride had a 25-foot-high teardrop-shaped loop around which the passengers traveled. It is said that the apparatus was eventually removed due to numerous complaints of back and neck injuries. (Publisher unknown, 1901.)

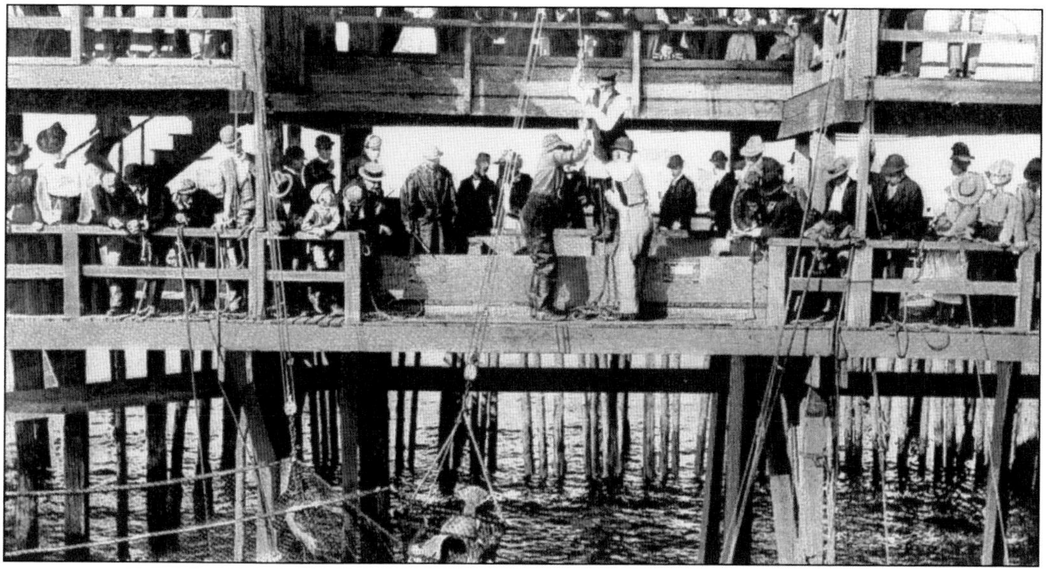

Hauling the Net. One of the highlights of a visit to the pier was witnessing the twice daily "Big Net Haul." The netting of fish from the sea was a very popular attraction for many years. Capt. John L. Young would often supervise this activity, and it was said that he could identify up to 48 different species of fish for the spectators. This operation was later moved to the Million Dollar Pier. (S. H. Knox, *c.* 1907.)

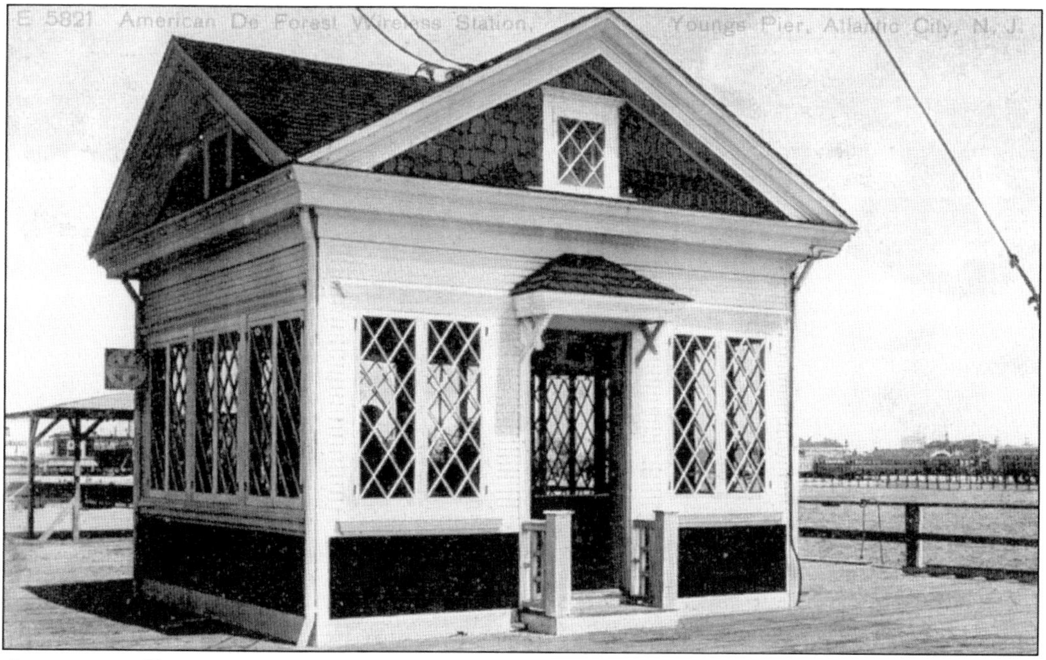

American DeForest Wireless Station. Situated at the end of Young's Pier, this small wireless station utilized a form of telegraphic technology invented by Lee DeForest, the "father of the radiophone." Designed for use in communications over great distances, the system was said to be capable of transmitting messages up to 40 words per minute without interference. This same technology was used very successfully during the 1904–1905 Russo-Japanese War. (Publisher unknown, *c.* 1910.)

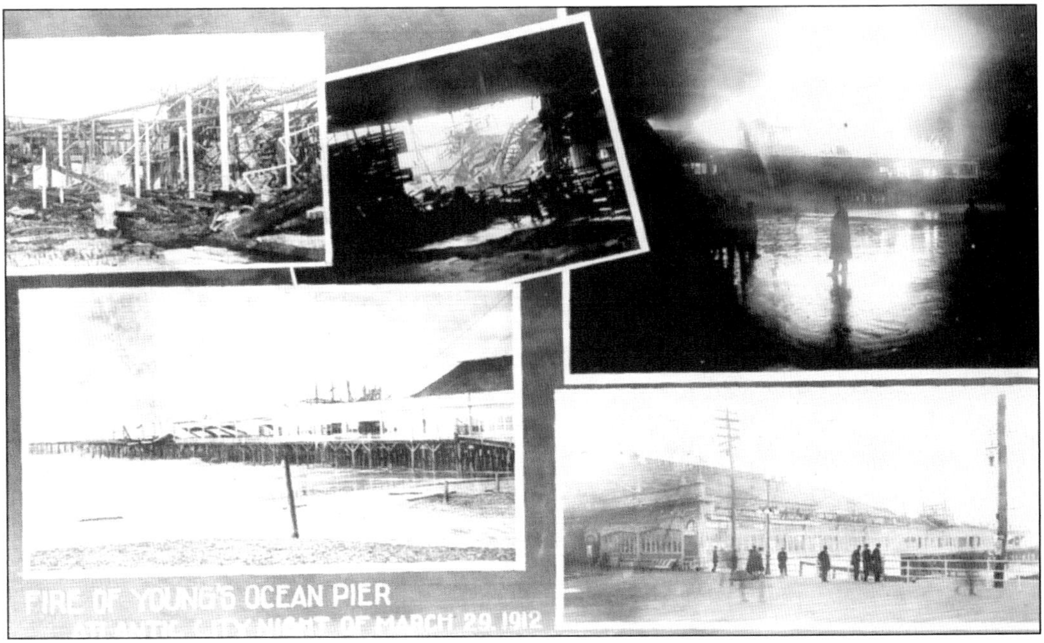

FIRE ON YOUNG'S PIER. March 29, 1912, saw a devastating fire that destroyed most of this fabulous pier. Only the boardwalk front was saved from the flames. Ever the entrepreneur, Capt. John L. Young sold tickets for 10¢ to people wishing to see the debris hauled away. After lying in ruins for many years afterward, the pier was finally rebuilt in 1922 and renamed the Central Pier. (Publisher unknown, 1912.)

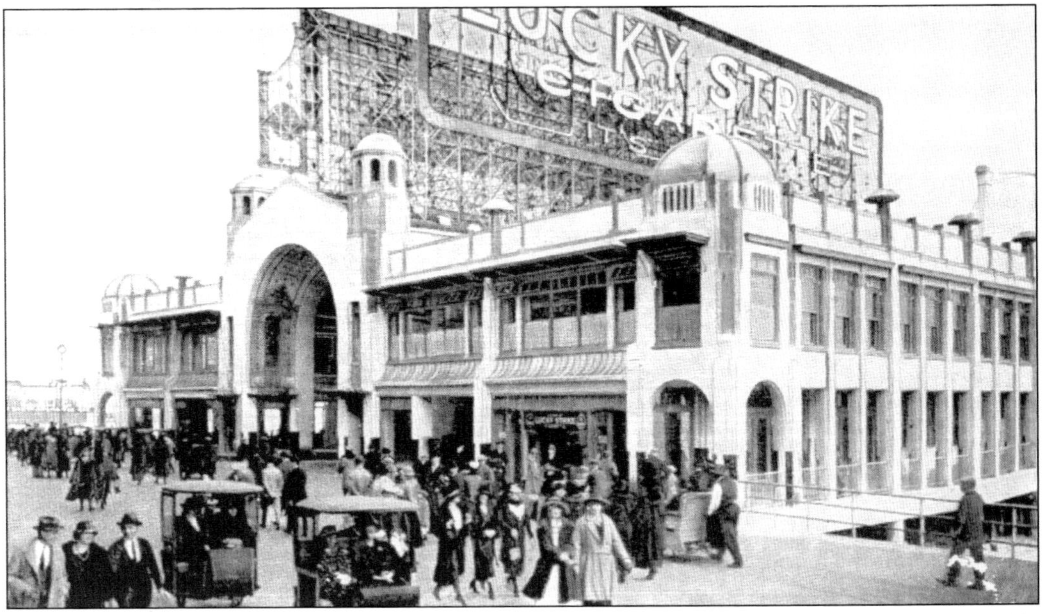

CENTRAL PIER. Central Pier was to eventually arise from the ashes of Young's Pier in 1922. Shorter in length than the original pier, it contained a variety of commercial exhibits, including a model home display. Organizations such as the Atlantic City Chamber of Commerce and the Convention Bureau had offices there as well. Despite damaging fires that struck again in 1929 and 1944, the pier continues to survive today. (Saltzburg, *c.* 1924.)

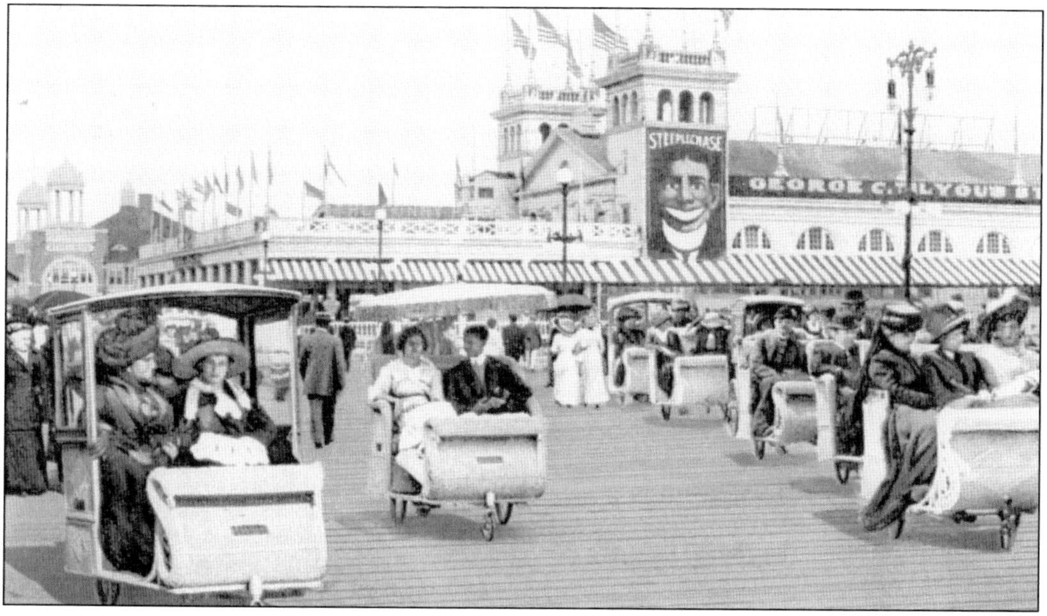

STEEPLECHASE PIER. Originally known as the Auditorium Pier, this pier located between Pennsylvania and North Carolina Avenues was purchased by George C. Tilyou in 1902. At first Tilyou continued the pier's focus on providing musical and theatrical performances, but in 1904, he changed the venue. He went on to create a copy of his very successful Coney Island Steeplechase Pier. Thus was born "the Mirth Place of the Nation." (Detroit Publishing Company, 1913.)

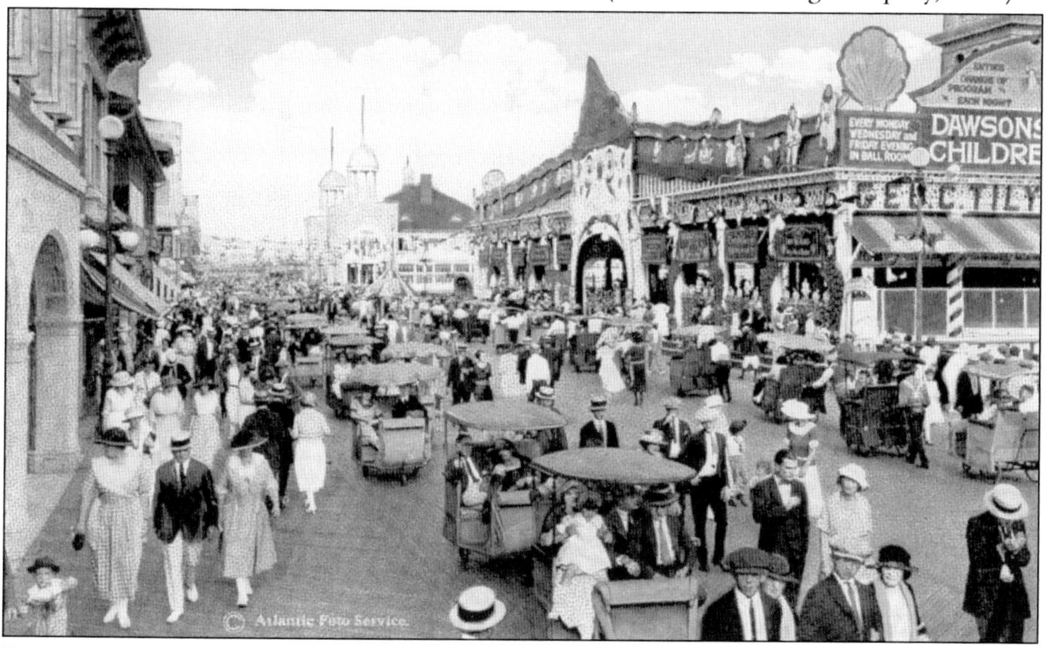

BOARDWALK NEAR STEEPLECHASE PIER. The entranceway to Steeplechase Pier was unmistakable. Patrons walked through the gaping mouth of a giant clown's face to enter a world of thrills and excitement. Rides such as the whirlpool, the whip, giant slides, a Ferris wheel, and others awaited those who ventured onto the pier. For those who wished, clown costumes called carnival suits could be rented to further enhance the experience. (Saltzburg, *c.* 1924.)

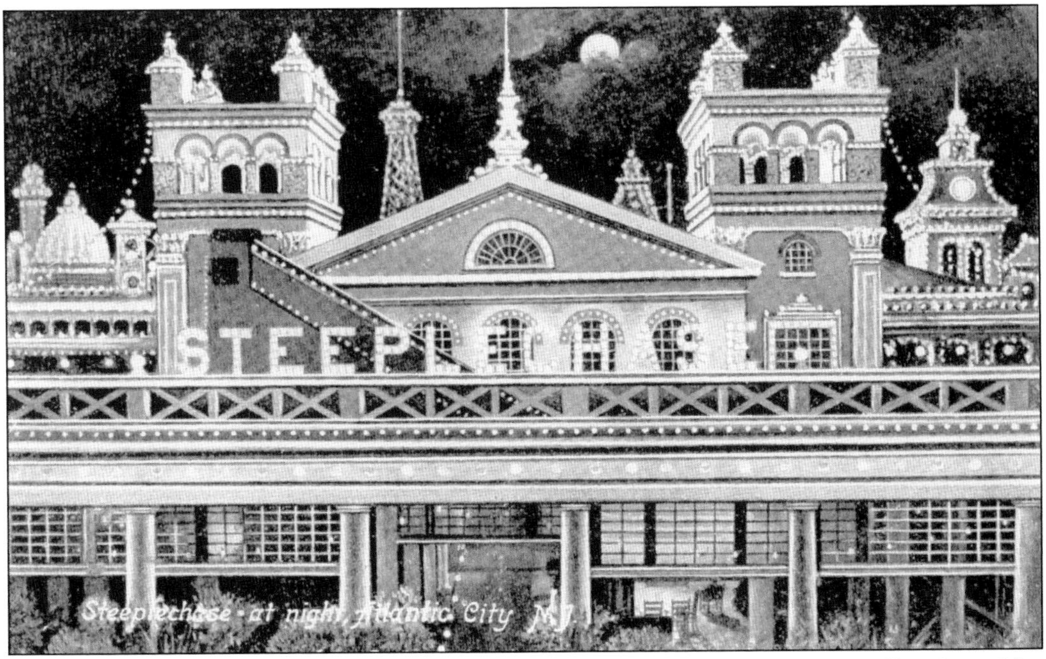

STEEPLECHASE AT NIGHT. Open day and night, the amusement piers were illuminated by many thousands of colorful electric lightbulbs after dark. As seen in this view, the Steeplechase Pier was no exception. The pier was open late into the evening in hopes of attracting as many customers as possible. Nighttime had its own appeal to many seeking thrills and excitement on the boardwalk. (Illustrated Postal Card Company, *c.* 1908.)

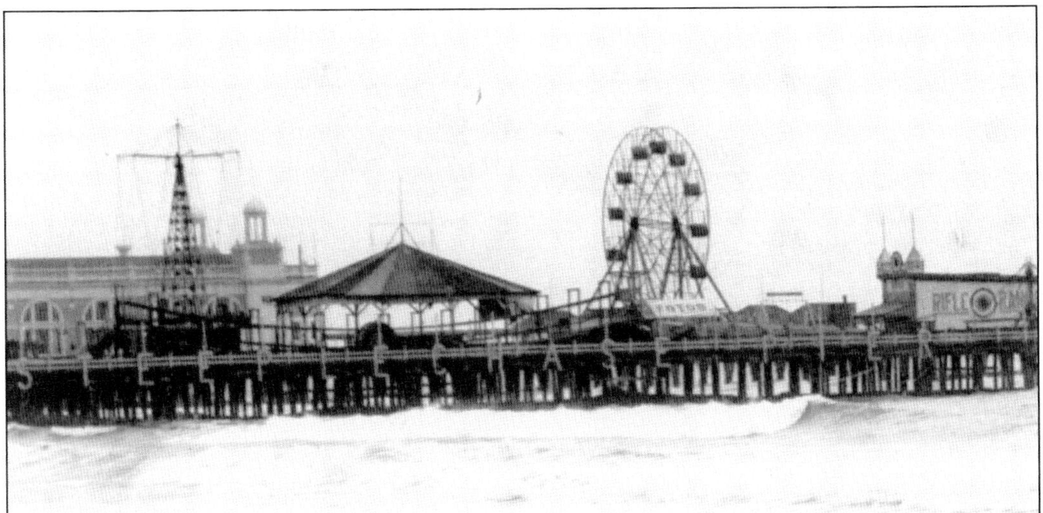

STEEPLECHASE PIER. This view shows some of the attractions found on the 800-foot-long Steeplechase Pier. Easily seen is the large Ferris wheel, a ride that first appeared on the Atlantic City Boardwalk in 1891. A fire destroyed the pier on February 14, 1932. It was later rebuilt, but it never again reached the height of its former glory. (Publisher unknown, *c.* 1910.)

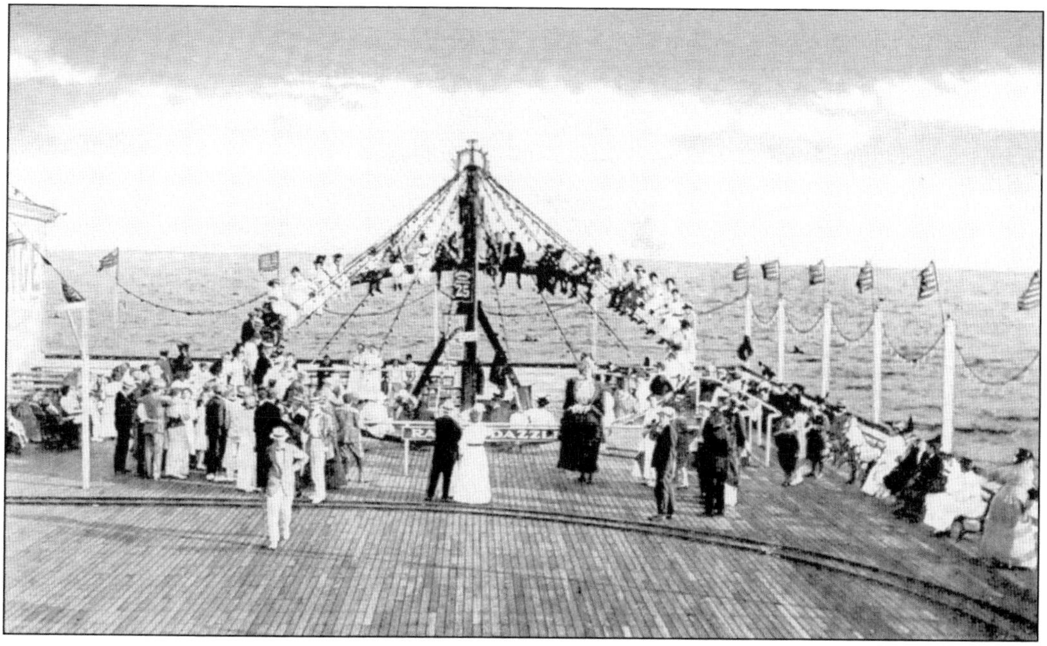

THE RAZZLE-DAZZLE. Located next to the rifle range, at the ocean end of Steeplechase Pier, was a thrill ride called the Razzle-Dazzle. Riders sat facing inward on the edge of a large-diameter wheel that tilted and spun them about, much to their delight. Also visible are the tracks for the Dragon Ride. Such entertaining rides helped bring back customers time and again to the pier. (Publisher unknown, *c.* 1910.)

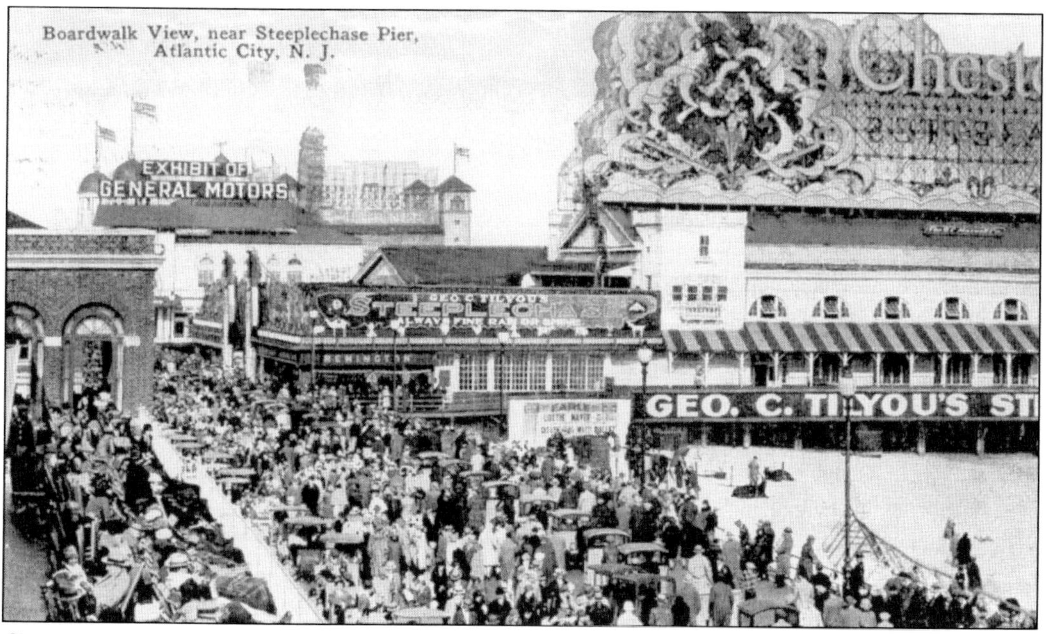

CHESTERFIELD SIGN. In 1926, an enormous electrical sign, the largest in the world at the time, was placed on top of a pier building. This sign had 26,000 multicolored lightbulbs illuminating each side of its 215-foot length. Advertising Chesterfield cigarettes, the sign only lasted six seasons, as it was destroyed in the disastrous pier fire of 1932. (Sithens, *c.* 1928.)

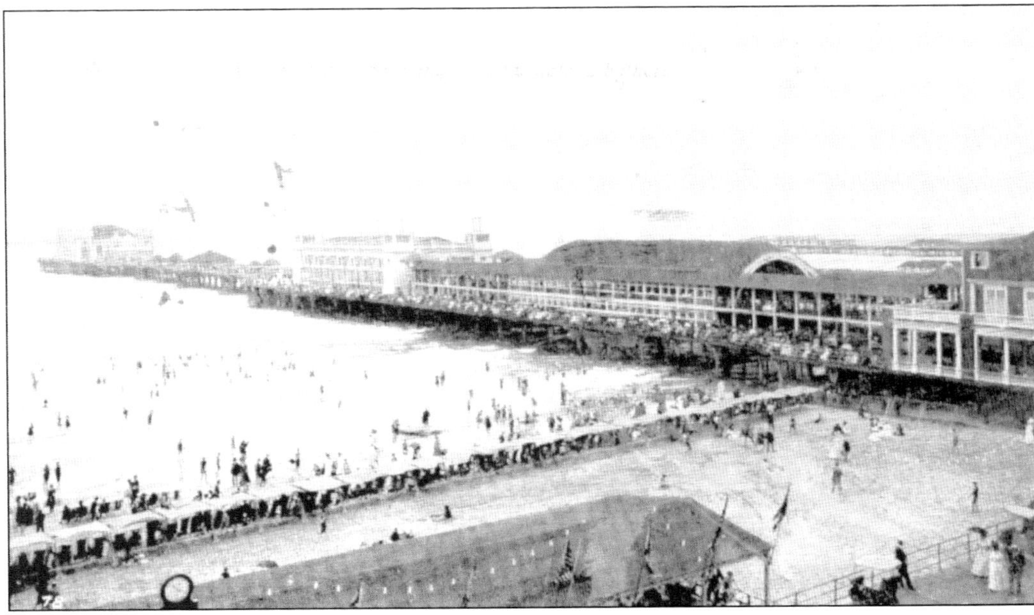

Steel Pier. Situated at Virginia Avenue and the boardwalk, Steel Pier is undoubtedly the best known of all the amusement piers. Opening to the public on June 18, 1898, the pier was named for the iron pilings upon which it was built. Lengthened several times, the pier eventually stretched 1,780 feet into the ocean. Over the years it has featured all types of entertainment and amusement, becoming known as the "Showplace of the Nation." (Chilton, *c.* 1908.)

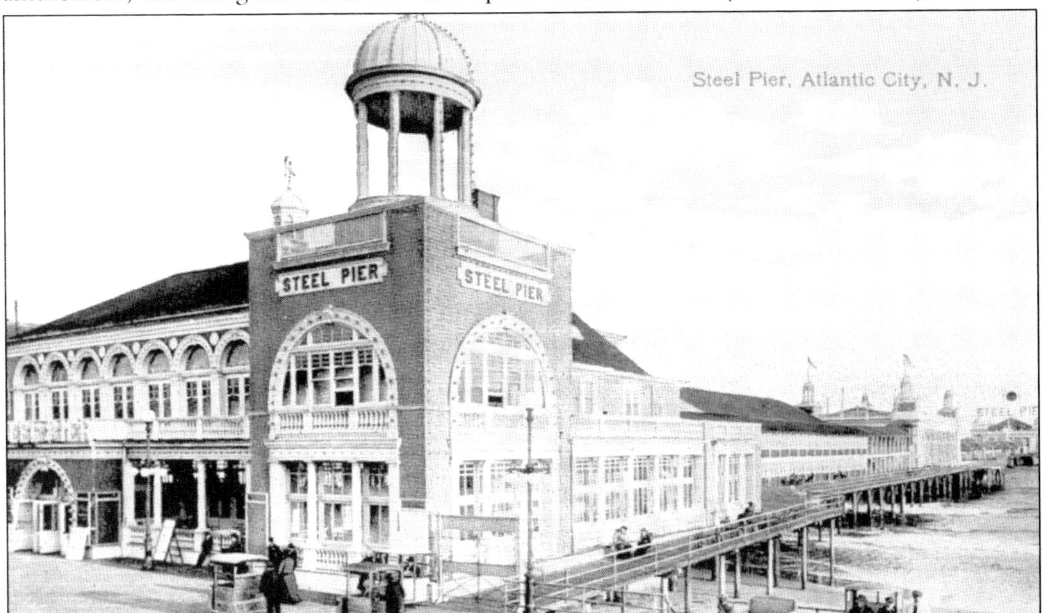

Entrance to Steel Pier. In 1916, customers paid an admission fee of 10¢ during the day and 15¢ at night. This entitled them to experience all the wonders that Steel Pier had to offer. Daily attendance during the summer months would often number in the tens of thousands. The entrance seen here was replaced after a devastating three-alarm fire in 1924 that ravaged the front portions of the pier. (Post Card Distribution Company, *c.* 1916.)

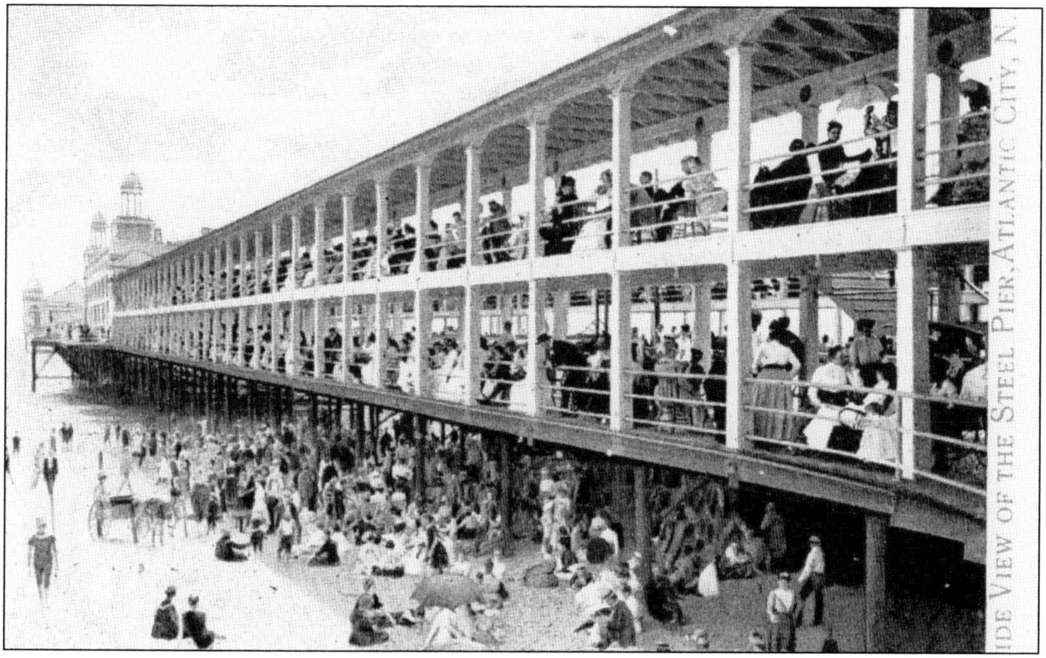

A SIDE VIEW OF THE STEEL PIER. One of the more tranquil activities on the pier in the early years was to simply sit in the shade and enjoy the cool ocean breeze while gazing down at the bathers on the beach below. This was a pleasant way to spend time between attending some of the many activities and performances that were scheduled. (Publisher unknown, *c.* 1906.)

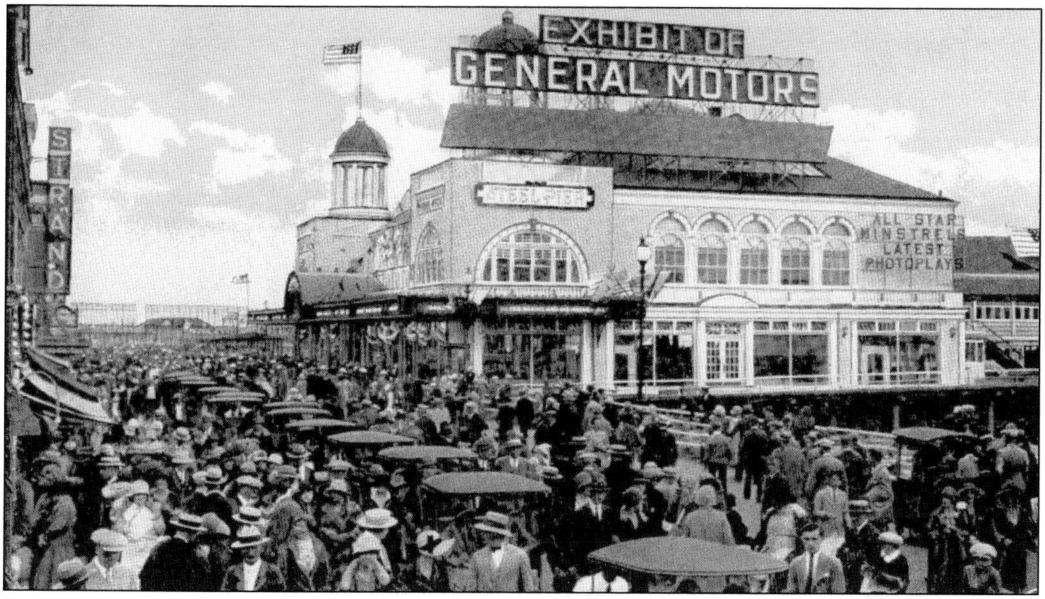

GENERAL MOTORS AT STEEL PIER. A large sign above the entrance to the pier advertises the General Motors Exhibit. In 1926, extensive renovations on Steel Pier provided 20,000 square feet of space for this commercial exhibit. Taking advantage of the large crowds attracted to the pier, General Motors displayed its latest car models to the curious. Later Ford utilized the space, with General Motors returning after World War II. The exhibit continued operating until April 15, 1968. (Saltzburg, *c.* 1930.)

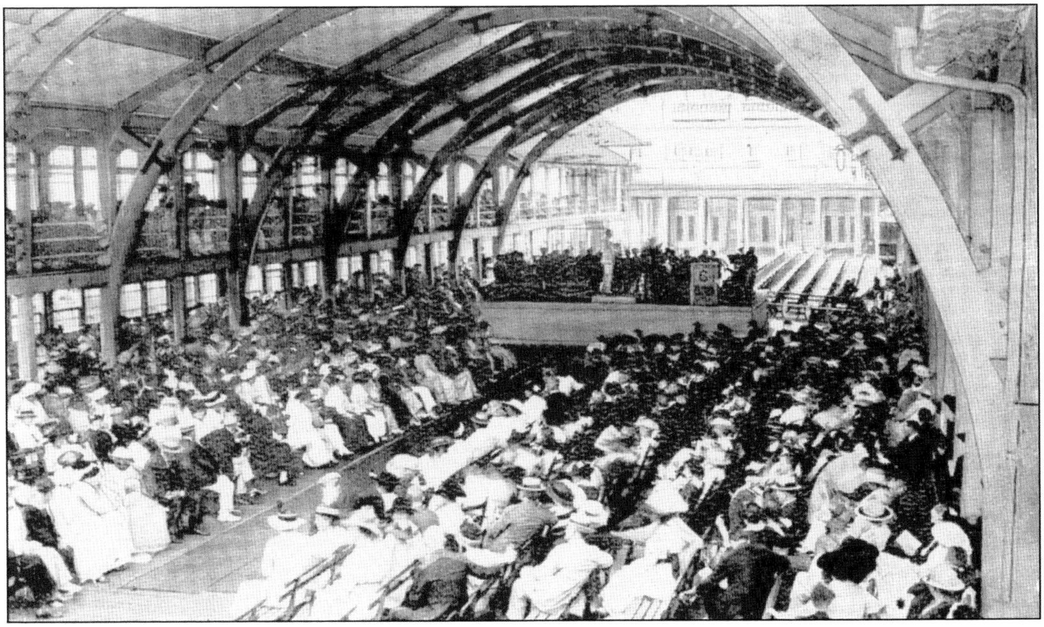

VESSELLA'S BAND. First conducting his brass band at Steel Pier in 1902, the Italian maestro Oreste Vessella would continue to play concerts here for many years. Famous for his long black hair, he had so many fervent female devotees that he hired a bodyguard to help protect his locks. He always preferred to perform music by Italian composers for his admiring audiences. (Virginia Post Card Company, *c.* 1916.)

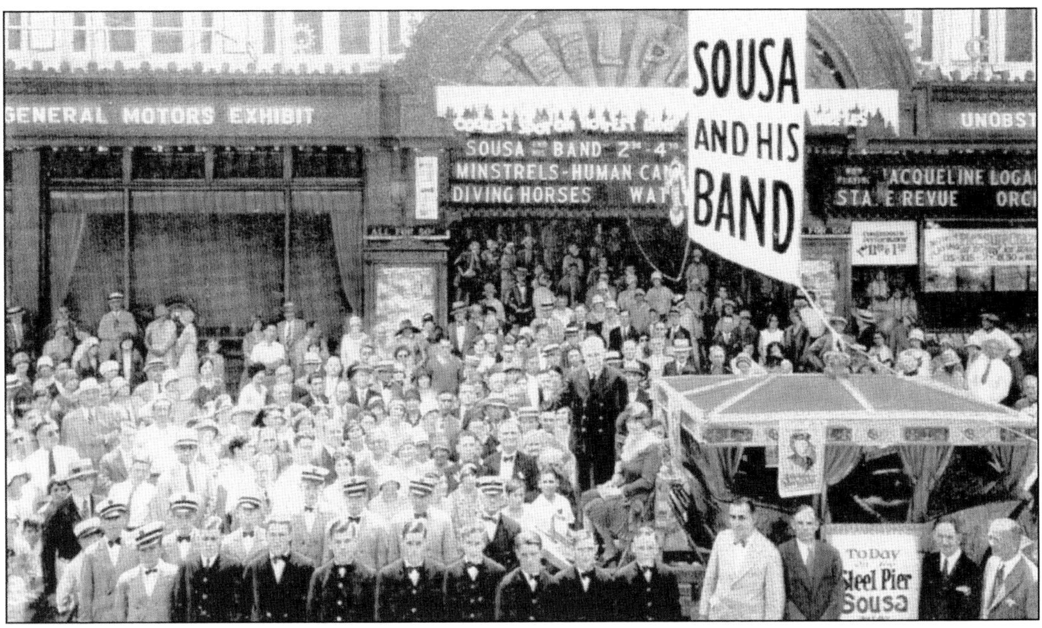

SOUSA AT STEEL PIER. John Philip Sousa, famous bandleader and composer, poses with his band at the entrance to Steel Pier. Married to the daughter of an Atlantic City Boardwalk photographer, Sousa performed for many years during the summer at both the Steeplechase and Steel Piers. Sousa died on March 6, 1932, at the age of 77. (Saltzburg, *c.* 1925.)

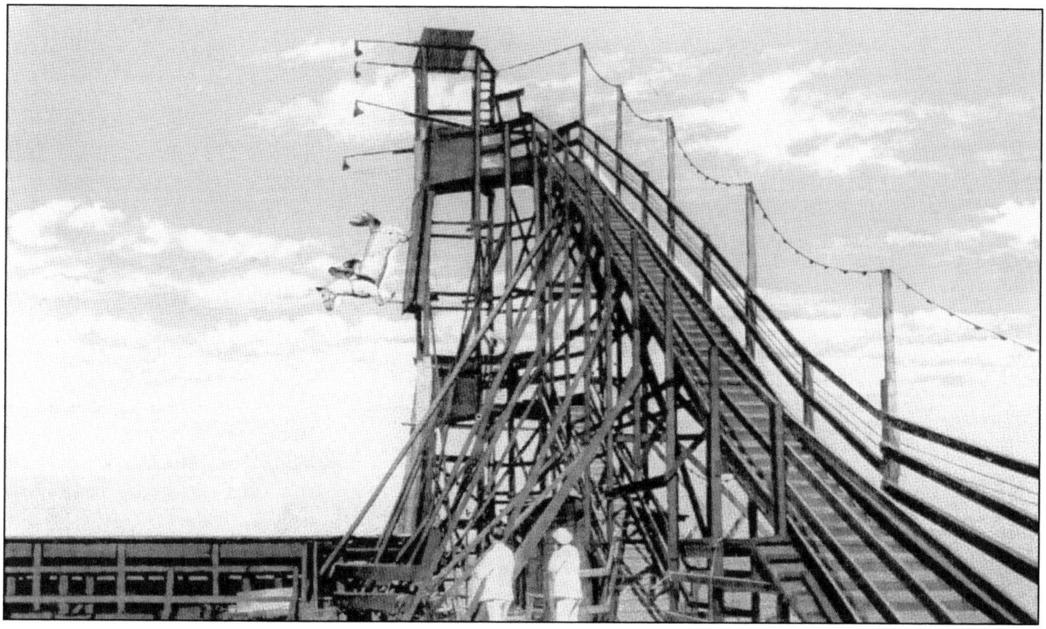

A THRILL A MINUTE. The most famous of all Atlantic City attractions was the World Famous Diving Horse. This act was developed by William F. Carver, an associate of "Buffalo Bill" Cody, and was brought to Steel Pier in 1929. Performances continued until 1978. The stunt involved a horse and rider plunging into a 12-foot-deep pool of water from a tower platform 40 feet high. (Saltzburg, *c.* 1930.)

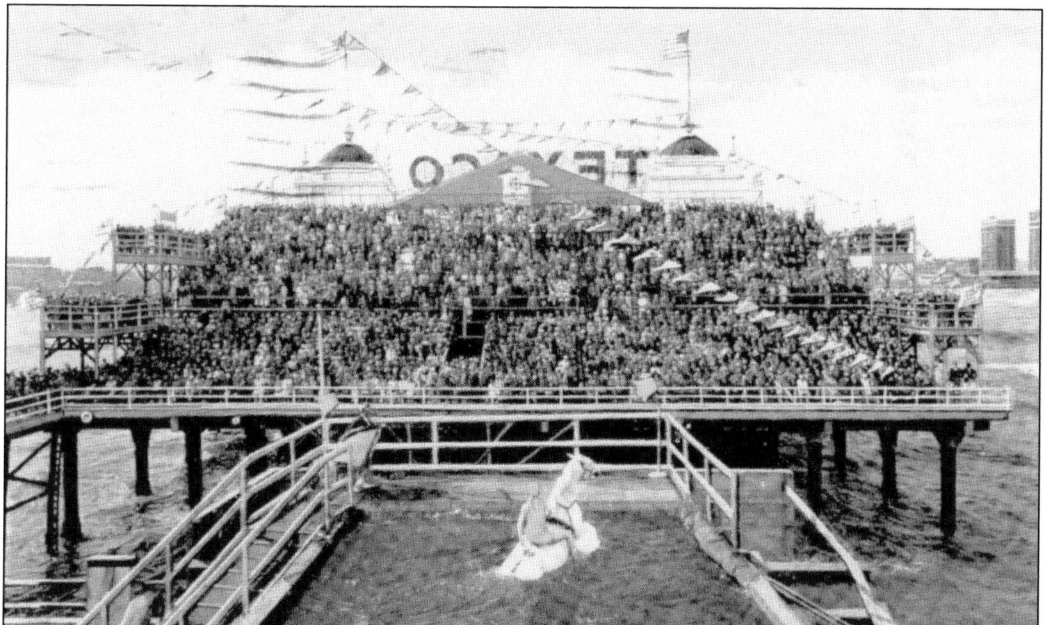

CROWDED STANDS. Over the years many different riders performed this renowned act. The most celebrated rider was Sonora Webster Carver, who dove here for 14 years, 11 of these after being blinded in a jump. Here her sister Arnette Webster French is emerging from the pool on the back of the horse John the Baptist as a huge crowd looks on. (Saltzburg, *c.* 1930.)

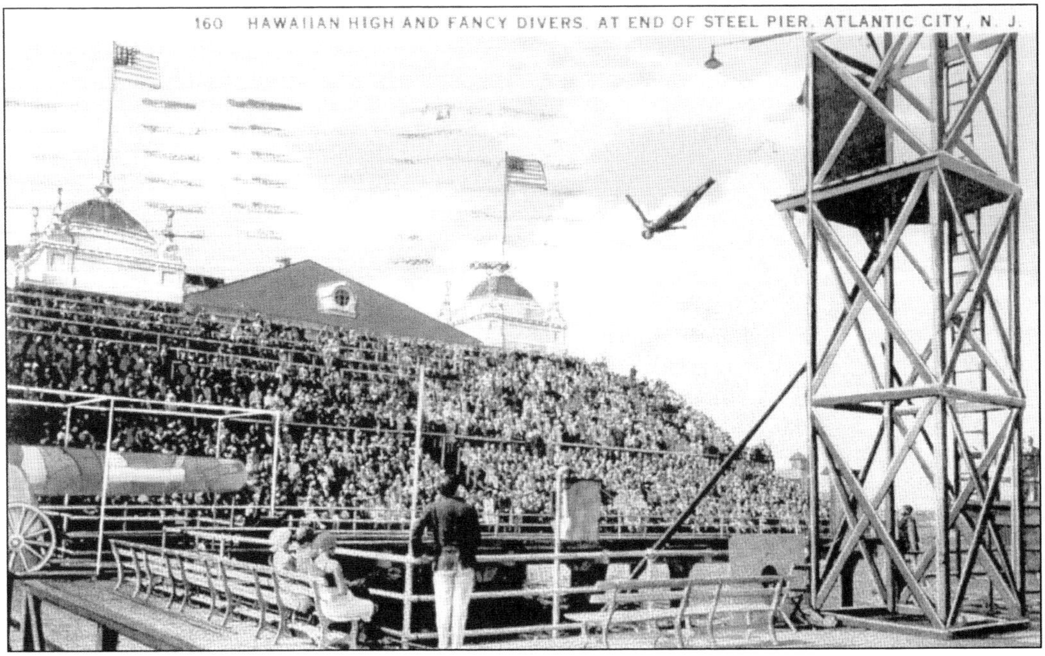

HIGH DIVERS. Another attraction at the end of the pier was the water circus. Here spectators were thrilled by the daring Hawaiian Divers or they laughed at the antics of a comedy diving team. Before gaining fame playing Tarzan in the movies, Johnny Weismuller performed at Steel Pier as part of a water comedy act. (Saltzburg, *c.* 1930.)

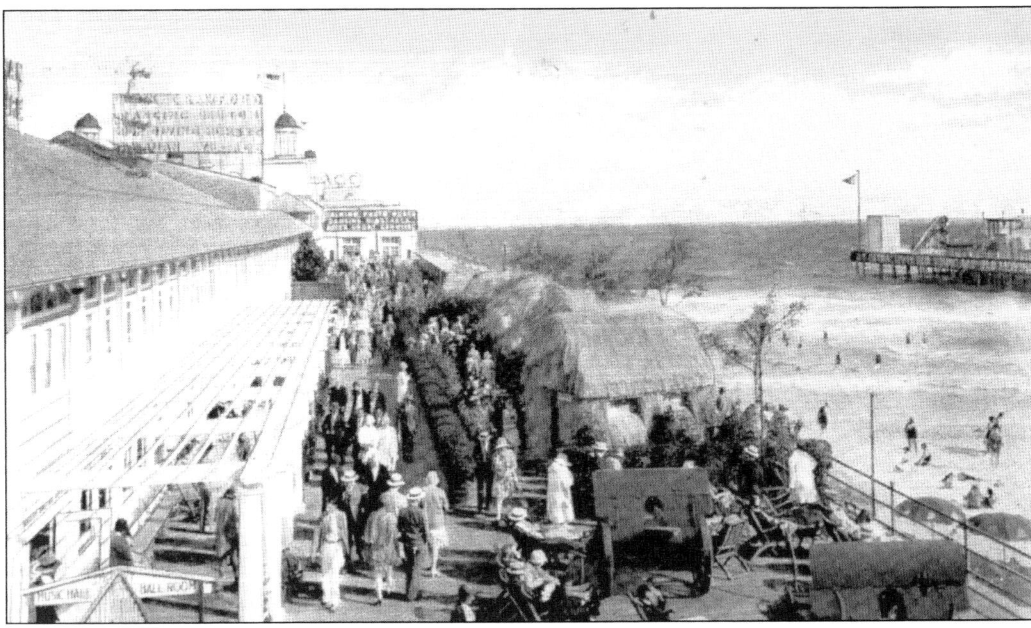

HAWAIIAN VILLAGE. Yet another unusual exhibit was the Hawaiian village. Set up along one side of the pier, it consisted of several palm-thatched huts with a few small palm trees added for atmosphere. A little touch of the tropical paradise was brought to the Jersey shore as musicians, singers, and hula dancers performed. (Saltzburg, *c.* 1930.)

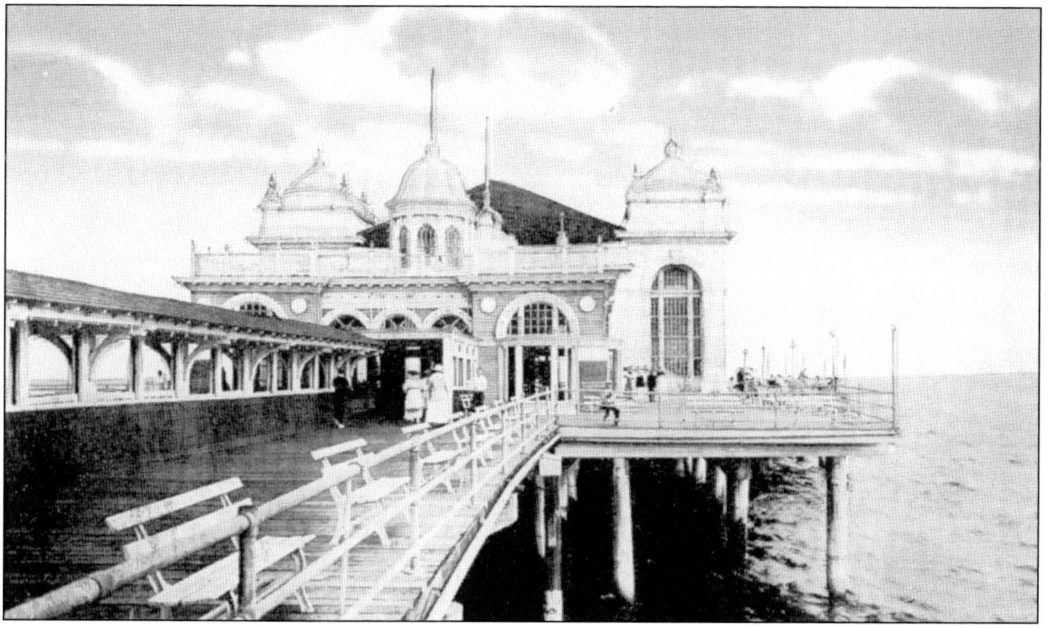

Music Hall. At the ocean end of Steel Pier was the building called the Music Hall or Marine Ballroom. Over the years countless musical performances were held here, helping to make the pier the "Showplace of the Nation." The hall seen here was rebuilt and expanded in 1930 to accommodate larger audiences. (Virginia Post Card Company, *c.* 1920.)

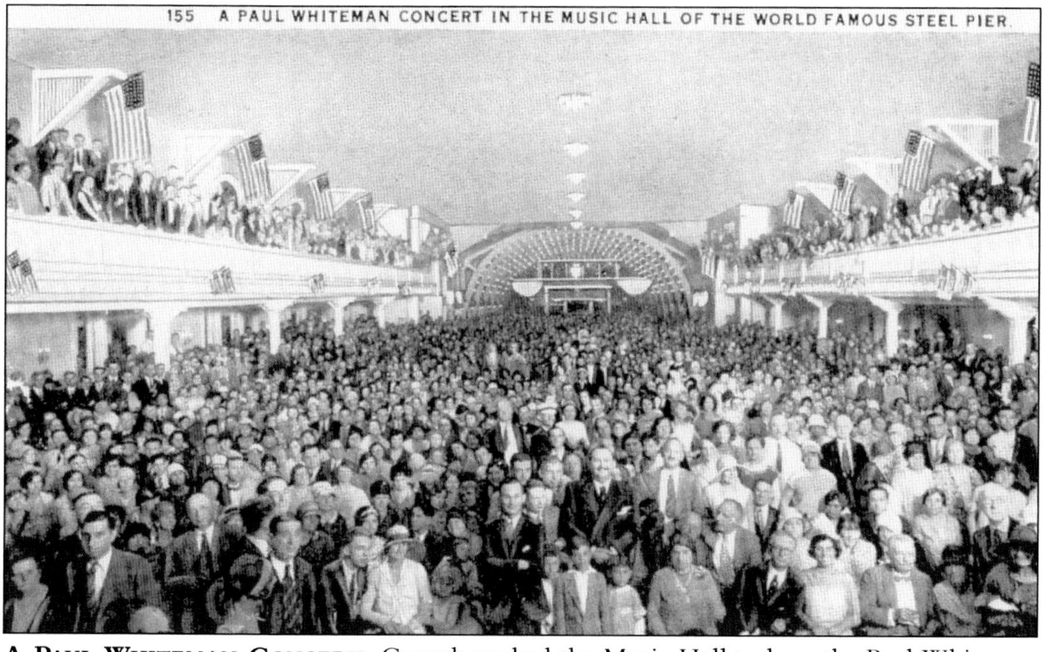

A Paul Whiteman Concert. Crowds packed the Music Hall to hear the Paul Whiteman Band perform. Billing himself as the "King of Jazz," Whiteman revitalized dance music and the dance orchestra after World War I. During the 1920s, his was the most popular dance band in the nation. The band's signature tune was George Gershwin's "Rhapsody in Blue." Paul Whiteman died in 1967 after a long musical career. (Saltzburg, *c.* 1929.)

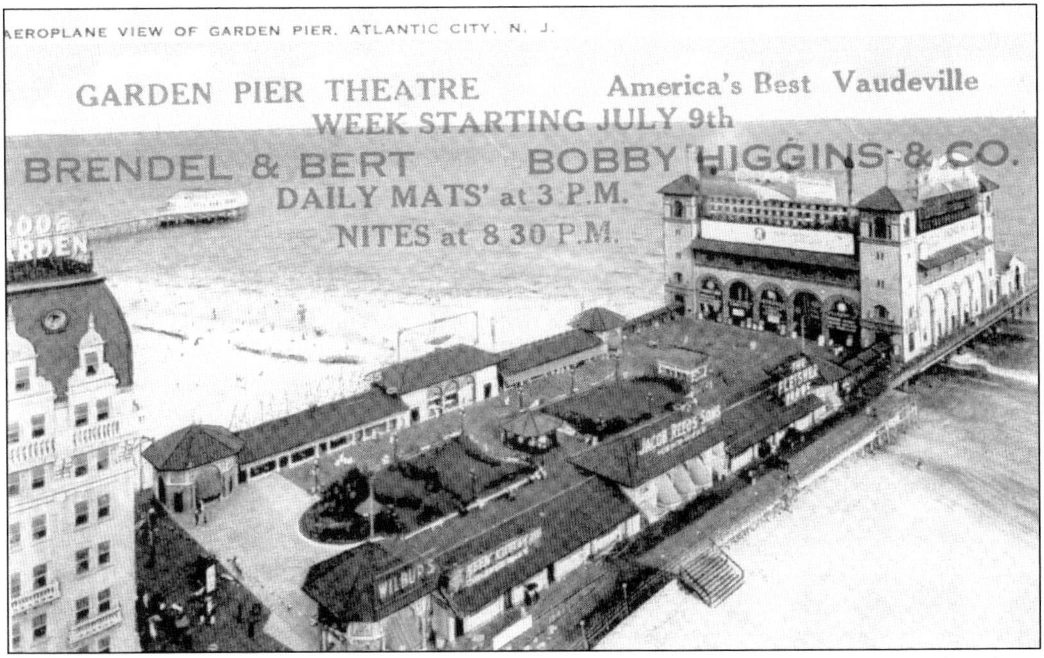

The New Garden Pier. Opening on July 19, 1913, at New Jersey Avenue, the 700-foot-long Garden Pier had its buildings designed in the Spanish Renaissance style. In future years the pier would see both financial difficulties and decline. However, the pier continues to exist. Present-day visitors can find the Cultural and Art Center as well as the Atlantic City Historical Museum located here. (Post Card Distribution Company, *c.* 1914.)

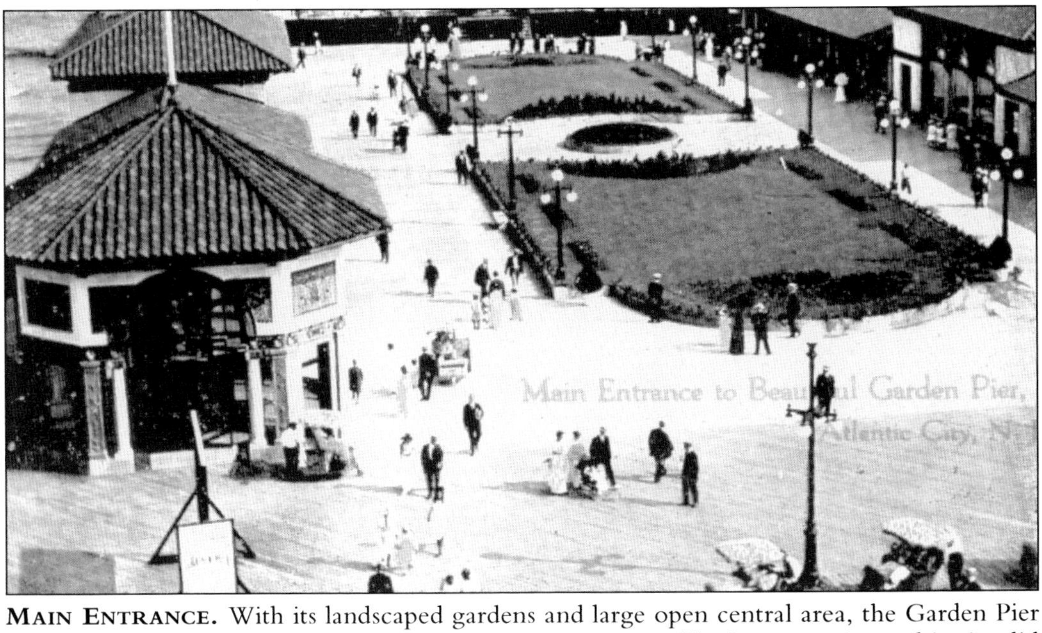

Main Entrance. With its landscaped gardens and large open central area, the Garden Pier had a different ambiance than the other amusement piers. Unlike its competitors, this pier did not offer thrill rides, nor did it have a carnival-like atmosphere. Instead it became famous for its theatrical and vaudeville entertainment. Before the construction of Convention Hall, it was also the site of a number of major conventions. (National Post Card Company, *c.* 1920.)

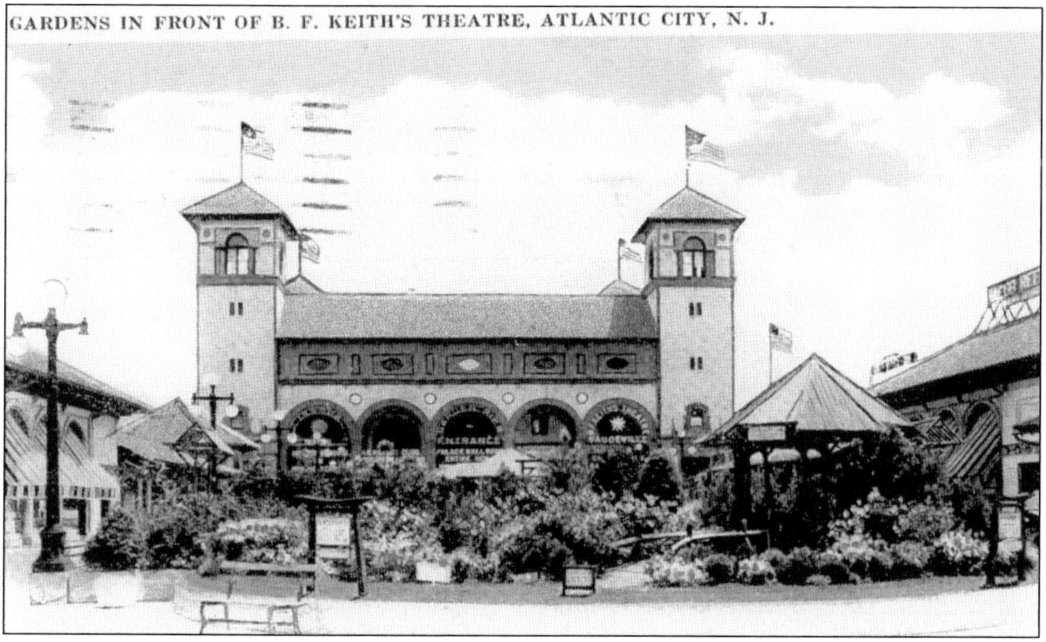

GARDENS IN FRONT OF THEATRE. Garden Pier was named for its luxurious flower gardens seen here in front of the theater building. The B. F. Keith's Vaudeville Theatre and Palace of Dancing would host many of the nation's top entertainers. Included among those who performed here were Eddie Cantor, Rudy Vallee, Paul Whiteman, Harry Houdini, and Gypsy Rose Lee. The famous silent film star Rudolph Valentino began here as a tango instructor. (Sithens, *c.* 1926.)

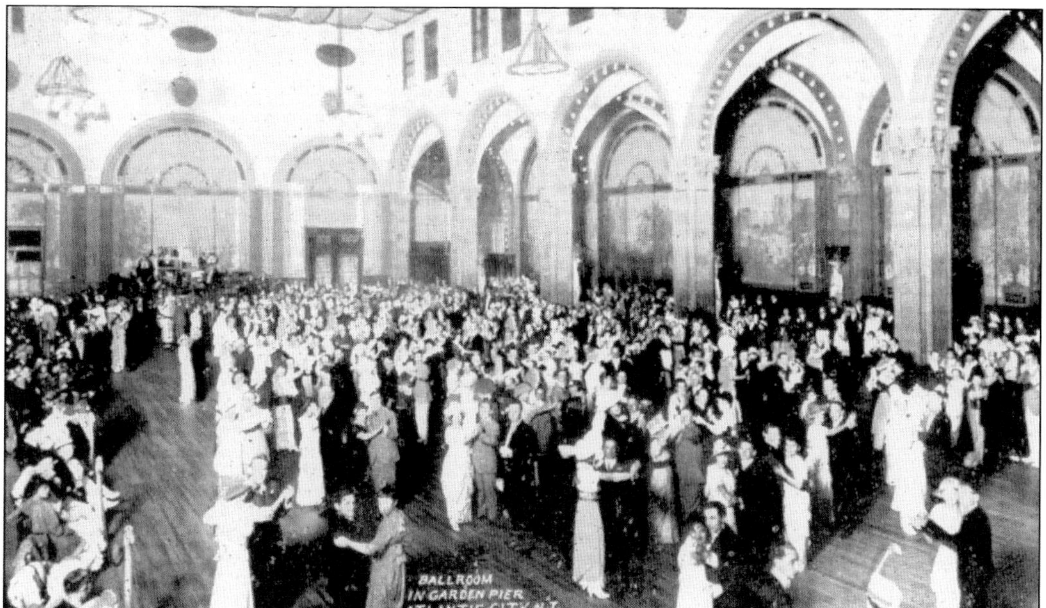

BALLROOM. The hardwood floor of the large ballroom was often filled with couples enjoying themselves, dancing to the sounds of a big-name orchestra or dance band. In 1920, the Garden Pier advertised dancing 8:30 to 11:00 every evening. This form of nightly entertainment was very popular at the time. (Post Card Distribution Company, *c.* 1920.)

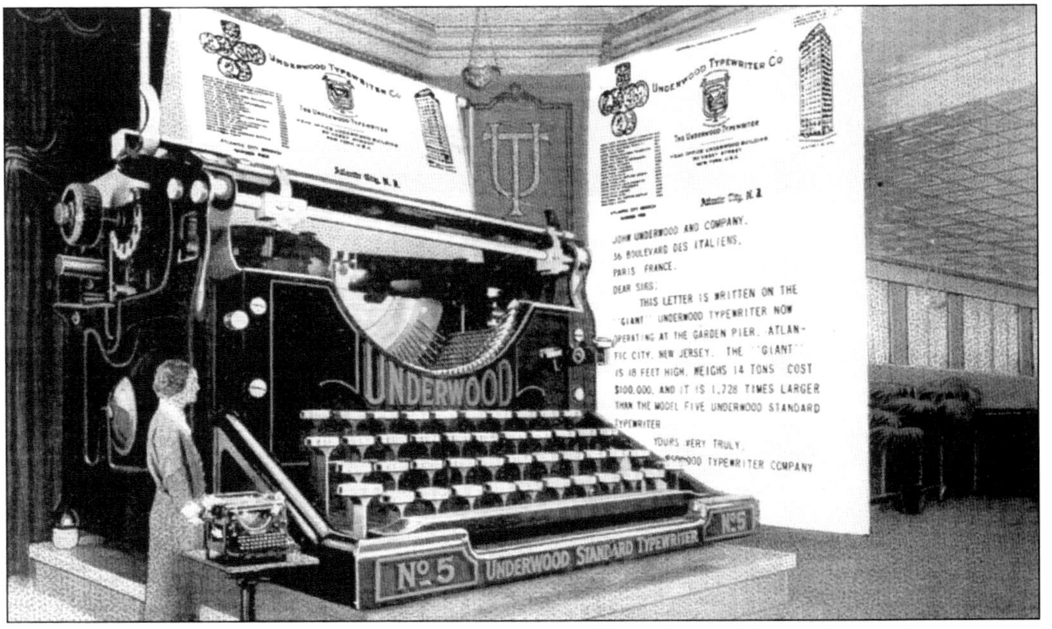

GIANT TYPEWRITER. This giant 14-ton, 18-foot-tall, 21-foot-wide Underwood typewriter was exhibited in a pavilion on Garden Pier starting in 1916. A working typewriter, 1,728 times actual size, it printed out messages by remote control on paper that was 9 feet wide and over 12 feet high. During World War II, this device was scrapped as part of the war effort. (Publisher unknown, *c.* 1929)

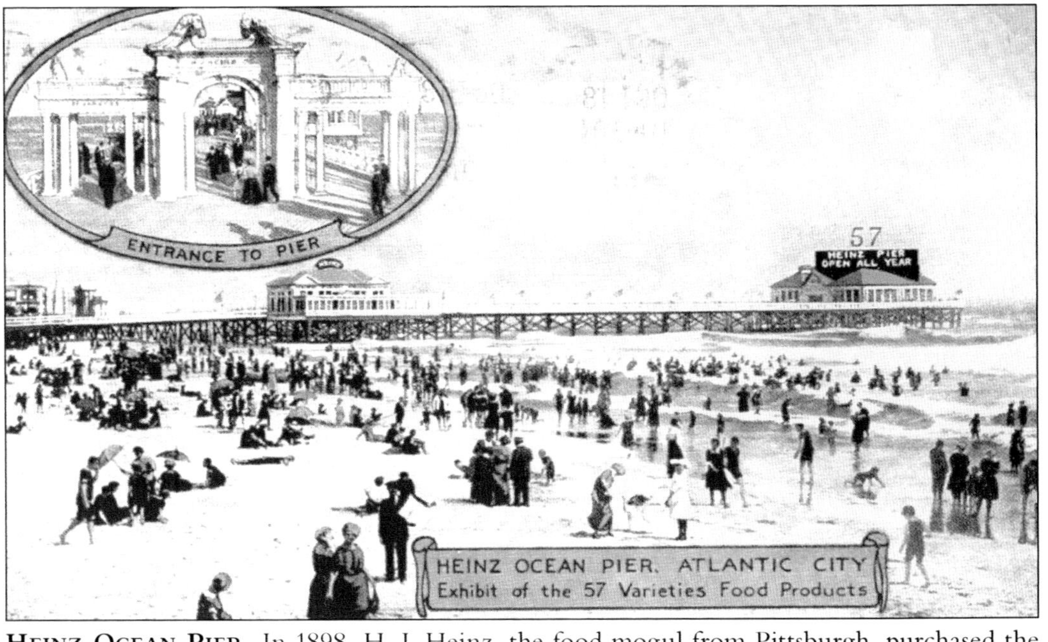

HEINZ OCEAN PIER. In 1898, H. J. Heinz, the food mogul from Pittsburgh, purchased the Iron Pier at Massachusetts Avenue. The Iron Pier, which had been built in 1886, received its name from the fact that it was the first amusement pier in the city constructed on iron pilings. The pier extended outward from the boardwalk for 600 feet. It was located farther north than any of the other great piers. (Publisher unknown, *c.* 1915.)

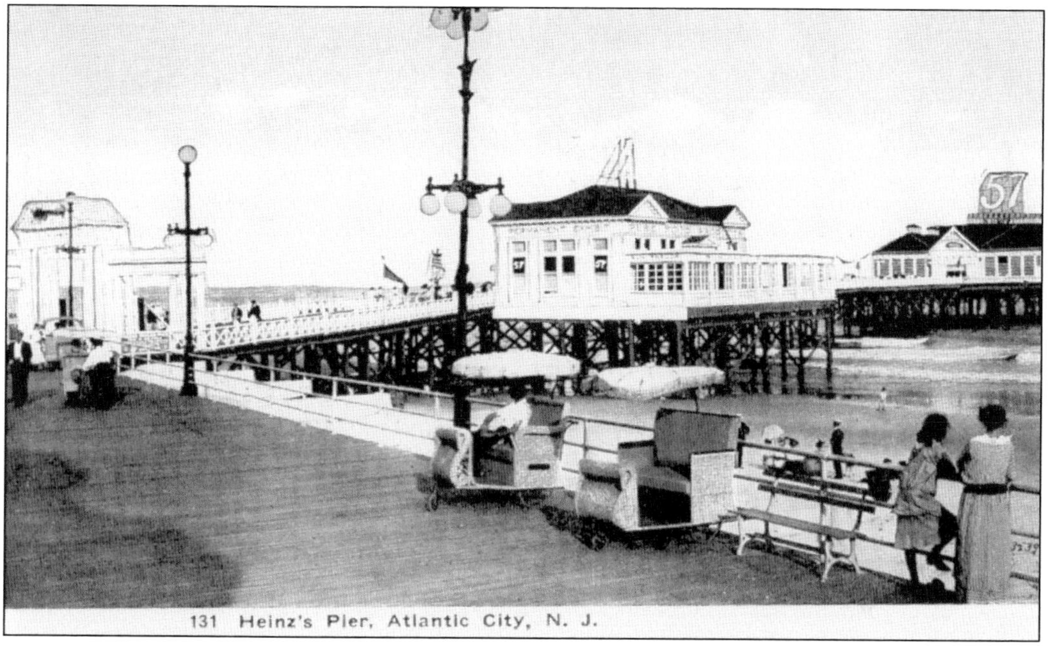

HEINZ PIER. After taking over ownership, Heinz enlarged the pier somewhat and changed its entertainment focus. Previously well known for theatrical productions, Heinz transformed it into a showcase for his company's many food products. A large "57" sign on the roof of the building at the end of the pier helped instill the slogan "57 varieties" in visitors' minds. (Publisher unknown, *c.* 1915.)

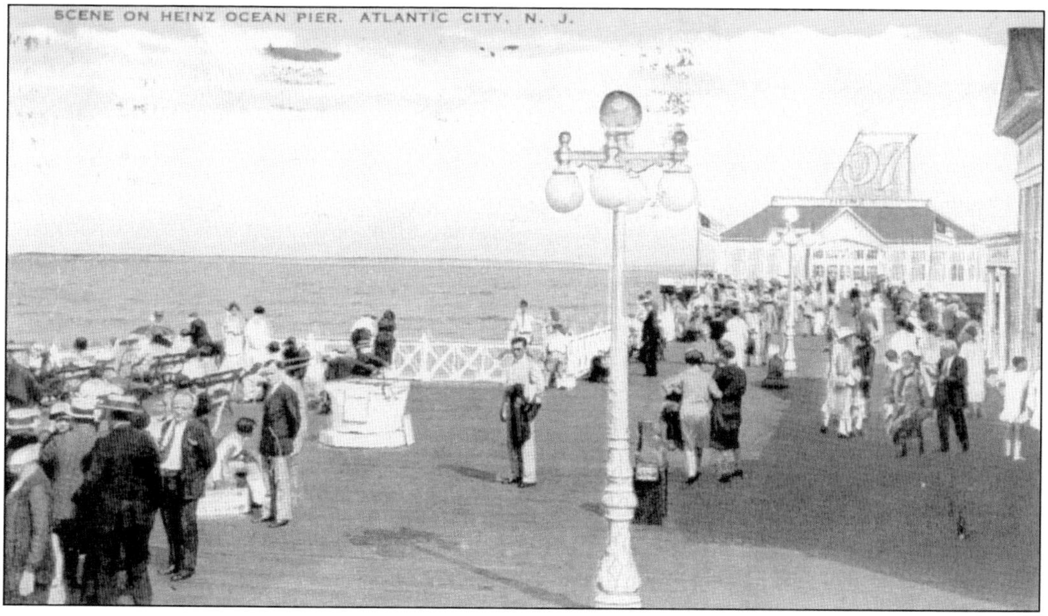

SCENE ON HEINZ PIER. To help entice visitors, there was no charge for entrance to the pier. Once on the pier, people could stop by the permanent kitchen exhibits and view cooking demonstrations and receive free samples of hot and cold Heinz food products. A special and memorable treat, especially for the children, was getting a free souvenir miniature pickle pin. (Sithens, *c.* 1928.)

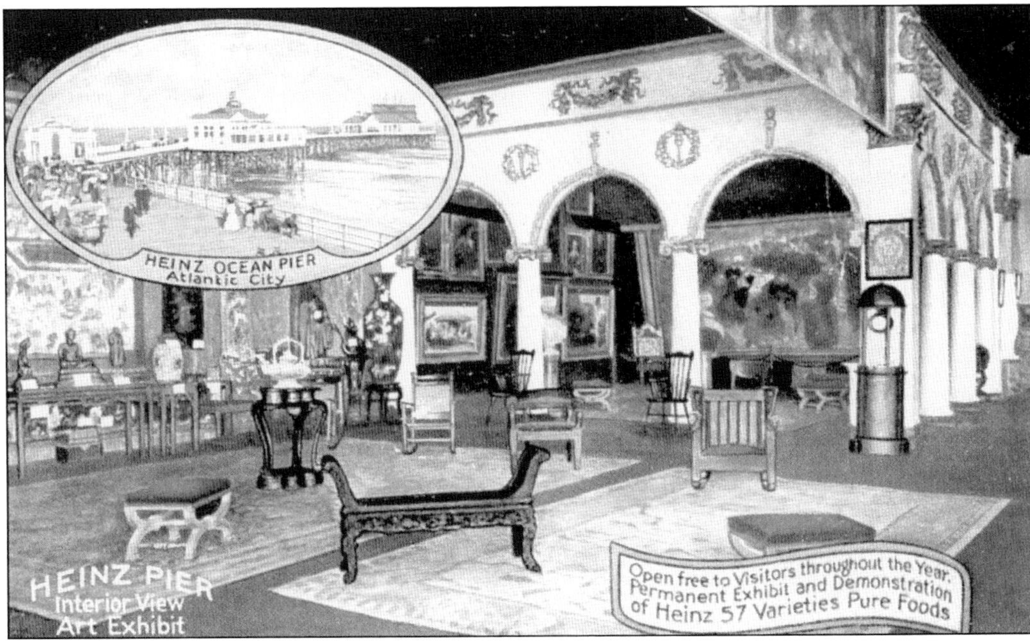

ART EXHIBIT. One exhibit on the pier was a display of some of the personal art collection of H. J. Heinz. Here in this ornate and lavishly decorated room were many oil paintings for the public to view and admire. A particular favorite for many on the pier was a large dramatic painting titled *Custer's Last Stand.* (Publisher unknown, *c.* 1908.)

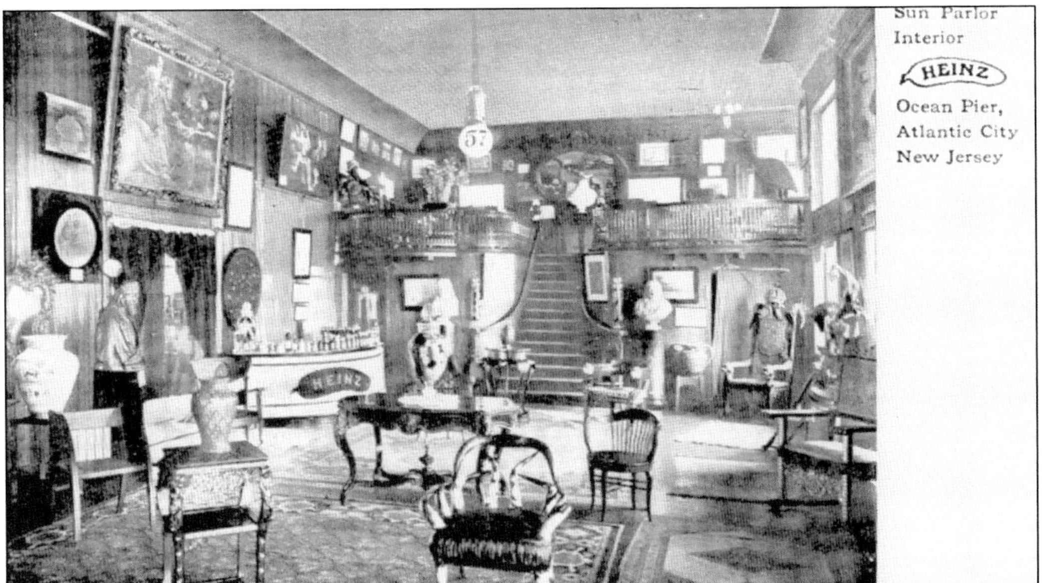

SUN PARLOR. Yet another room on public exhibit was the sun parlor. This room was filled with numerous chairs and small tables adorned with busts and statuary. Additional artwork and tapestries on the walls added to the decor. Unfortunately, the pier was severely damaged in the great hurricane of 1944, and its remains had to be completely removed the following year. (Publisher unknown, *c.* 1905.)

Five

The Beach

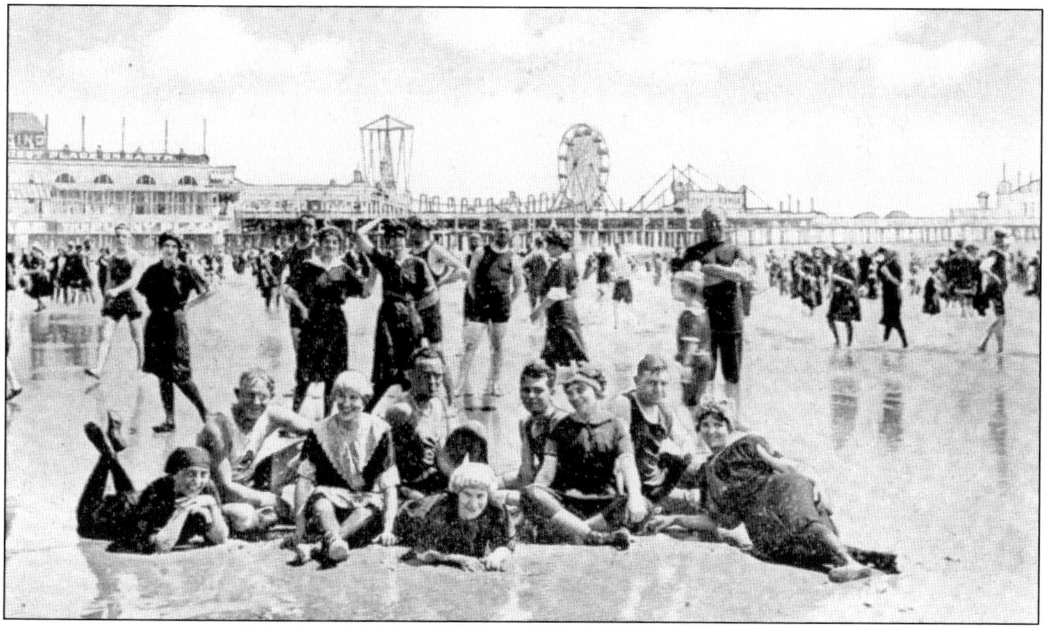

On the Beach. Nature provided its own lure to attract visitors to Atlantic City—the approximately four miles of gently sloping beaches. The white sands and the cool ocean waters helped draw people to these shores from nearby cities during the hot summer months. The people seen here posing for the camera were among the many having an enjoyable day in the sun. (National Post Card Company, *c.* 1919.)

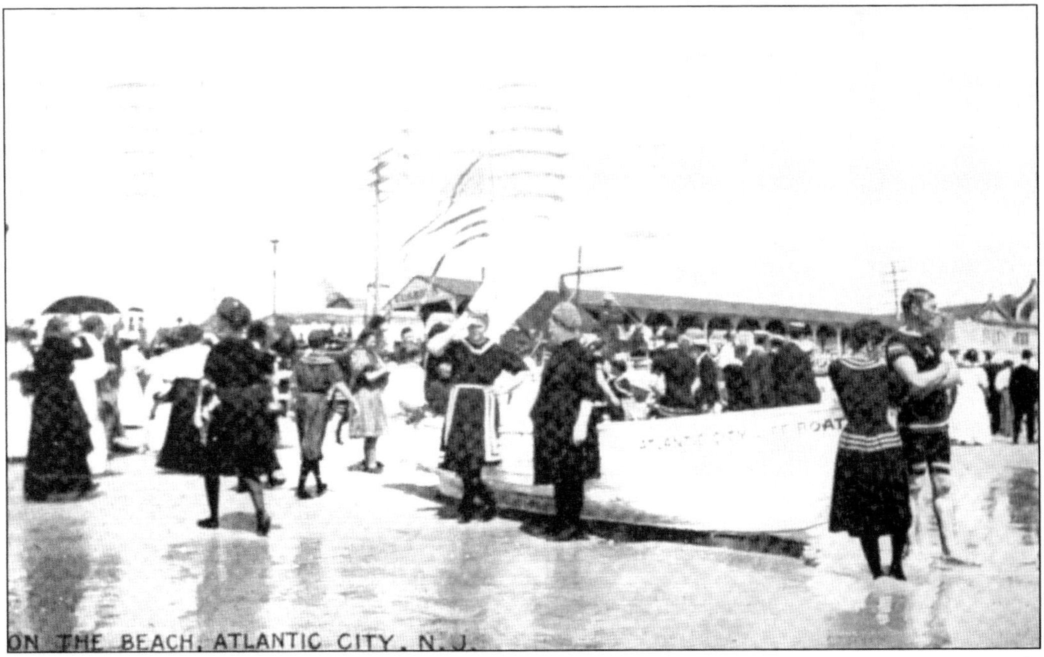

A Day On the Beach. During the peak months of July and August, the numbers of people on the beach swelled enormously. Some years it was estimated that as many as 10 million people came to enjoy the beach. Beachgoers such as these may have arrived by special excursion train from New York or Philadelphia to enjoy a day of sand, surf, and cool ocean breezes. (I. and M. Ottenheimer, *c.* 1910.)

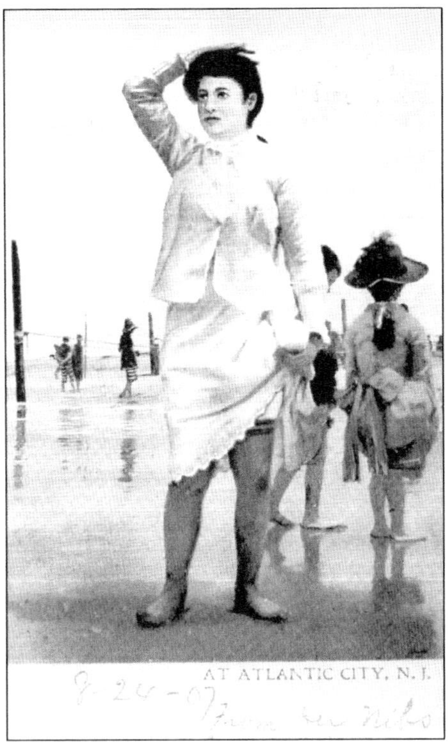

At the Water's Edge. To help ensure the well-being of beachgoers, several types of beach safety devices were introduced. One of the earliest was the patented "lifeline for surf bathing" developed by Capt. William Tell Street. This apparatus consisted of cables, running from posts on the beach to anchoring points out beyond the breakers; these could be grasped by anyone in danger. (Illustrated Post Card Company, *c.* 1904.)

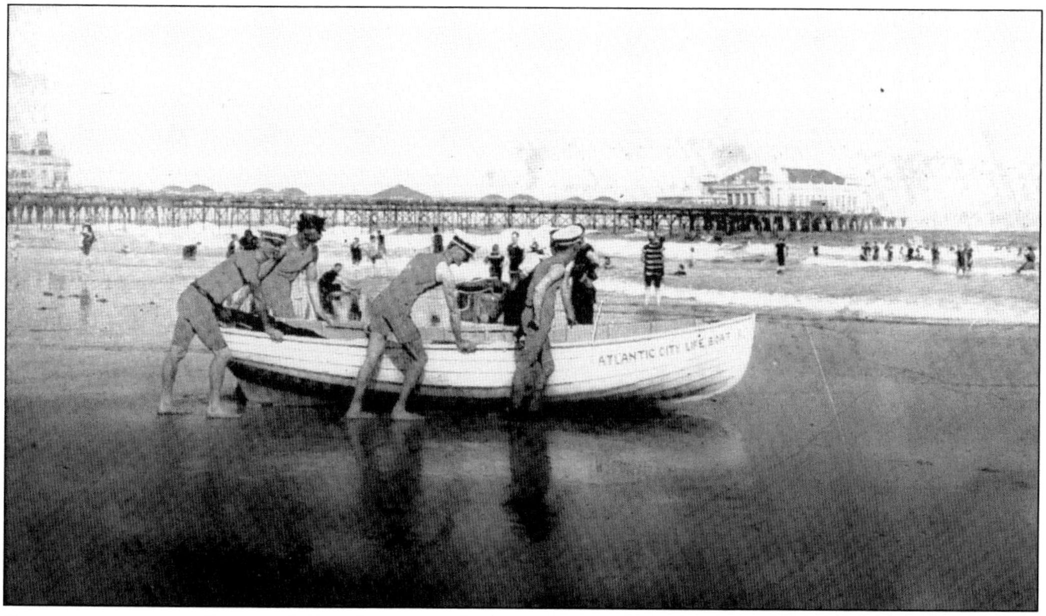

LIFEBOAT AND CREW. The first regularly trained paid beach patrol was established on August 24, 1891, and took to the beaches beginning in June 1892. Before that, volunteers and privately funded lifeguards protected bathers. Ever since its inception, the Atlantic City Beach Patrol has been a very highly regarded organization. Lifeboat drills had to be constantly practiced to ensure the proficiency of the lifesaving crew. (Ottenheimer, *c.* 1910.)

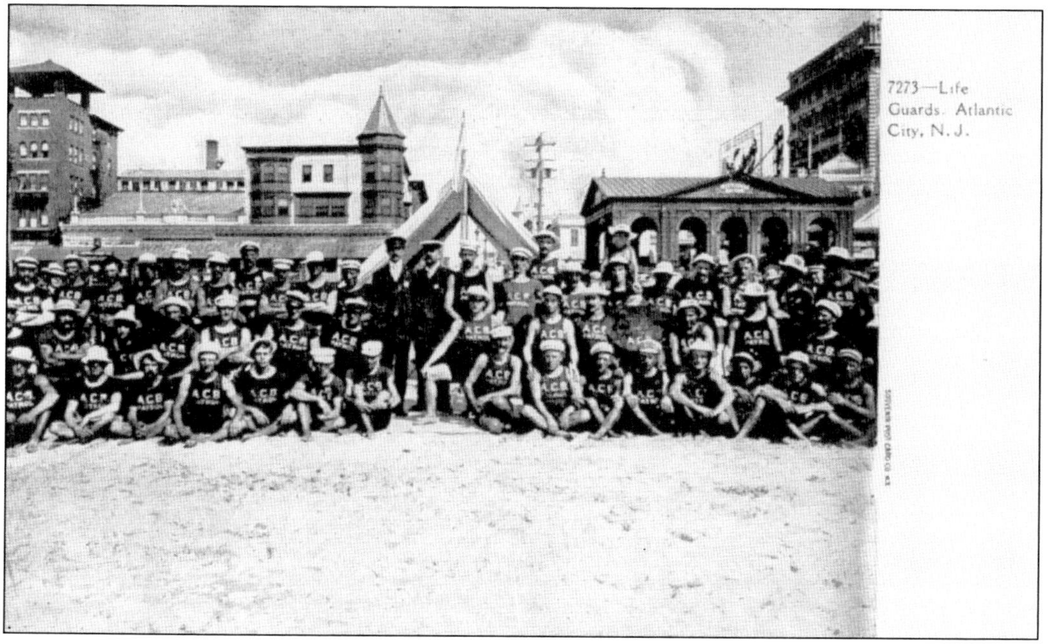

LIFE GUARDS. Proud to be members of the Atlantic City Beach Patrol, a group of lifeguards pose on the beach at South Carolina Avenue. These dedicated young men ensured that the waters were safe for swimmers. The first female lifeguards appeared during World War II. After the war they were to disappear from the beaches until relatively recent times. (Souvenir Post Card Company, *c.* 1905.)

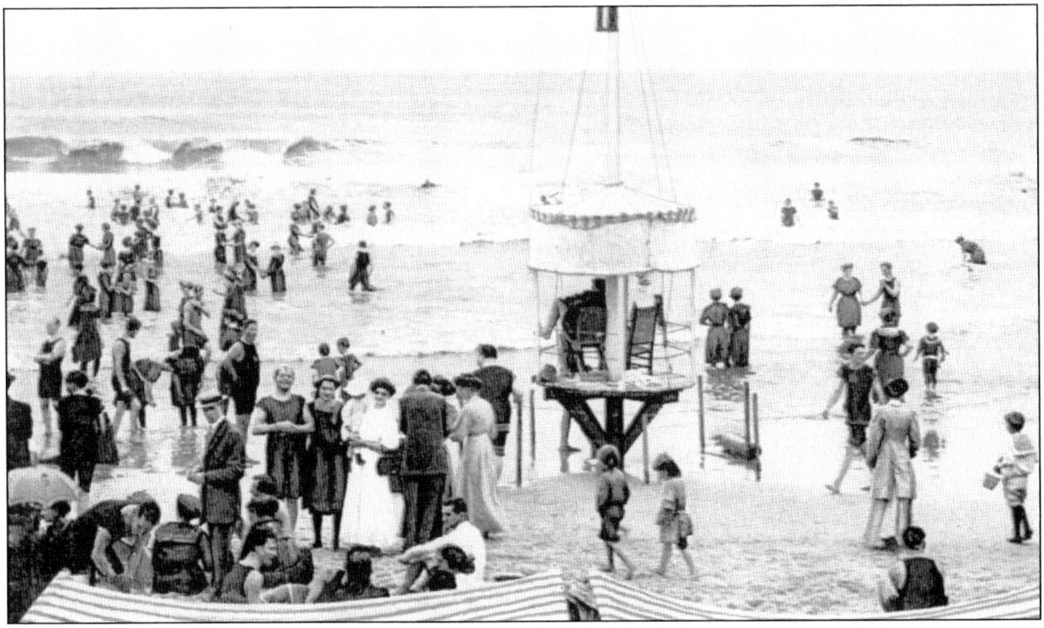

LIFESAVING LOOKOUT. During the early 1900s, splashing and wading in the ocean was referred to as bathing. A lifeguard seated under the canopy of a lifesaving lookout keeps a careful watch over those in the water. With its gradually sloping shoreline and skilled beach patrol, Atlantic City boasted of having some of the safest beaches in the nation. (Detroit Publishing, 1908.)

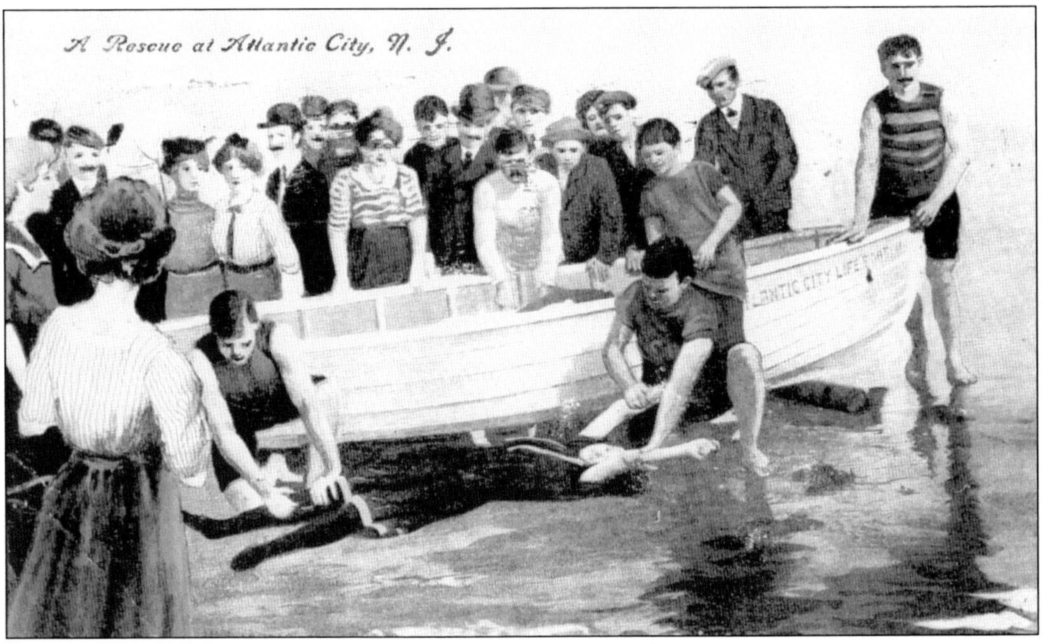

A RESCUE. A pair of lifeguards practice their lifesaving techniques while a group of onlookers observe. Between 1913 and 1951, records show that 50,611 people were rescued from the water, while only 29 drownings were reported. This is a remarkable tribute to the competence and skills of the well-trained Atlantic City Beach Patrol. (Illustrated Post Card Company, 1907.)

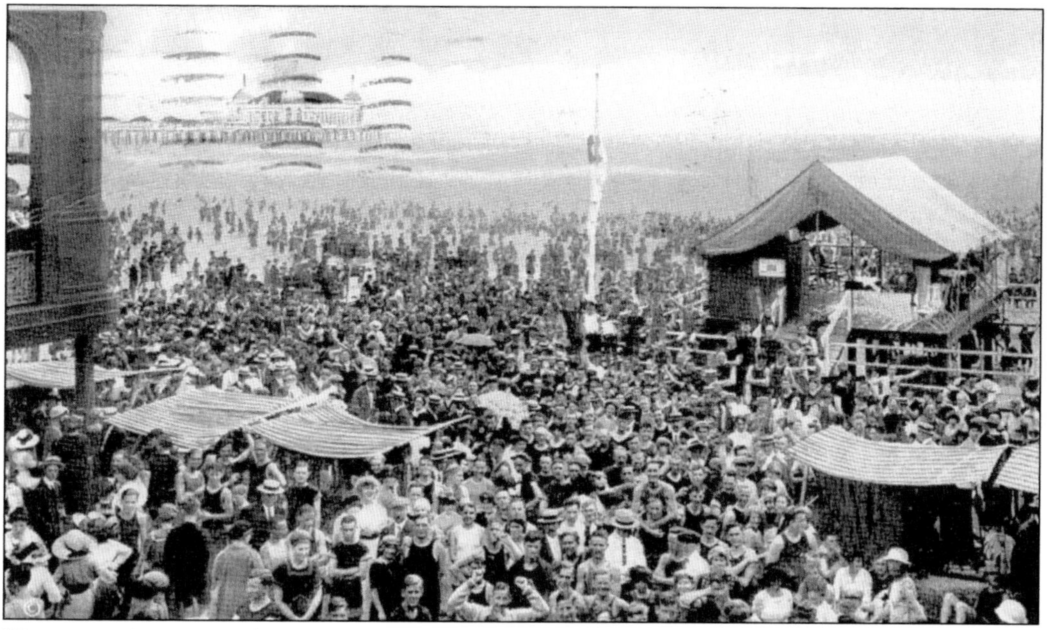

Hospital Tent. In this view of the beach at South Carolina Avenue, a large crowd is seen gathered near a hospital tent. Such tents, provided by the city, were furnished with first aid supplies and manned by medical personnel to further ensure the welfare of those on the beach. (Post Card Distribution Company, *c.* 1916.)

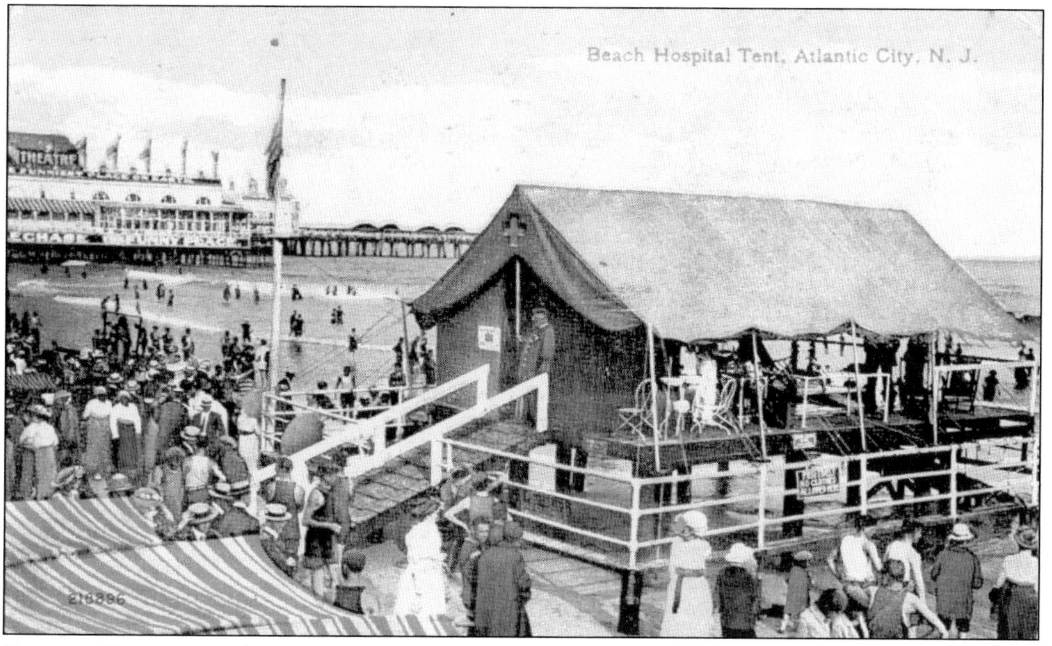

South Carolina Avenue Hospital Tent. The city installed hospital tents at various locations. In 1905, the first hospital tent was erected here at South Carolina Avenue. Two years later another was opened on the beach at Mississippi Avenue, while smaller tents were installed at the Missouri and Maryland Avenue beaches. Around 1913, a new tent was placed at Morris Avenue. (Post Card Distribution Company, *c.* 1912.)

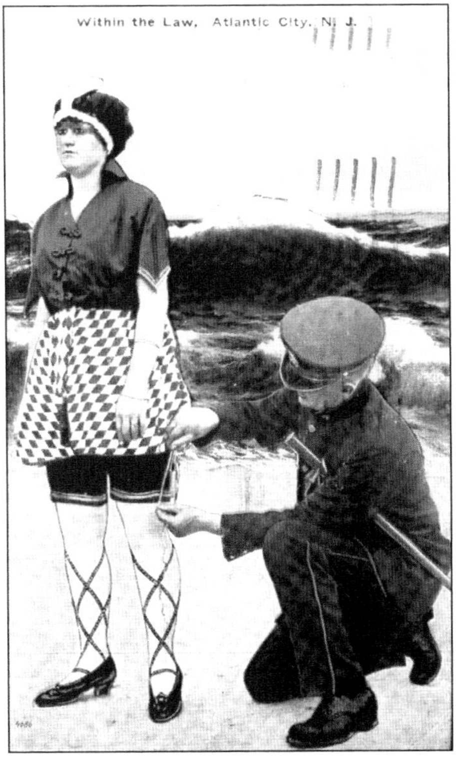

WITHIN THE LAW. Armed with a tape measure, a censor checks the length of a woman's bathing suit. Beachgoers both male and female could be fined or arrested if they broke the rules designed by city officials to protect public decency. One ordinance, in effect until repealed in 1940, required men to always wear a shirt or top while on the beach. (P. Sander, *c.* 1919.)

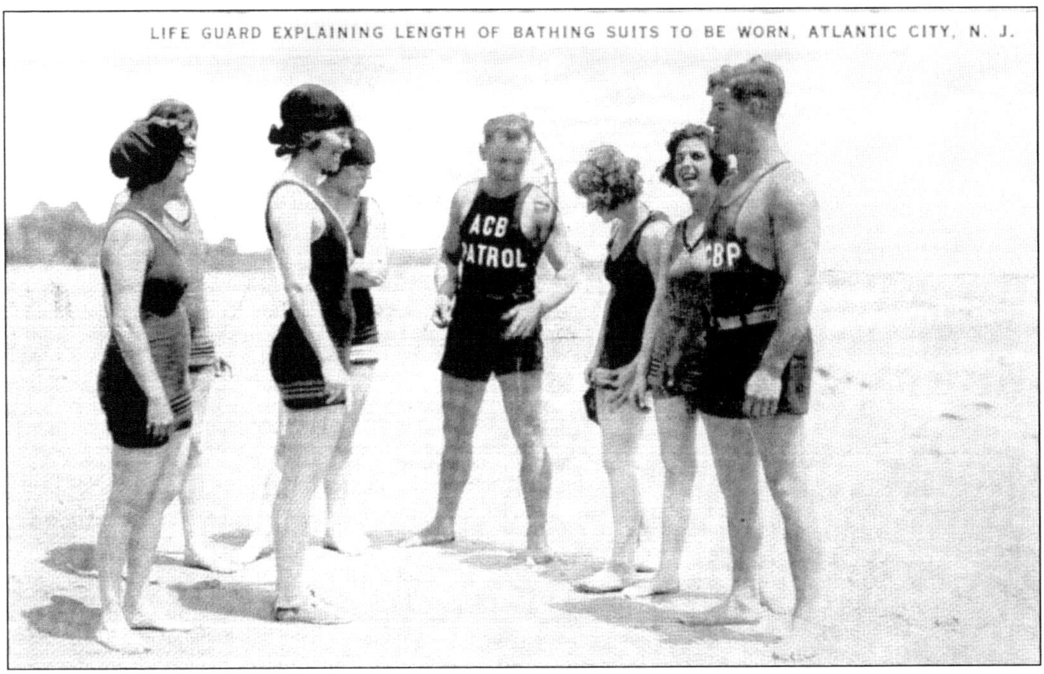

BATHING SUITS. Two lifeguards pause to explain the rules governing proper bathing suit attire to a group of young ladies. As beach fashions changed over the years, from ankle-length skirts and bloomers to the one-piece suits of the 1920s, so did the laws regulating them. Of course there were always those willing to try to push the limits of modesty. (I. Robbins and Sons, *c.* 1923.)

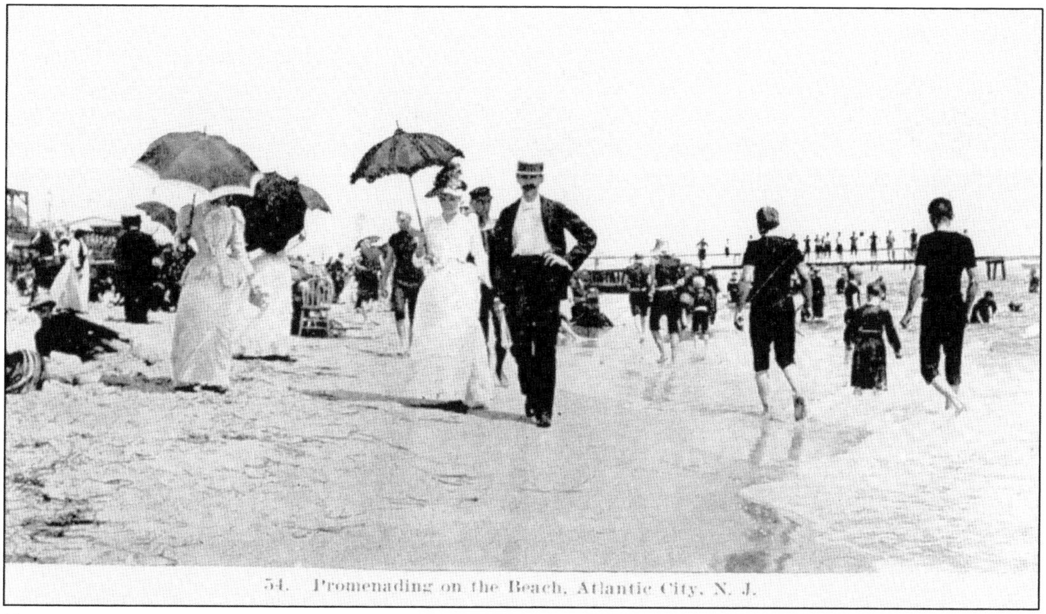

PROMENADING ON THE BEACH. Not everyone came down to the seaside to bathe in the ocean. In the early part of the 20th century, many came merely to enjoy a leisurely stroll or promenade on the sands while dressed in their finest attire. For females, walking under a parasol to protect themselves from the sun was considered the proper ladylike thing to do. (I. and M. Ottenheimer, 1909.)

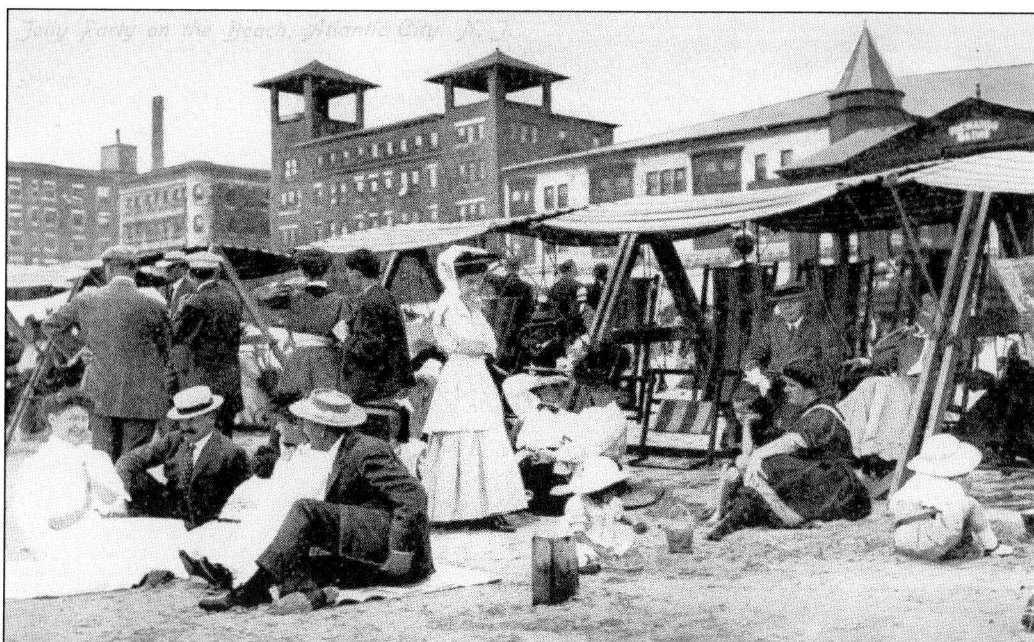

JOLLY PARTY ON THE BEACH. Throughout the summer months the Atlantic City beaches were usually crowded with people seeking the enjoyment of the sand and ocean breezes. Here beachgoers stake out a small plot of sand to call their own as they enjoy a day in the sun. Take note of how the people are dressed for a relaxing day on the beach. (L. Beard, *c.* 1909.)

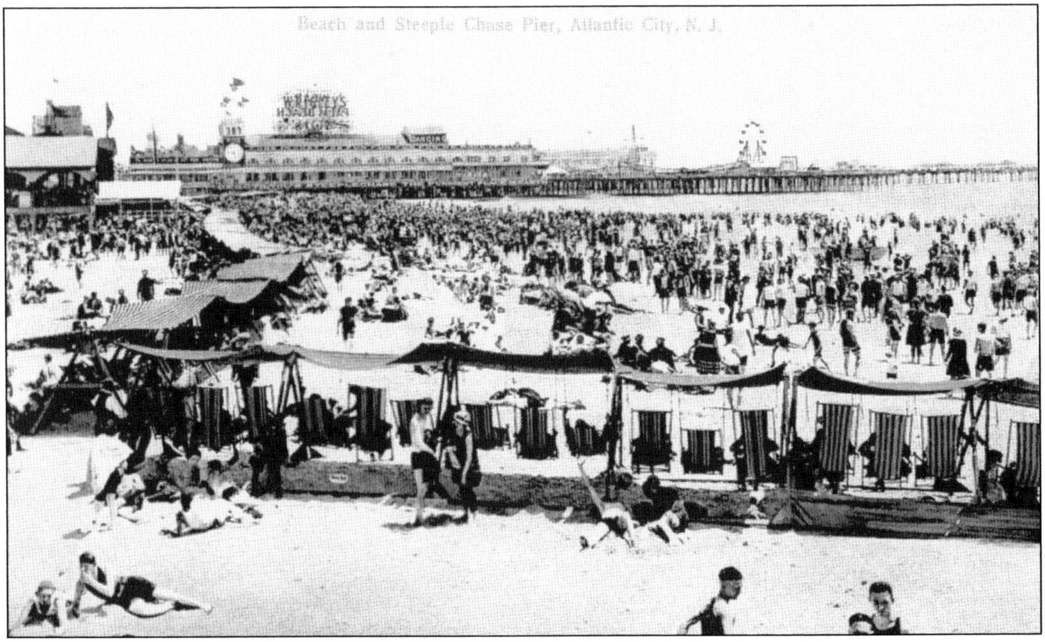

BEACH AND STEEPLECHASE PIER. Here is seen a long row of shaded canvas swings extending along the beach. Renting one of these for a nominal fee allowed a person to be shaded from the sun while lazily swaying back and forth. It was a comfortable way to sit and watch all of the beach activities taking place around them. (A. C. Bosselman, *c.* 1918.)

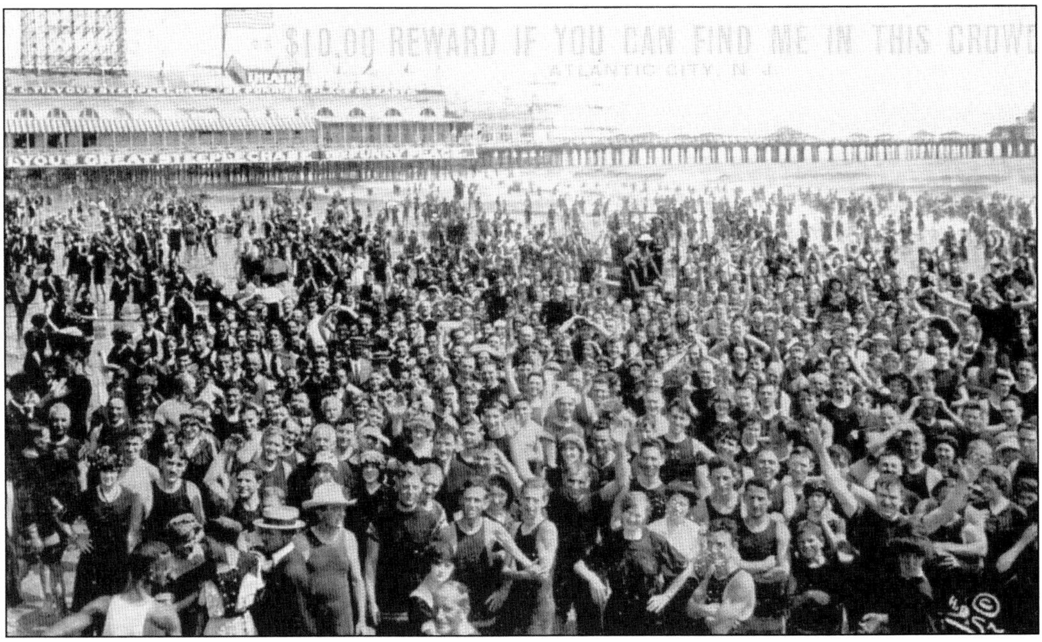

"$10.00 REWARD IF YOU CAN FIND ME." People seeking to escape the oppressive heat in the larger cities would flock to the seaside in vast numbers. Weekend crowds on Atlantic City's beaches could reach into the tens of thousands. Postcards, such as this one, poked fun at the fact that a person could easily get lost among the masses. (Atlantic Post Card Company, *c.* 1916.)

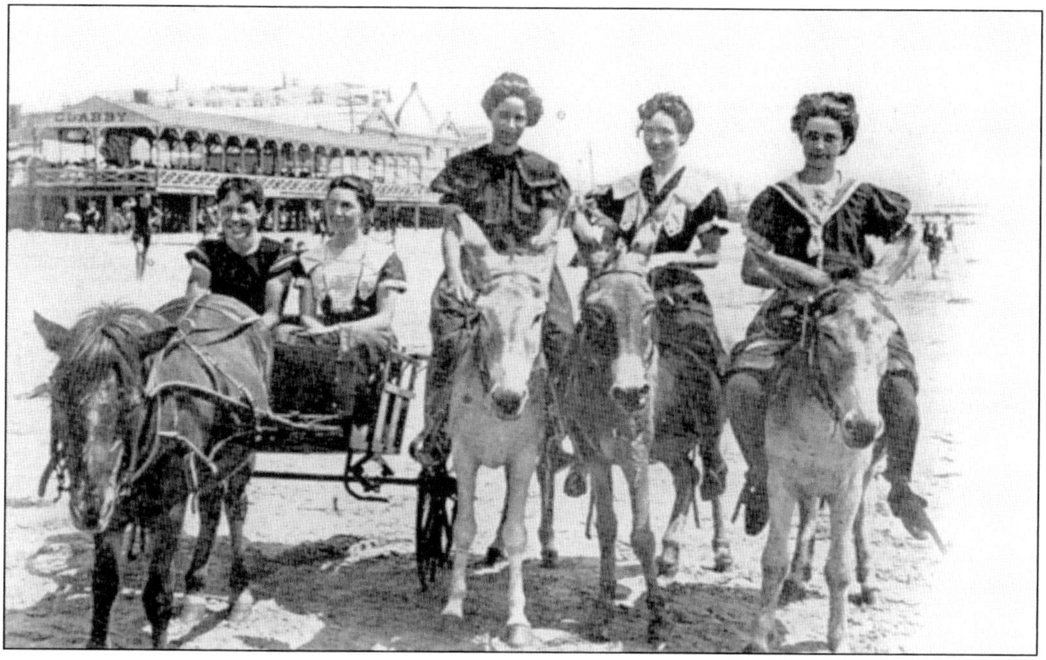

JACKS, QUEENS UP! One common theme of beach postcard views from the early 1900s was that of people photographed sitting on a pony cart or atop a donkey. Here three young ladies and a couple pose for the photographer. Horses and donkeys were a common sight on the beach in those days. (Publisher unknown, *c.* 1904.)

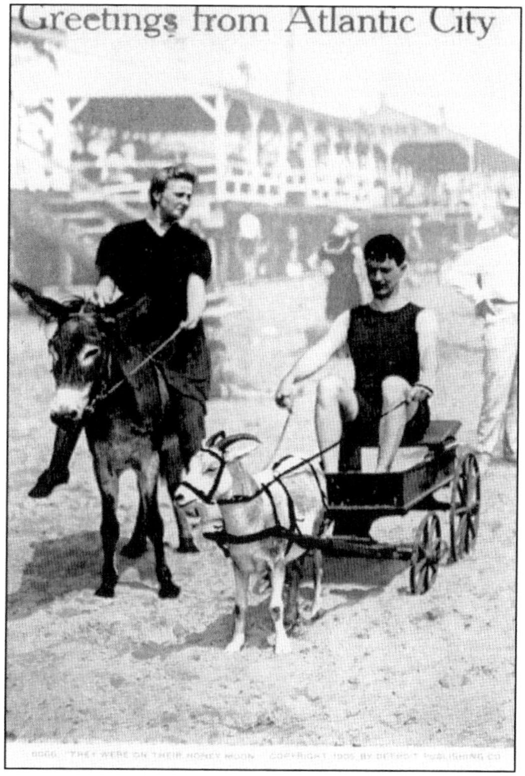

ON THEIR HONEYMOON. A young man and woman, identified as honeymooners, are photographed sitting on competing means of transport. Atlantic City, with its many diverse offerings, has been a popular destination for newlyweds over the years. (Detroit Publishing, 1905.)

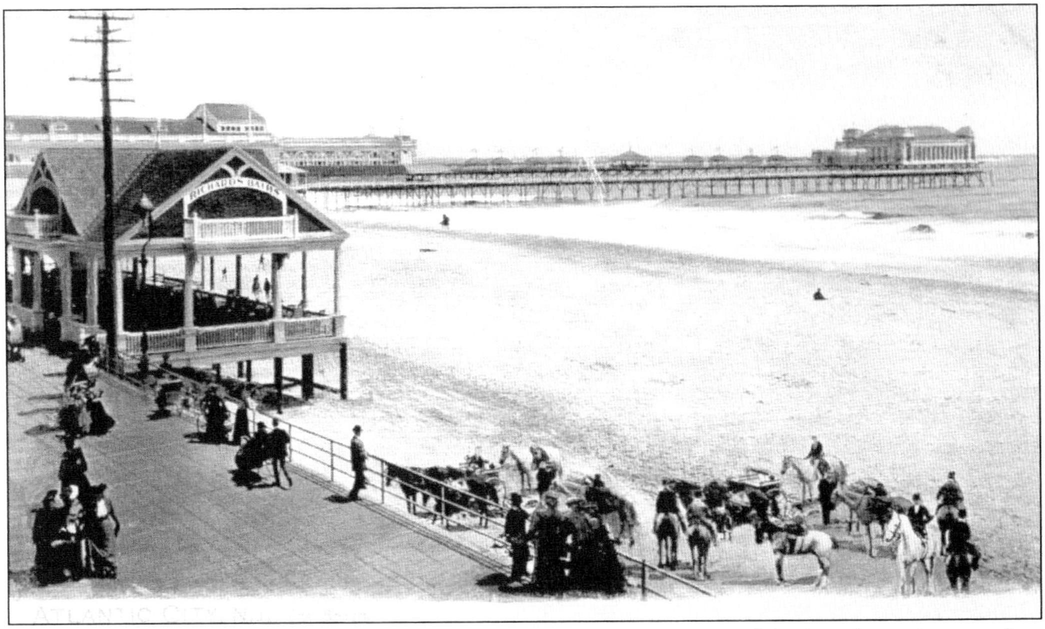

The Beach. An early-morning horseback ride on the packed sands of the beach was just another type of recreation in which people could engage themselves. Horses could be rented by the hour from nearby stables. After taking a ride, a group of English-style equestrians take a pause at the edge of the boardwalk. (Raphael Tuck, *c.* 1904.)

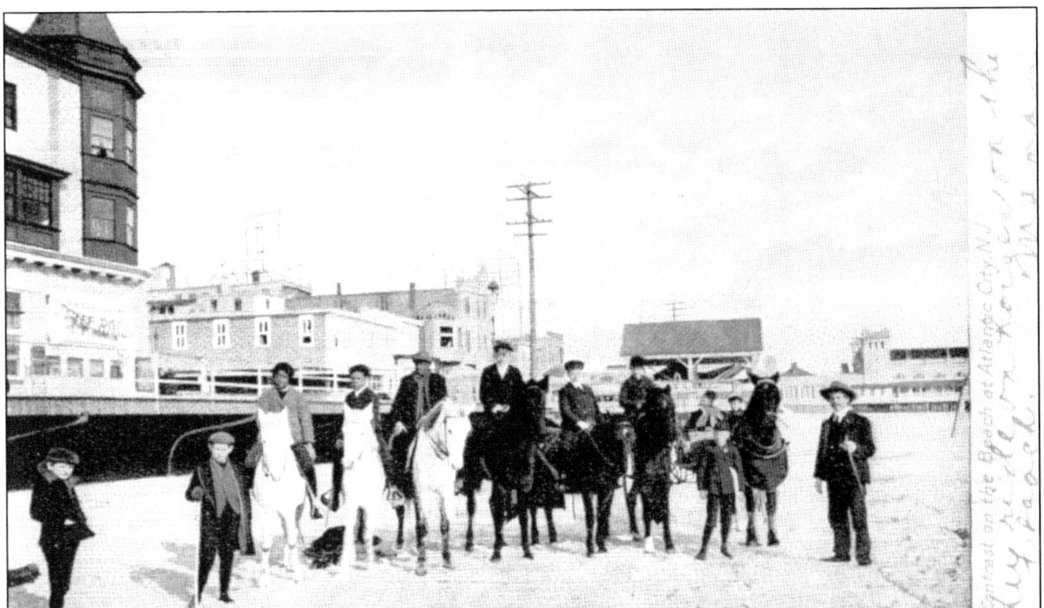

A Contrast on the Beach. A group of young boys on horseback pose for the postcard photographer. Riding on the beach could be an exhilarating and enjoyable pastime. However, doing this was an off-season activity. On July 25, 1905, a city ordinance went into effect that prohibited horseback riding on the beach between June 1 and October 1. (H. C. Leighton, *c.* 1904.)

CAST UP BY THE SEA. Popular on the beach for many years were the works of sand art produced by a handful of artists. Here a talented sand sculptor works on his elaborate carving of a woman and child. Such artwork would have been created within sight of the people walking the boardwalk. These artisans existed on the coins thrown down to them by appreciative admirers of their work. (J. J. Taylor, 1906.)

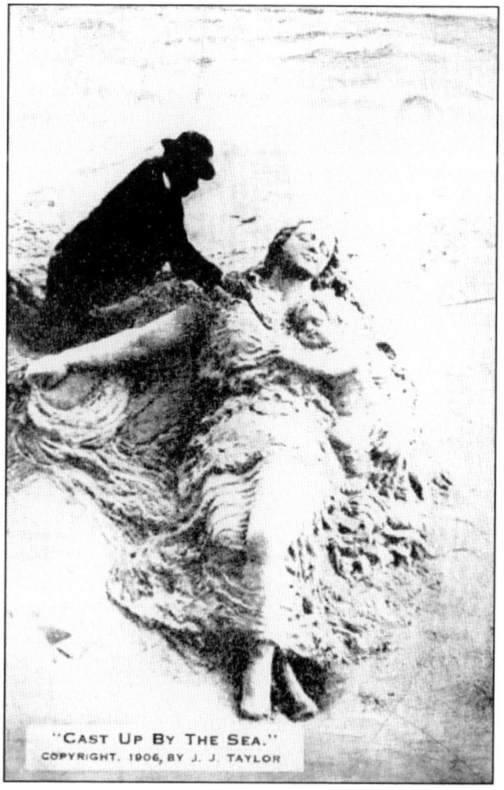

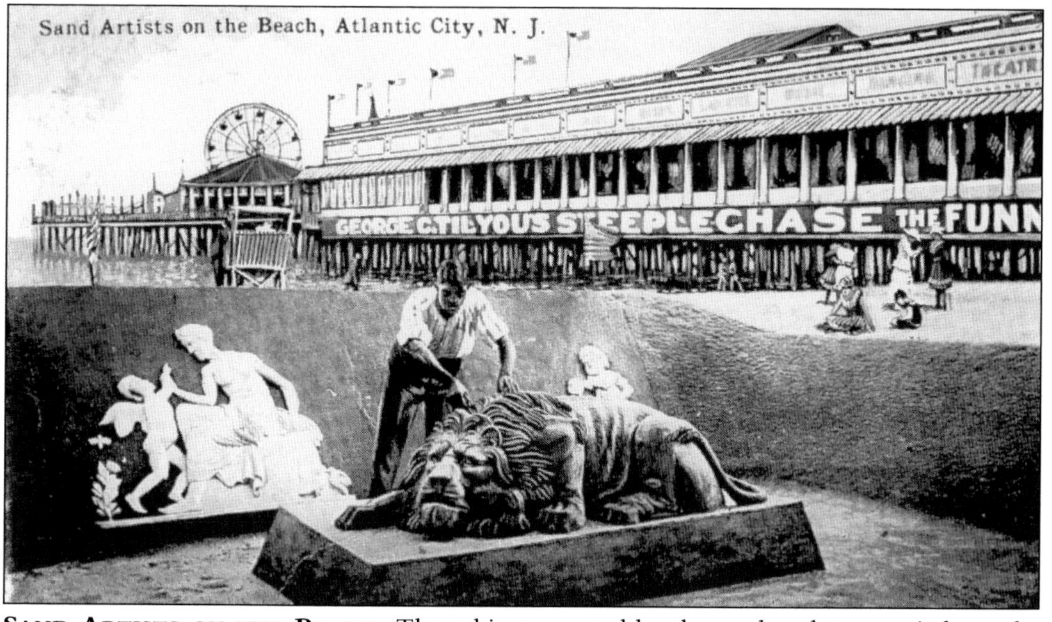

SAND ARTISTS ON THE BEACH. The subjects created by the sand sculptors varied greatly. Although classical and patriotic themes were traditional favorites, other representations included fish, caricatures of famous people, religious images, and automobiles, among others. Here the artist is seen completing his carving of a reposing lion. In the background can be seen the Steeplechase Pier. (Sithens, *c.* 1912.)

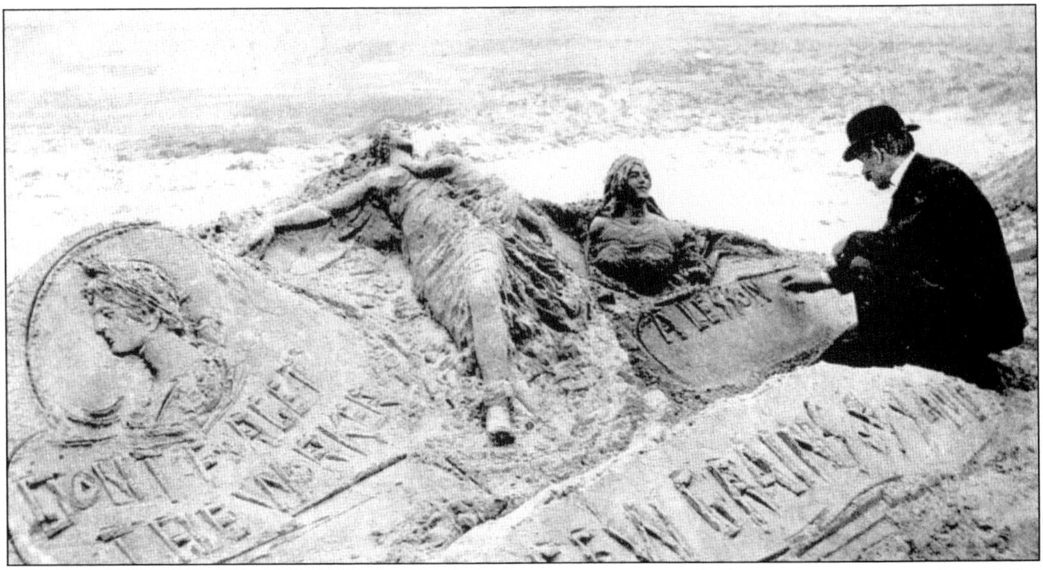

THE SAND MAN. Putting the final touches on his work entitled "A Few Grains of Sand," a sand artist completes his sculpture. To help ensure the durability of their creations, some were not above adding a little cement to their sand mixture. This rather unique form of artistry began with Philip McCord in 1897 and continued over the years until 1944, when the city commission officially banned the practice. (Detroit Publishing, 1900.)

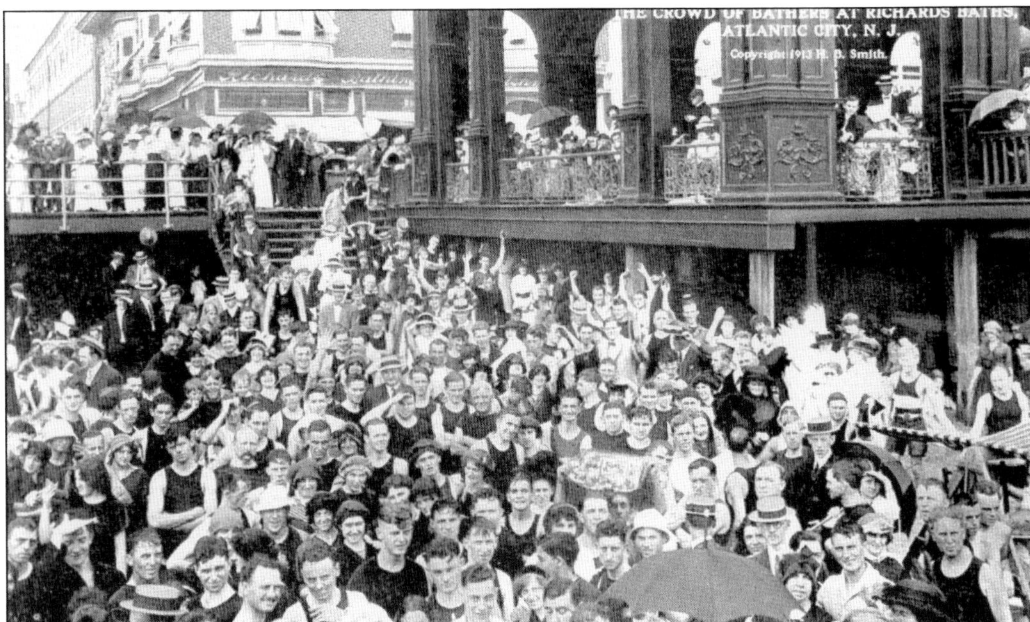

CROWD OF BATHERS. A huge crowd of seemingly happy beachgoers gather at the steps leading from the boardwalk to the beach at South Carolina Avenue. On the far side of the boardwalk is Richards Bath's, one of the largest bathhouses in the city. It was operated for many years by longtime state senator Emerson L. Richards. This landmark bathhouse was torn down in 1958. (Post Card Distribution Company, 1913.)

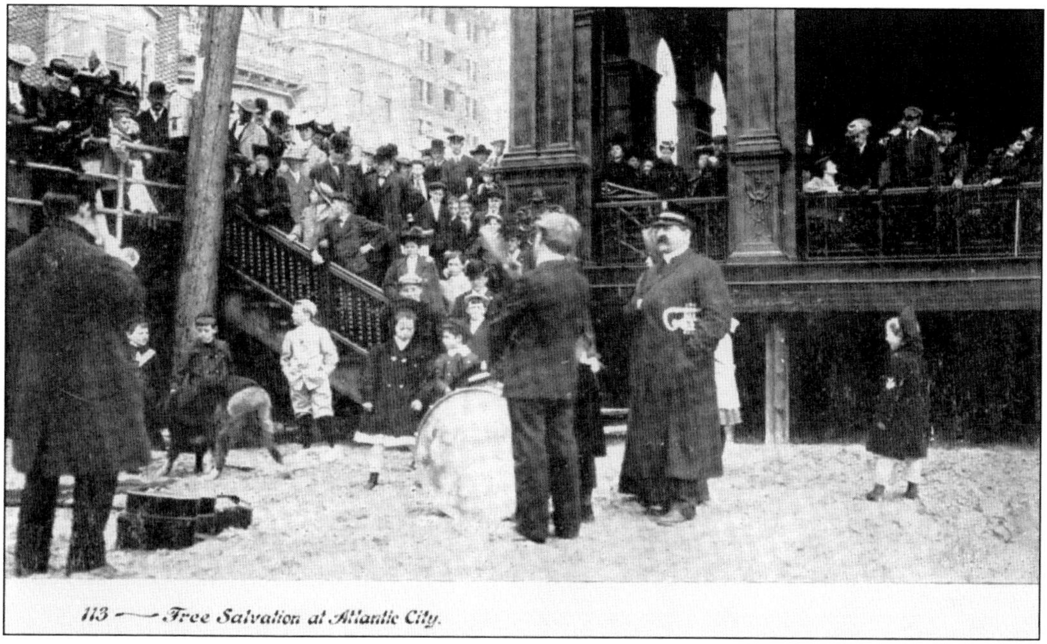

FREE SALVATION. At the South Carolina Avenue beach entrance, members of the Salvation Army with their musical instruments attract a crowd. Begun in 1865 as the Christian Mission, the group changed its name to the Salvation Army in 1878. The goals of this well-known organization are to provide social services to all those in need and to spread the gospel of Jesus Christ. (J. Murray Jordan, *c.* 1905.)

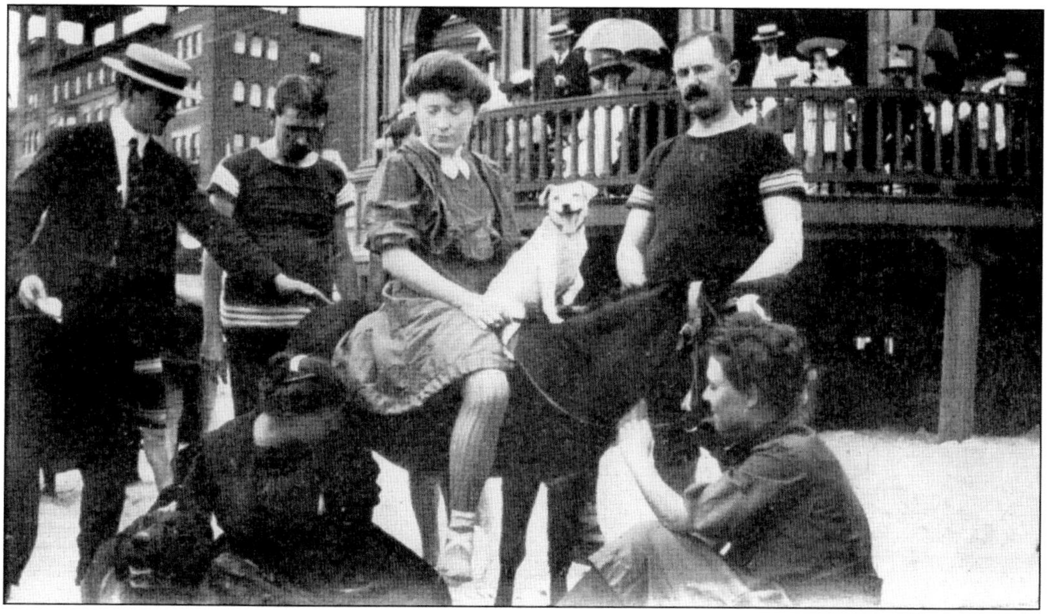

A FAMILY PARTY. People on the boardwalk pavilion, at the South Carolina Avenue beach entrance, look on as a family on the sands below poses for the camera. Even the family dogs, one sitting on the back of a donkey while the other sits on the ground, are included in the day's activities. The Dunlop Hotel, located on the boardwalk, can be seen in the background. (J. Murray Jordan, *c.* 1902.)

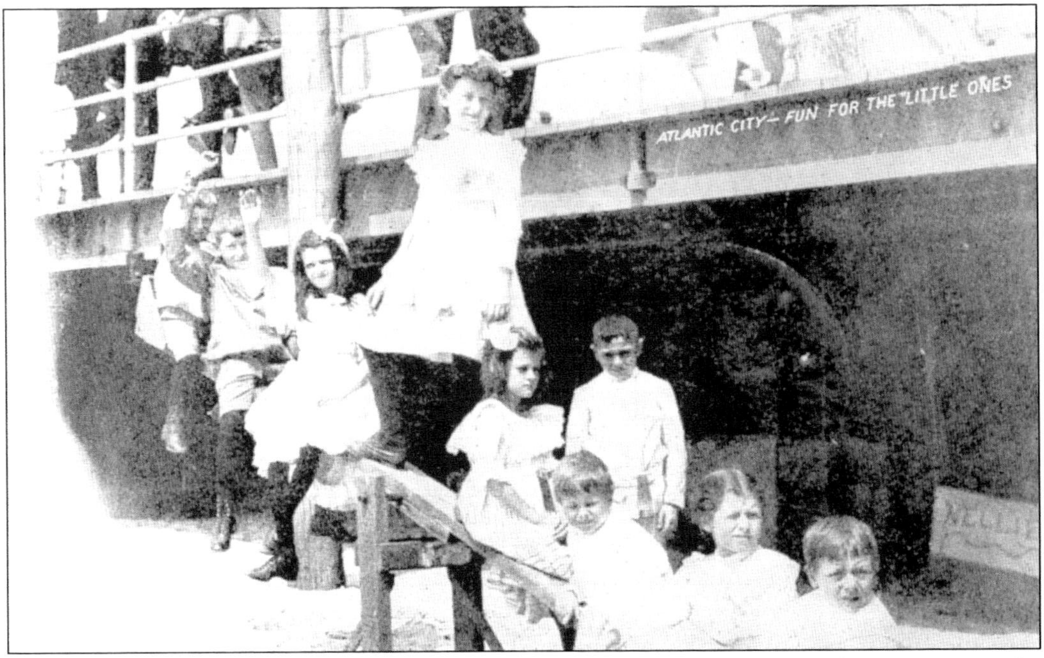

Fun for the Little Ones. A group of children sits on a seesaw that has been set up on the beach near the boardwalk. This apparatus provided another recreational activity they could take part in during a day of play on the sands. Fun and pleasures on the beach took many forms for both young and old. (J. Murray Jordan, *c.* 1905.)

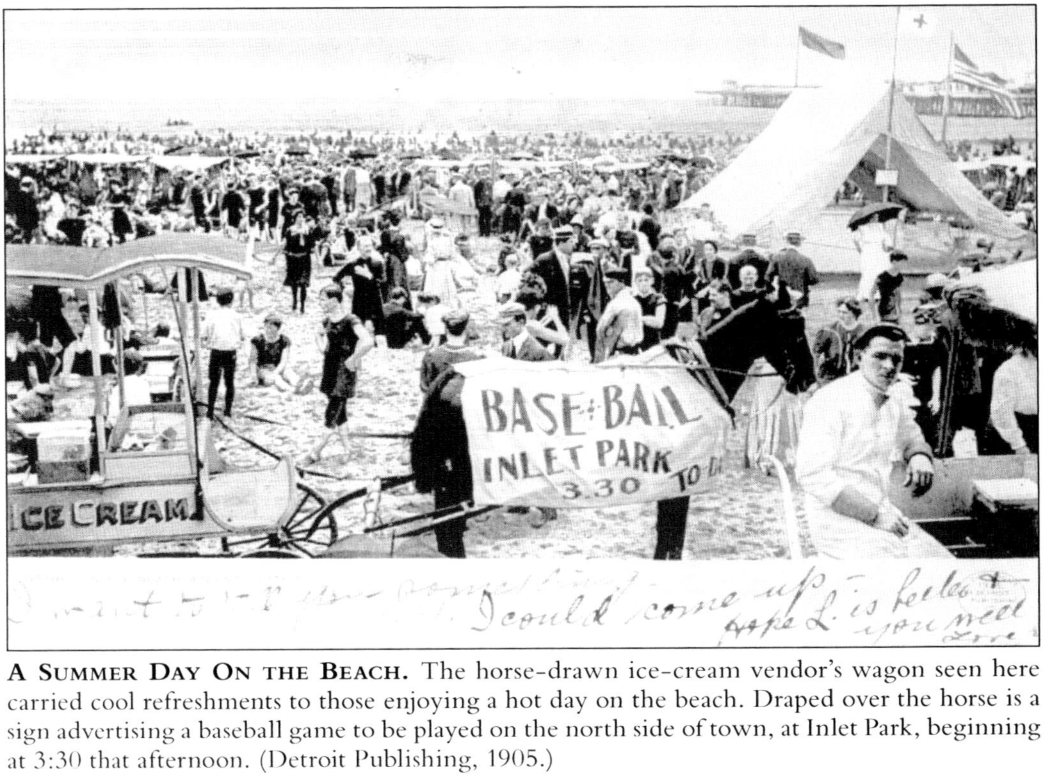

A Summer Day On the Beach. The horse-drawn ice-cream vendor's wagon seen here carried cool refreshments to those enjoying a hot day on the beach. Draped over the horse is a sign advertising a baseball game to be played on the north side of town, at Inlet Park, beginning at 3:30 that afternoon. (Detroit Publishing, 1905.)

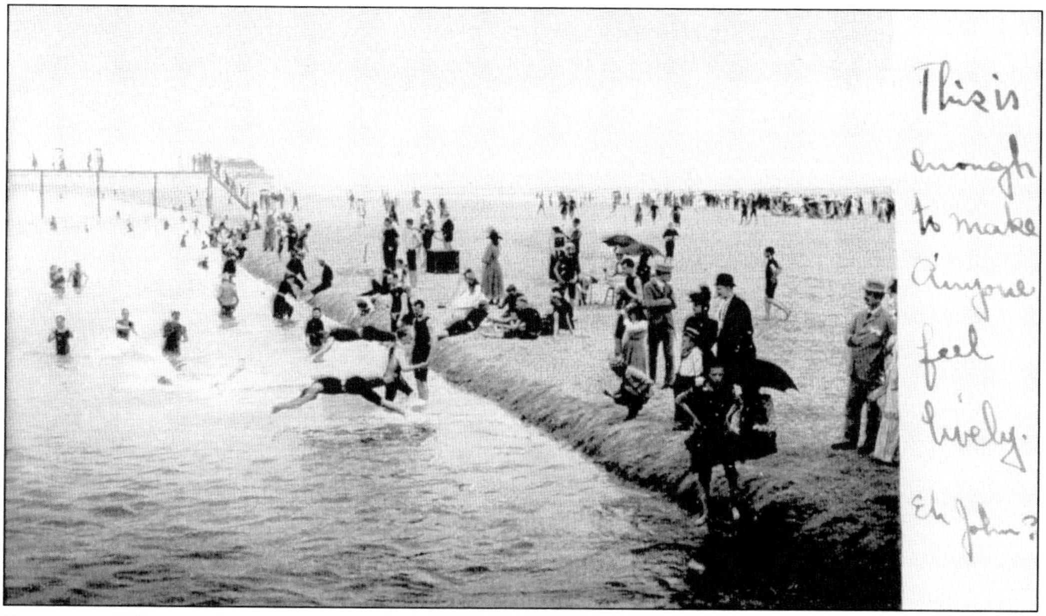

Smooth Water Bathing. Bathers are seen enjoying swimming and splashing about in a gully carved into the beach. These shallow, water-filled trenches were sometimes created by the ocean's receding tides, and they made ideal places to frolic in the warm salt water. As the sender of this postcard wrote to a friend back home, "this is enough to make anyone feel lively." (H. C. Leighton, *c.* 1905.)

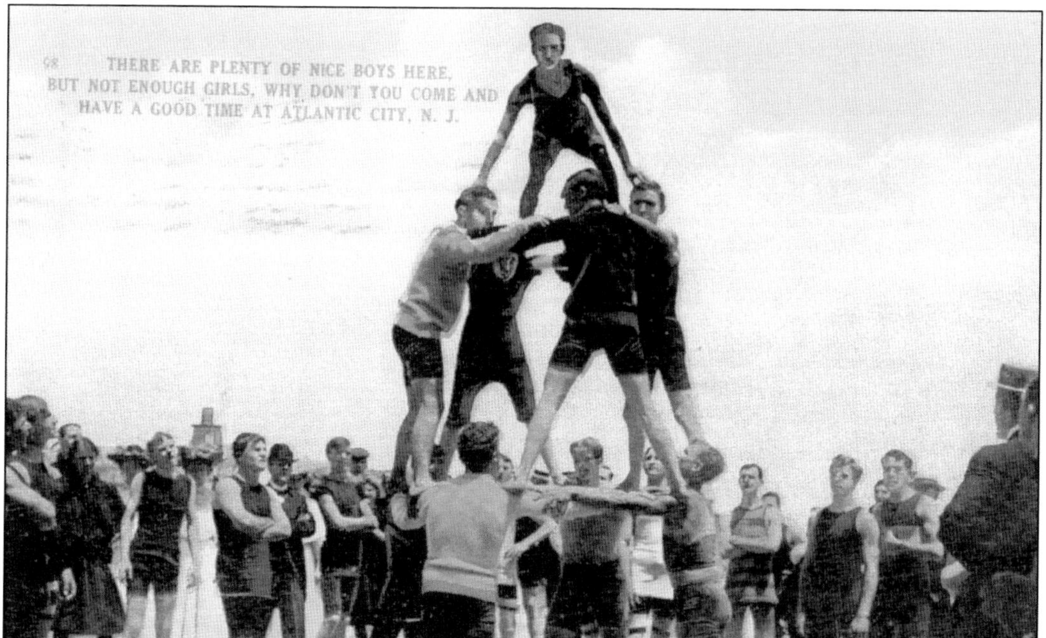

Plenty of Nice Boys Here. A group of boys demonstrate their acrobatic skills by constructing a human pyramid on the beach. Such an activity was a surefire way to attract a crowd and perhaps even the attention of some pretty young ladies on the beach as well. (Atlantic Postcard Company, *c.* 1913.)

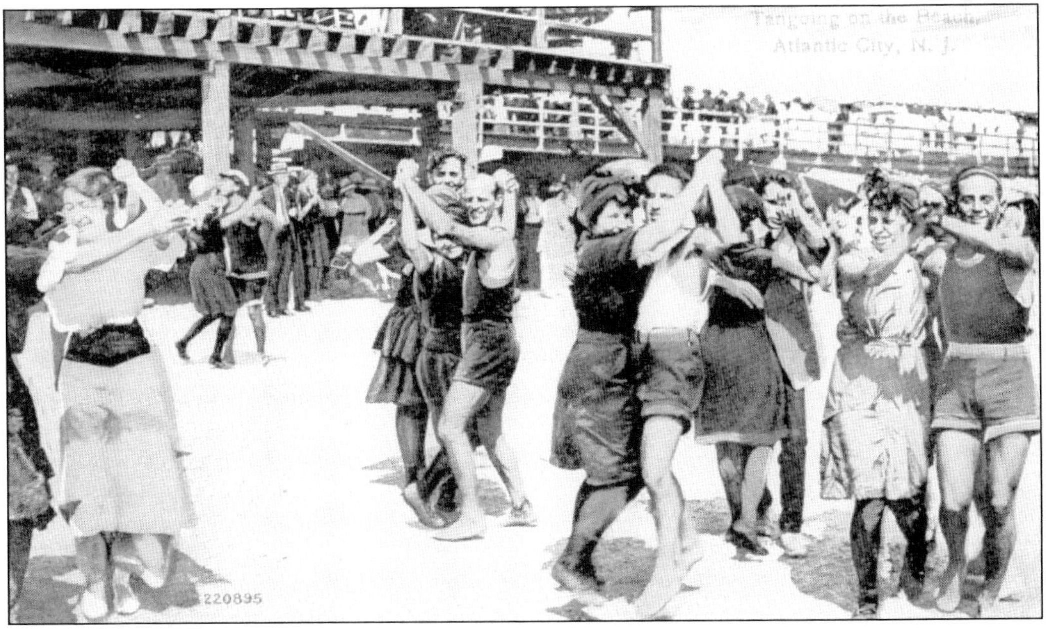

TANGOING. Couples practice their tango dance moves on the sand by the boardwalk. In 1913, with World War I only a year away, it was the "Year of the Tango." Couples all over the world wanted to learn this dance, which had originated in Argentina. The tango was only the third dance in history where the man and woman faced each other and held hands as they danced. (Post Card Distribution Company, *c.* 1913.)

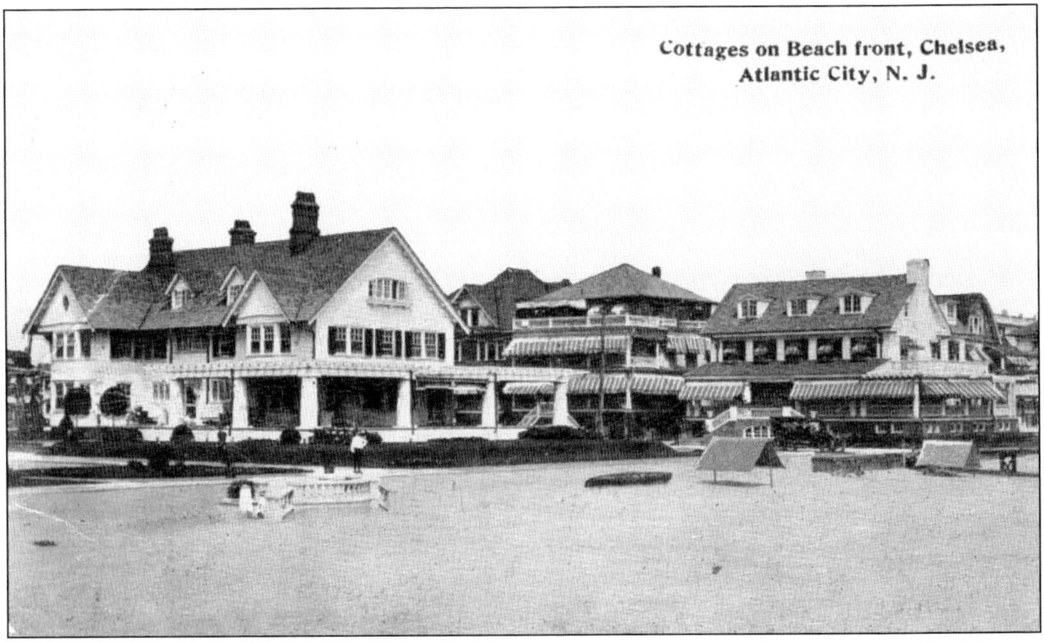

BEACHFRONT COTTAGES. During the early 1900s, stately homes sat beachfront in the Chelsea District. A much different atmosphere existed here compared to the beach just a little farther north, where the boardwalk and larger hotels existed. The beach here was far less crowded. (Post Card Distribution Company, *c.* 1912.)

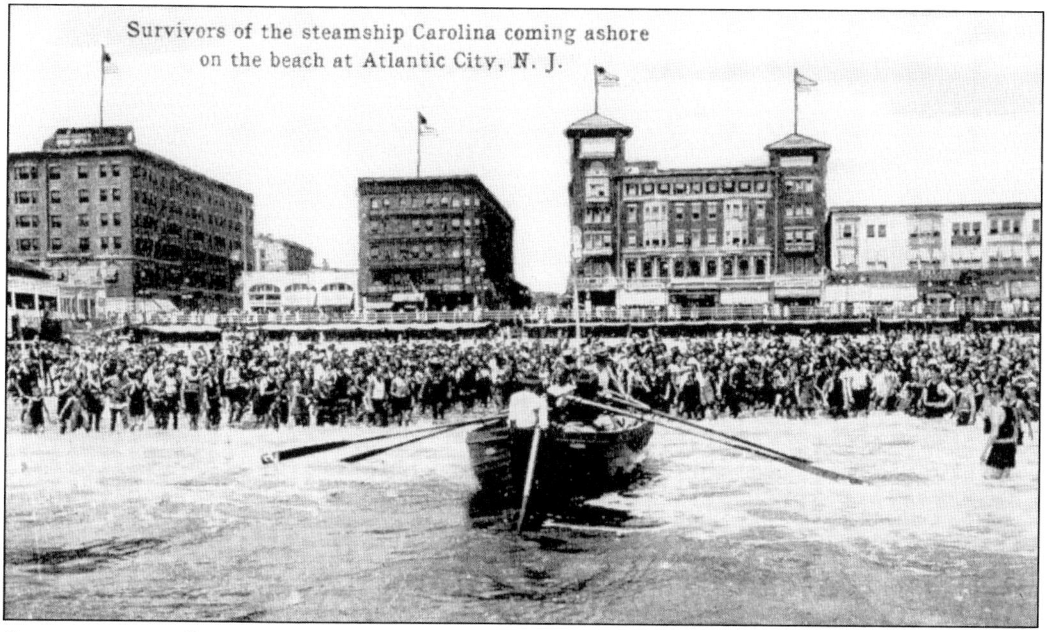

SURVIVORS OF STEAMSHIP *CAROLINA*. At 2:00 on the afternoon of June 4, 1918, a lifeboat carrying 28 survivors of the steamship *Carolina* rowed ashore at the South Carolina Avenue beach. They were greeted by hundreds of cheering beachgoers. Forty-four hours earlier the ship *Carolina* had been sunk by a German submarine about 75 miles off Cape Henlopen. (Virginia Avenue Post Card Company, 1918.)

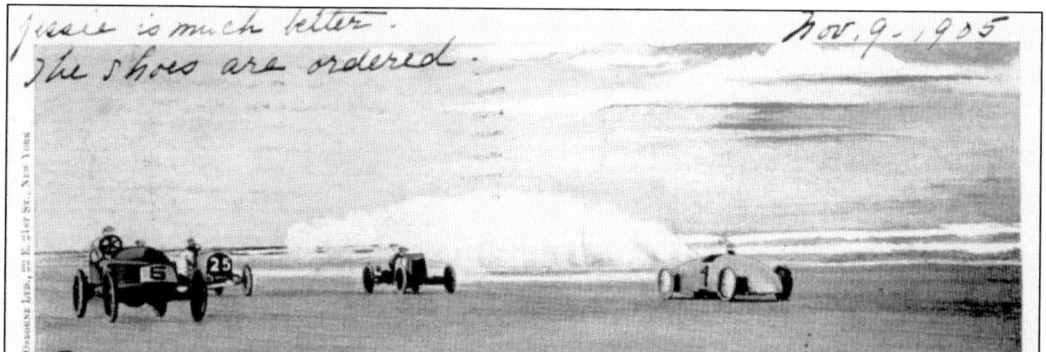

MOTOR RACING. The hard-packed sand between the high and low tide areas were utilized as a raceway on the Margate and Ventnor beaches. During a three-day period in early September 1905 and 1906, races were held on a two-mile-long course set up on the beach. The automobiles managed to average speeds up to 50 miles per hour during the competition. (Osborne, 1905.)

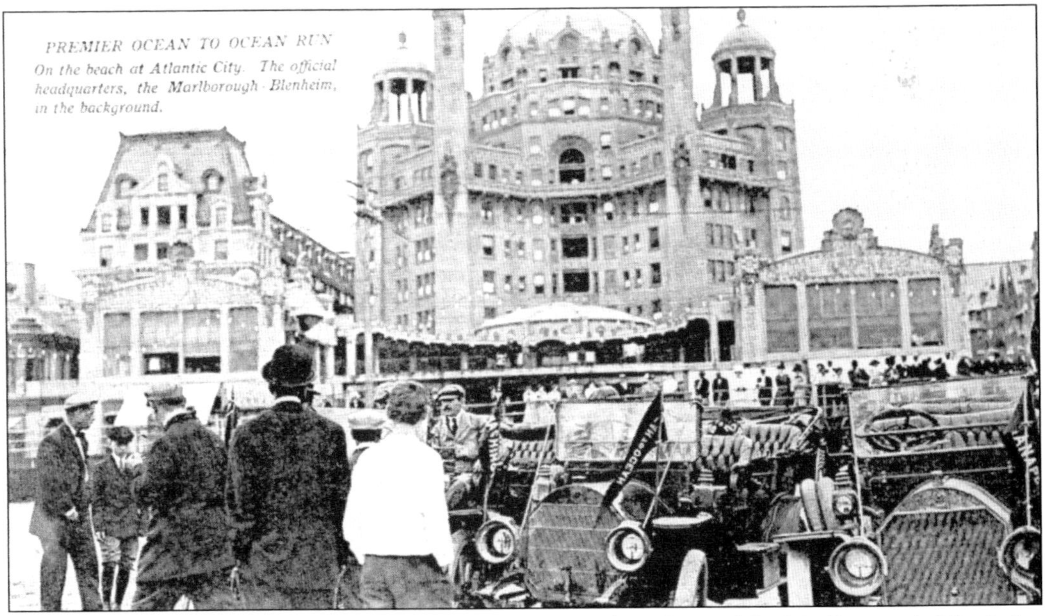

PREMIER OCEAN-TO-OCEAN RUN. Sitting on the beach in front of the Marlborough-Blenheim Hotel are several automobiles manufactured by the Premier Auto Manufacturing Company of Indianapolis, Indiana. This make of car was produced from 1903 until 1926. A regional distributor of these cars, John Guy Monihan organized an ocean-to-ocean road trip to advertise and promote these vehicles. (Publisher unknown, 1911.)

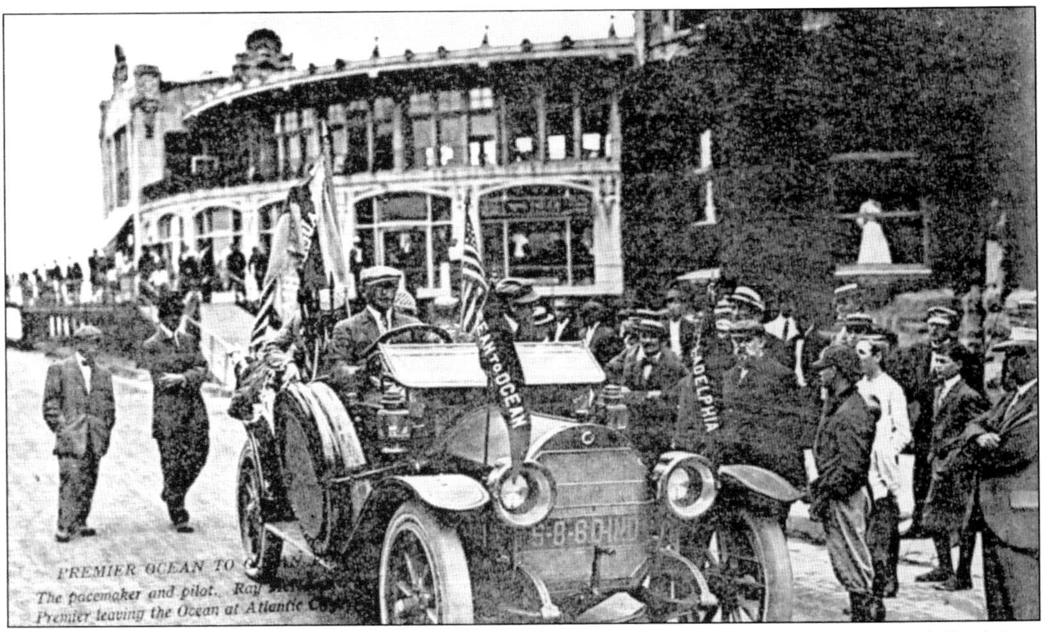

OCEAN-TO-OCEAN RUN. Decked out with flags and pennants, a Premier automobile drives off the beach as it begins its cross-country trip. A total of 40 people in 11 of these cars, and one truck, left from this beach on June 26, 1911. The caravan arrived in Los Angeles, California, on August 10 after traveling a distance of 4,731 miles. (Publisher unknown, 1911.)

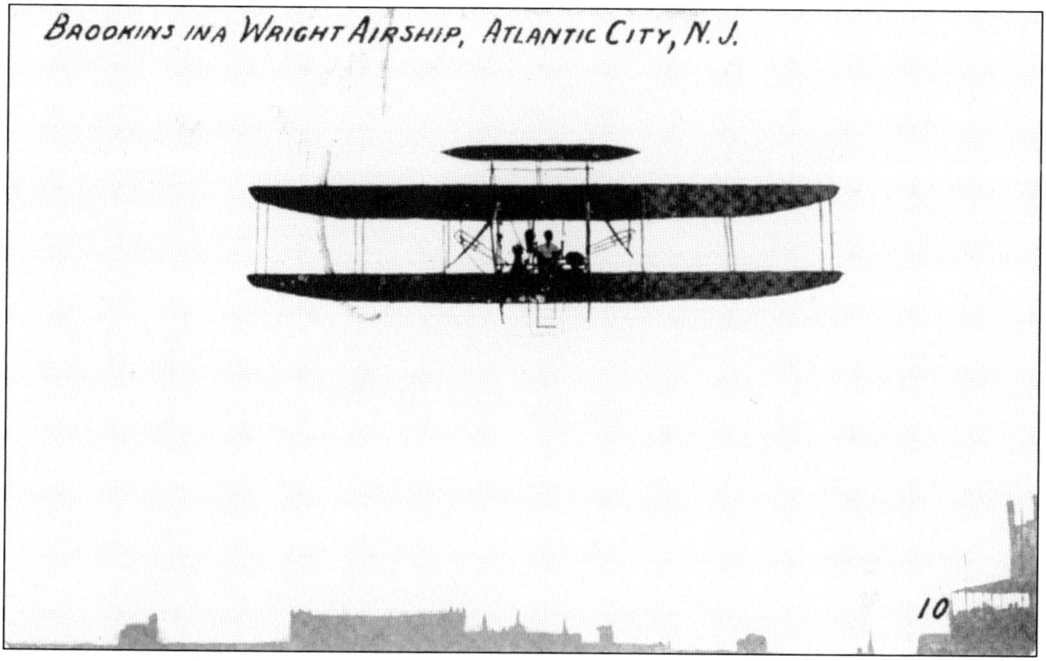

BROOKINS IN A WRIGHT AIRSHIP. On July 10, 1910, Walter Brookins became the first pilot to fly to an altitude of one mile, setting that record over Atlantic City in his Wright Brothers aeroplane. Brookins was considered to be the most skilled and daring member of the Wright Brothers' aviation team, when he flew in the 10-day-long Air Carnival held along the beach that year. (Ottenheimer, 1910.)

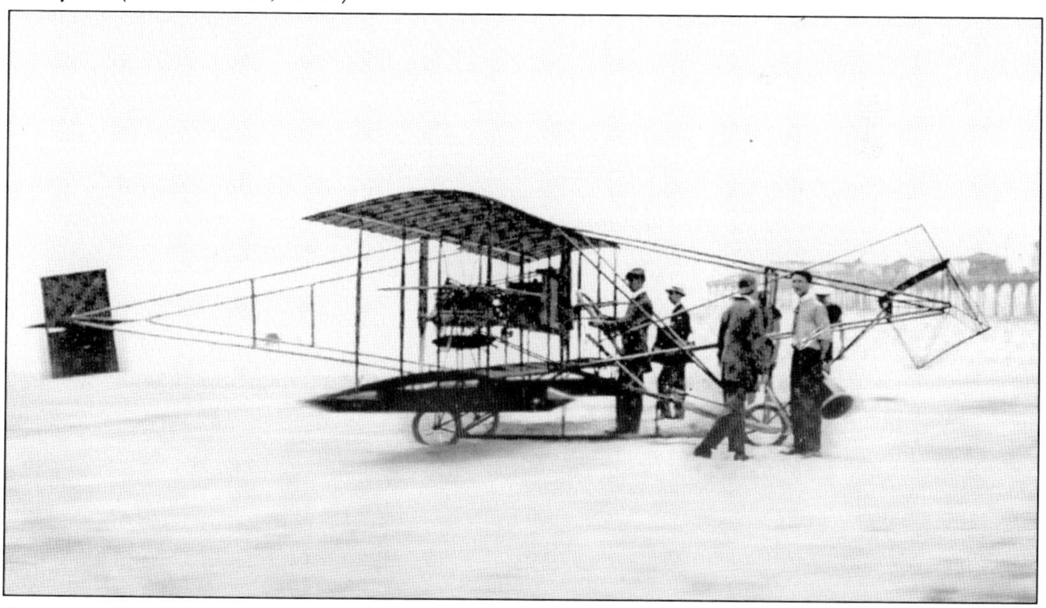

CURTISS AEROPLANE READY FOR FLIGHT. Another pilot who flew in the Air Carnival of 1910 was Glenn H. Curtiss, the "Henry Ford of aviation." While beach crowds looked on, Curtiss managed a record-breaking flight of 50 miles back and forth over the ocean in one hour and 14 minutes. He also demonstrated the possibilities of aerial bombing by dropping oranges on a yacht below him. (I. and M. Ottenheimer, 1910.)

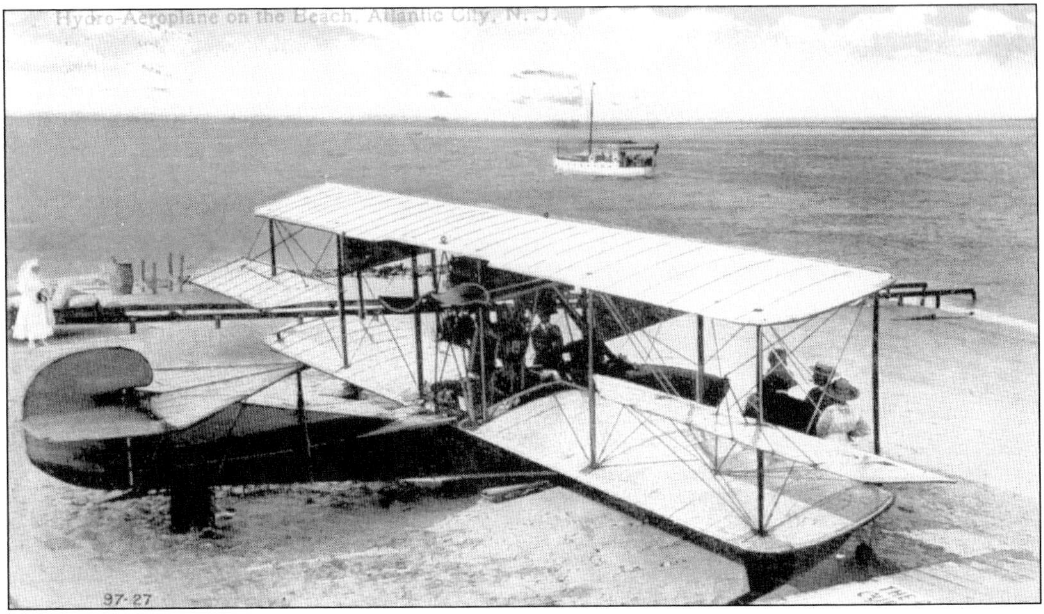

HYDRO-AEROPLANE ON THE BEACH. Glenn Curtiss was granted the first local airplane license for passenger flight on June 8, 1911. He went on to open an air station on the beach at the inlet end of the boardwalk near Hackney's. Here seaplanes that took passengers on aerial sightseeing trips took off and landed. Such flights provided an exciting and novel experience for many. (Post Card Distribution Company, *c.* 1919)

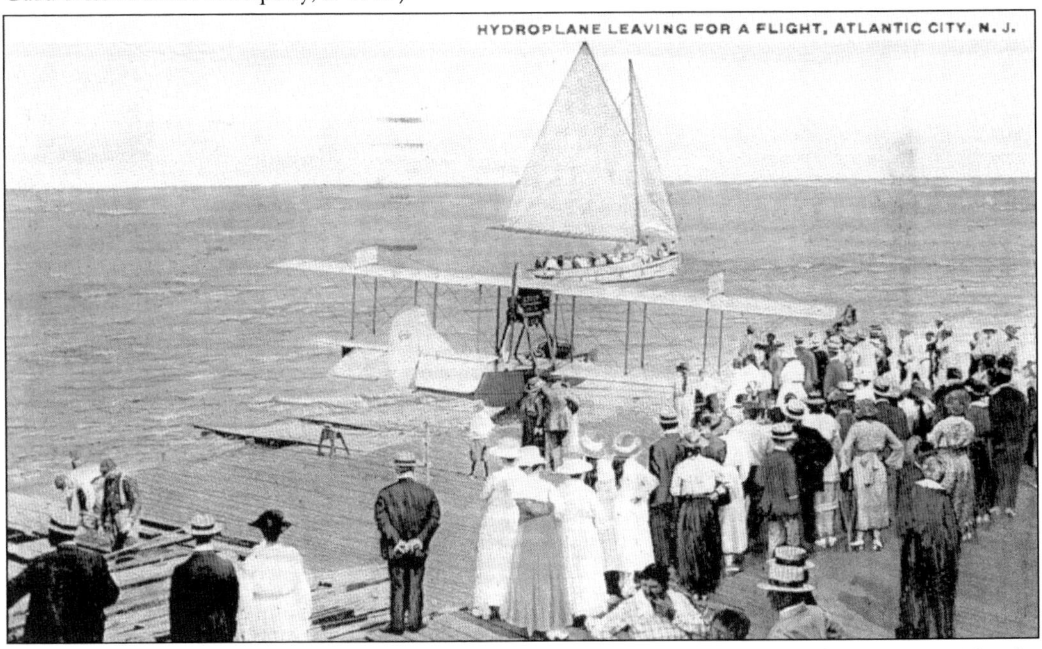

HYDROPLANE LEAVING FOR A FLIGHT. An early aviator by the name of E. K. Jacquith, the son of a wealthy Chicago banker, operated a flying school and gave rides from Mott's Hotel. Over the years he had landing platforms on the beach at Melrose and Madison Avenues. In 1920, patrons could board his single-engine seaplane for a $15 aerial sightseeing tour of Atlantic City. (I. Robbins and Sons, *c.* 1920.)

Six

The Inlet, Bay, and Ocean

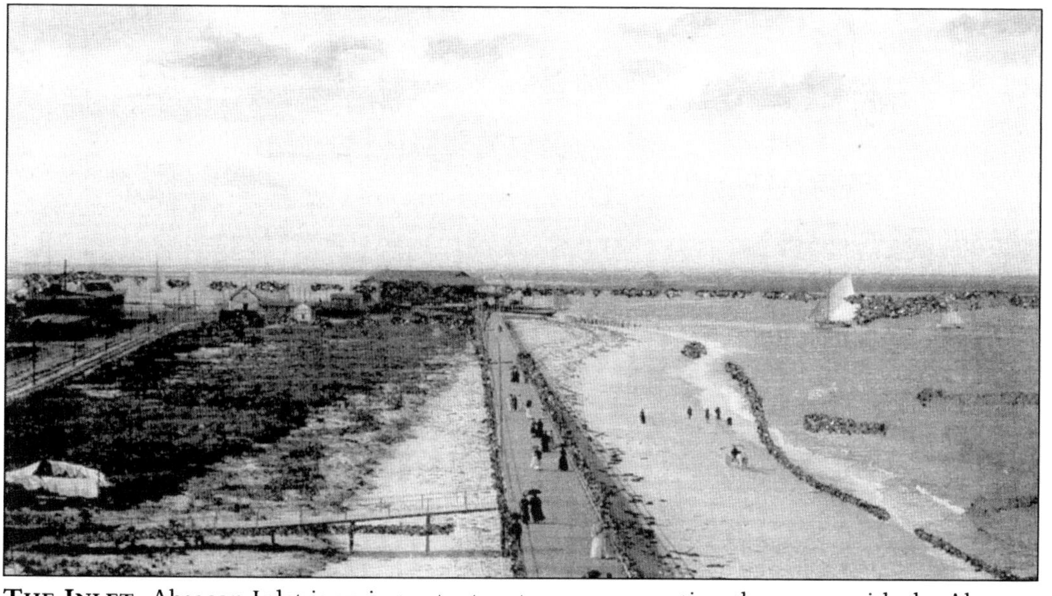

The Inlet. Absecon Inlet is an important waterway connecting the ocean with the Absecon Channel and inner bay. The name Absecon is derived from a Native American word meaning "bay" or "little water." The world's premier travel writer in the early 1900s, Harry Thurston Beck said of the inlet, "I have never seen anything that could compare with the savage beauty of the region." (Photo and Art Post Card Company, 1905.)

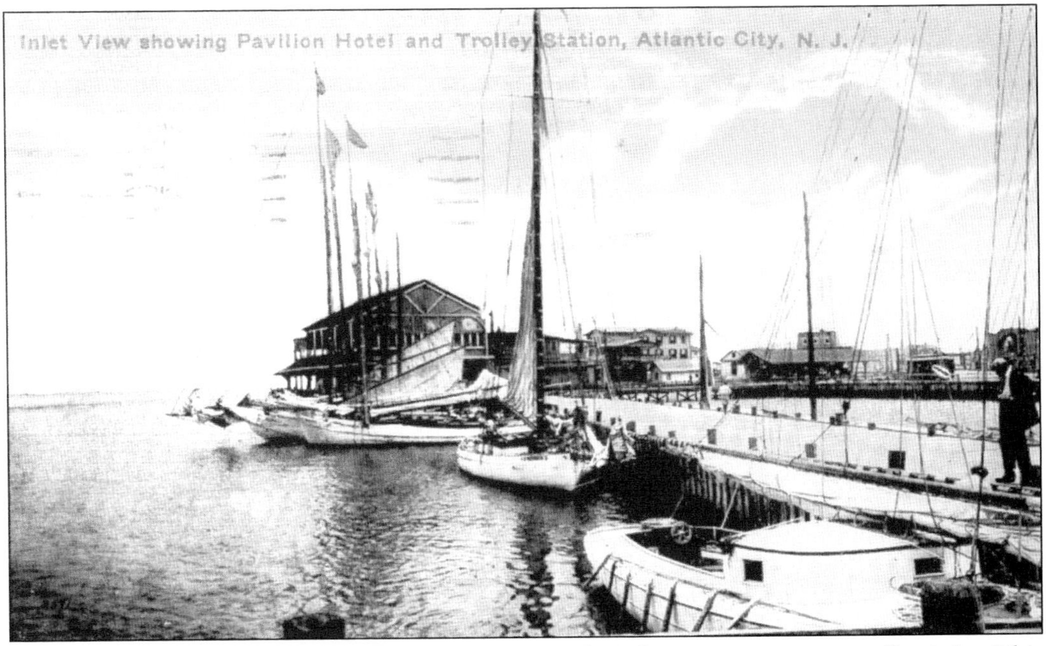

INLET VIEW. From early in Atlantic City's history, the inlet area was a center of activity. This view, looking toward the ocean, shows several of the important buildings that were once found here. The pavilion, Inlet Hotel, and the trolley station are among those visible. (National Post Card Company, *c.* 1914.)

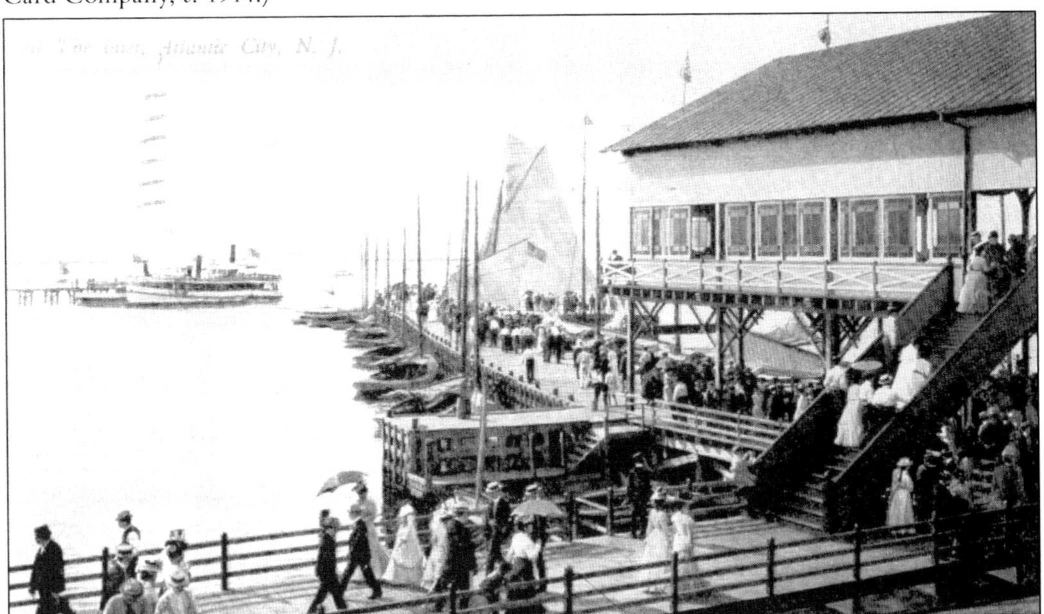

INLET PAVILION. One of the more prominent buildings in the area was the Inlet Pavilion. Standing right on the docks, it was only about one block from the northern end of the boardwalk. This open-air facility offered band concerts, dancing, and other forms of live entertainment. It was a place often frequented by ladies waiting for their men to return from a fishing excursion. (Rosin and Company, *c.* 1908.)

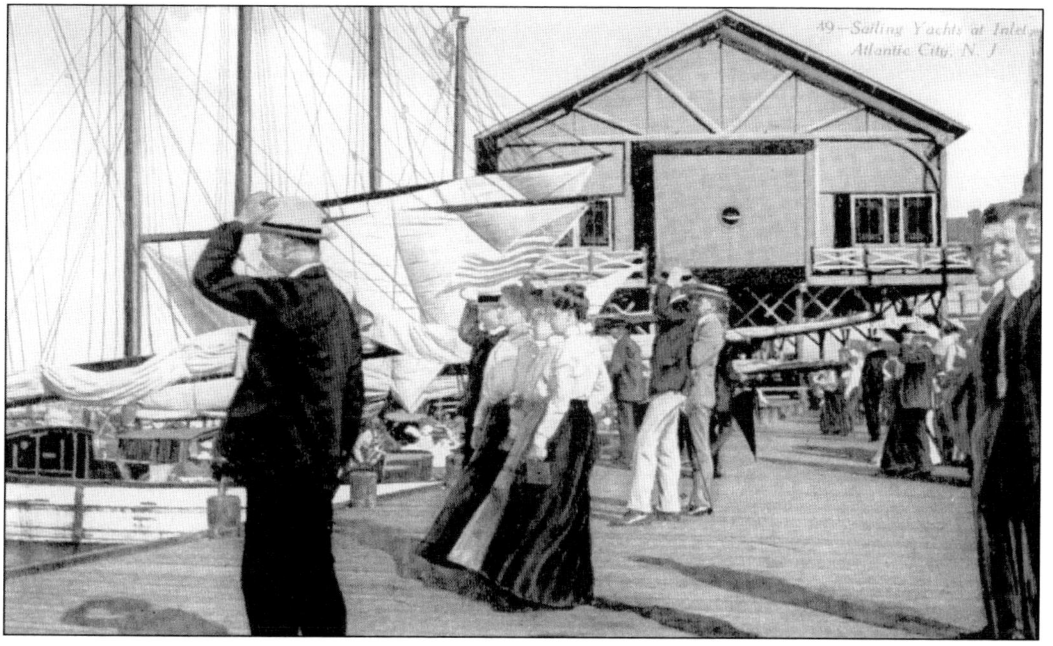

Sailing Yachts At the Inlet. Tied up to the wharf at the inlet was a small fleet consisting of a variety of vessels. Everything from sailing yachts to commercial fishing boats could be found moored here. All through the day the inlet waterfront would be bustling with people enjoying themselves in these nautical surroundings. (The Rotograph Company, *c.* 1910.)

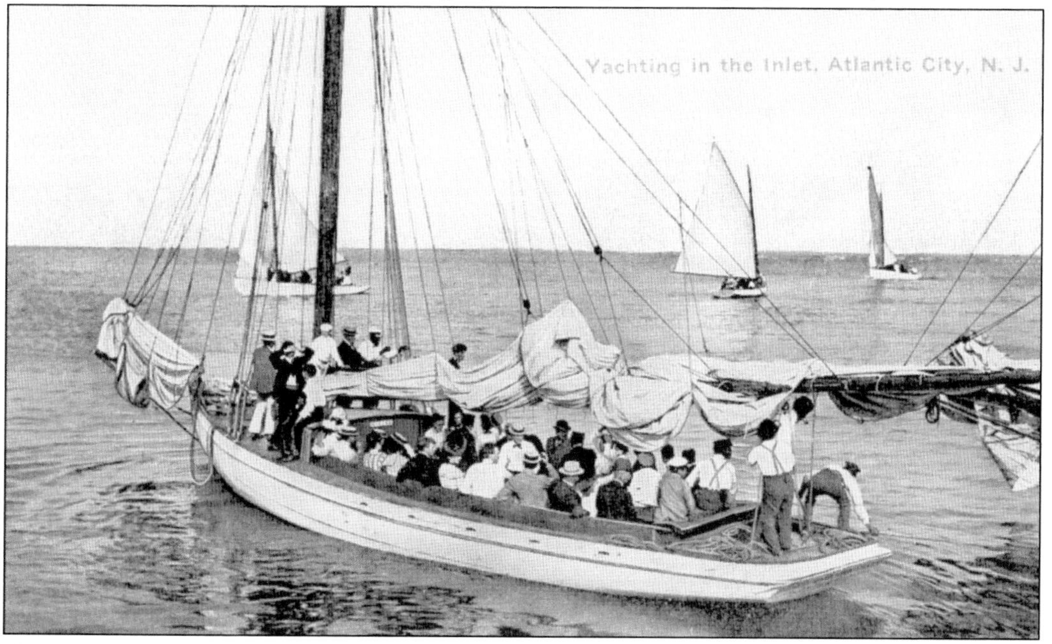

Yachting in the Inlet. Taking a voyage on a sailing yacht was a popular diversion during the early 1900s. Here a yacht is just leaving the dock with a full complement of passengers. As early as 1907, law prohibited yachtsmen from taking on more than 30 passengers at a time. At that time such vessels could be typically chartered for $5-10 per day or they might charge a rate of 25¢ per hour. (Koffman Brothers, *c.* 1908.)

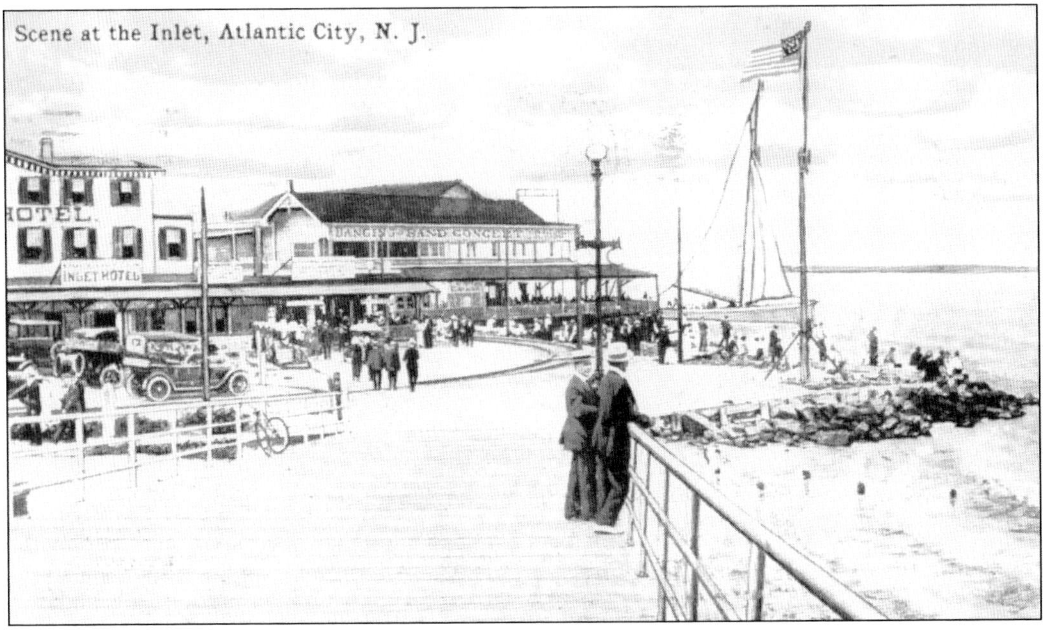

SCENE AT THE INLET. Two men stand at the northern end of the boardwalk where it terminates at the inlet. Here the trolley line can be seen curving around between the Inlet Hotel and the pavilion. Behind the pavilion were the docks where so many of the area's maritime activities took place. (Sithens, *c.* 1916.)

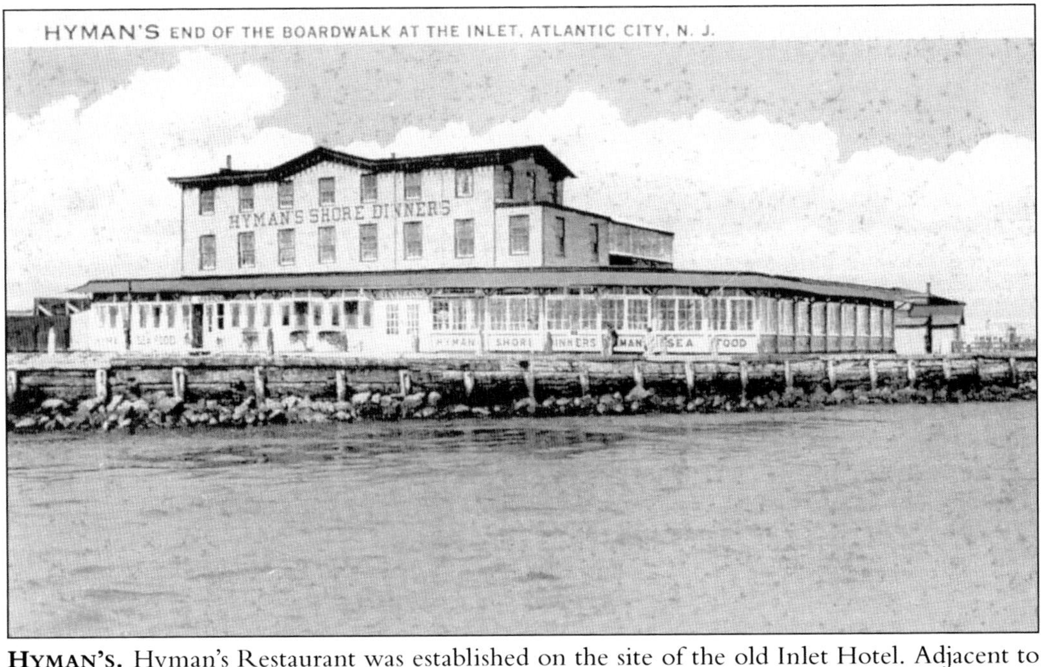

HYMAN'S. Hyman's Restaurant was established on the site of the old Inlet Hotel. Adjacent to the Yachtsmen's Association Pier and the trolley terminus, it was an ideal spot for a seafood eatery. Its large dining rooms had wonderful unobstructed views of the Absecon Inlet and ocean. Patrons could look forward to enjoying full-course seafood dinners served in a pleasant atmosphere. (Tichnor, *c.* 1924)

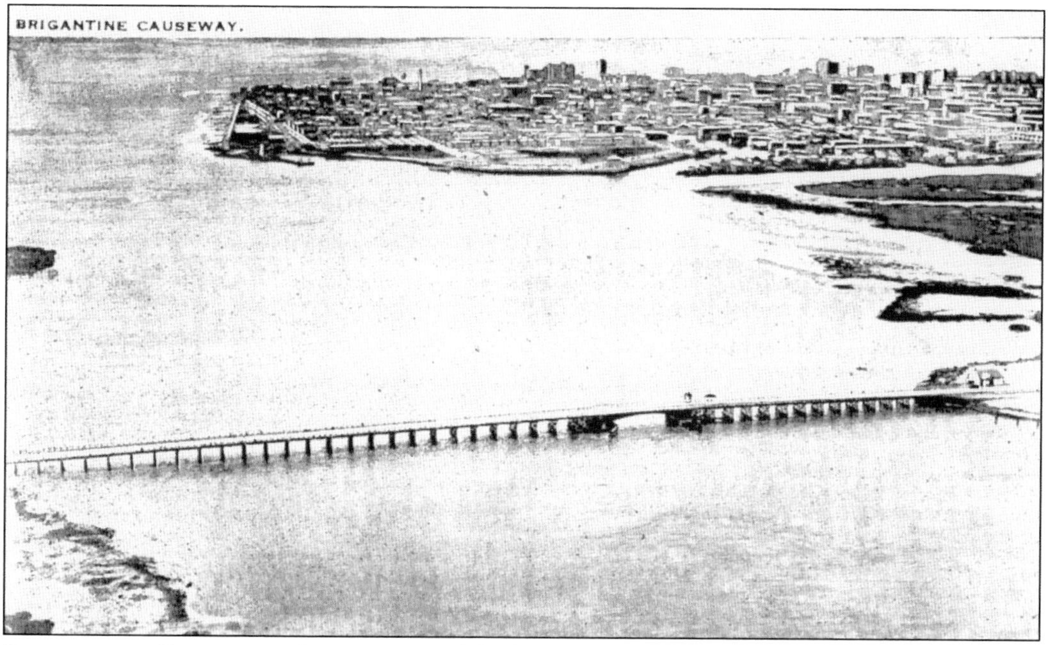

BRIGANTINE CAUSEWAY. Construction of the bridge connecting Atlantic City with its neighbor to the north, Brigantine, began in September 1923. The causeway, which crosses the Absecon Channel, opened in January 1924. This project was the work of the Island Development Company and cost over $960,000 to complete. (Sithens Postcard Company, *c.* 1926.)

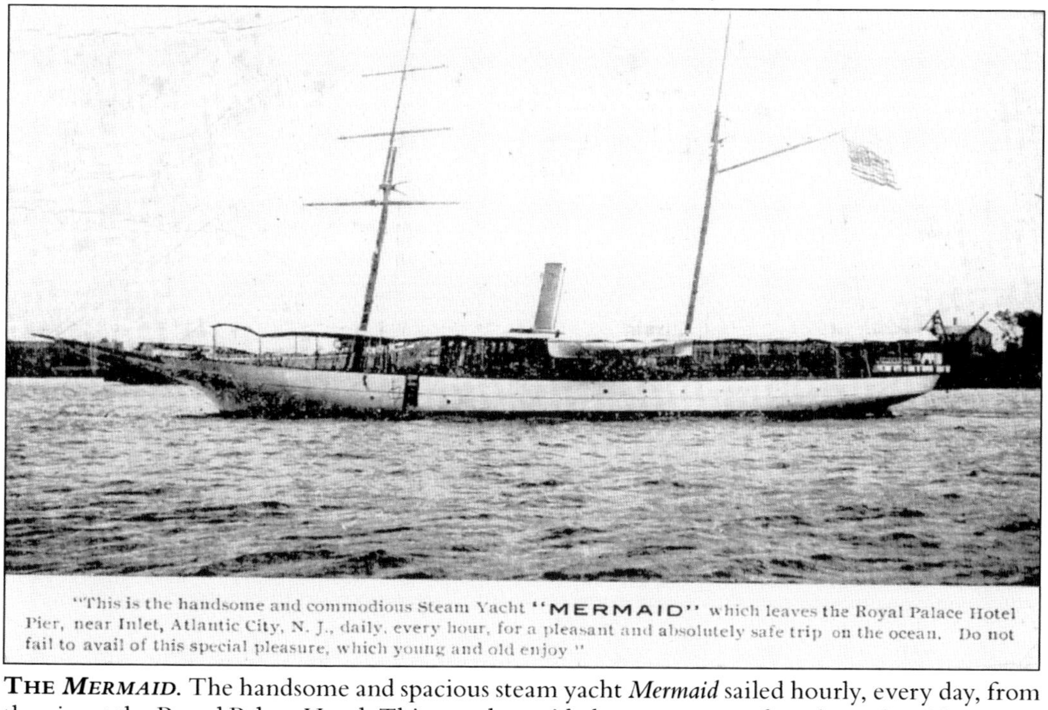

THE *MERMAID*. The handsome and spacious steam yacht *Mermaid* sailed hourly, every day, from the pier at the Royal Palace Hotel. This vessel provided passengers a safe and comfortable voyage out to the inlet and into the ocean on a short sightseeing tour. This excursion was proclaimed to be a "special pleasure, which young and old enjoy." (Publisher unknown, *c.* 1908.)

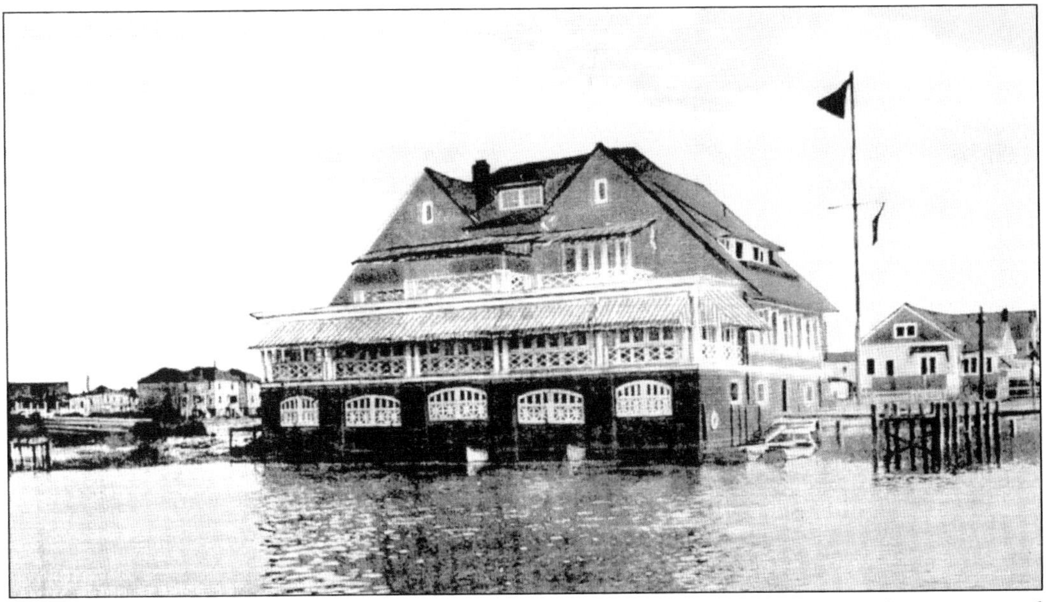

Chelsea Yacht Club. Situated at Aberdeen Place and the thoroughfare (now the Intracoastal Waterway), this yacht club was established on January 31, 1911. The building cost approximately $30,000 to construct. It had a library, lecture room, dance floor, and pool, billiard, and card rooms for its members and visiting yachtsmen to enjoy. On July 6, 1934, while being remodeled, a fire swept through the structure destroying it. (Sithens, *c.* 1920.)

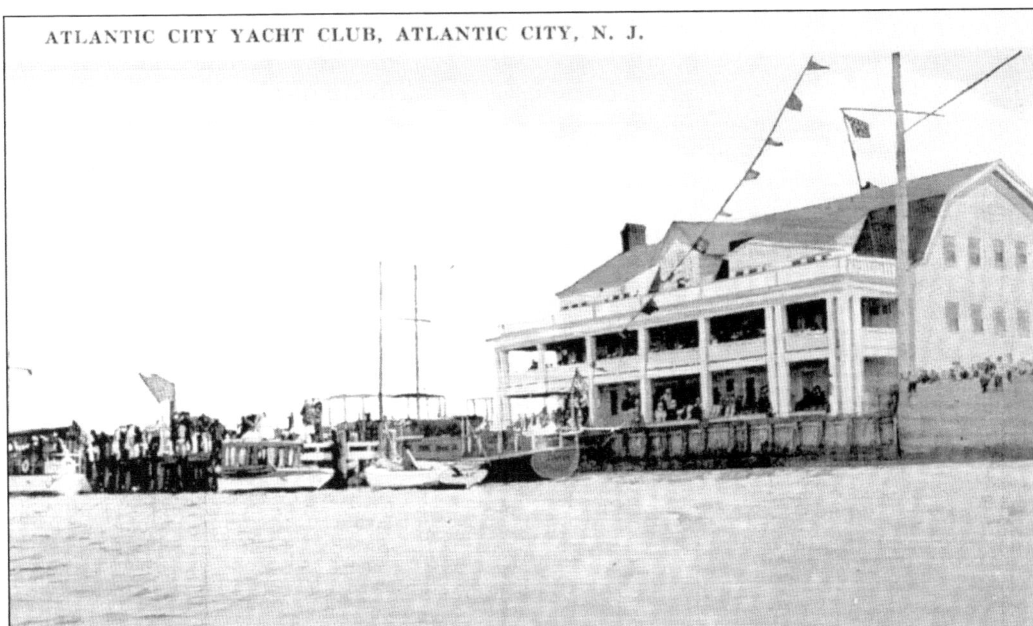

Atlantic City Yacht Club. The headquarters of the Atlantic City Yacht Club was located on New Hampshire Avenue at the inlet. Built right at the water's edge, this Dutch Colonial–style building, with its long porches, offered open views of the waterway. Organized in 1912, the club once had more than 500 members. This landmark structure was eventually demolished in 1936. (Sithens Postcard Company, *c.* 1920.)

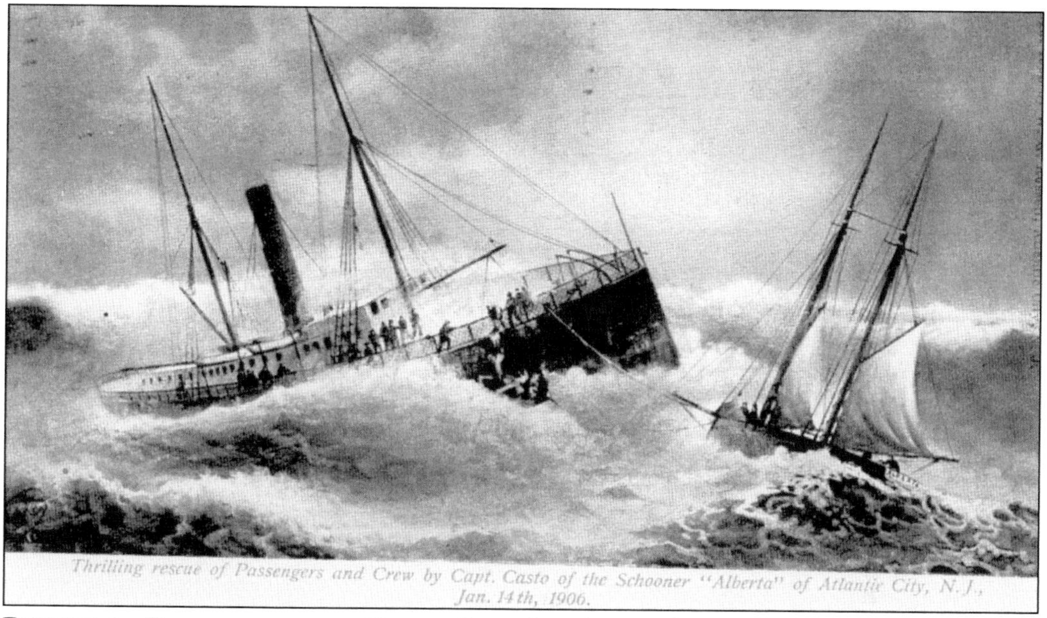

RESCUE OF PASSENGERS AND CREW. One of area's most famous sea stories dates back to a storm on January 14, 1906. The steamer *Cherokee*, grounded in fog two days earlier, became imperiled off Atlantic City. Braving very high seas, Capt. Mark Casto and six volunteers aboard the schooner *Alberta* sailed through 40-foot waves to rescue 61 passengers and crew from the stricken vessel. (W. G. Russell, 1906.)

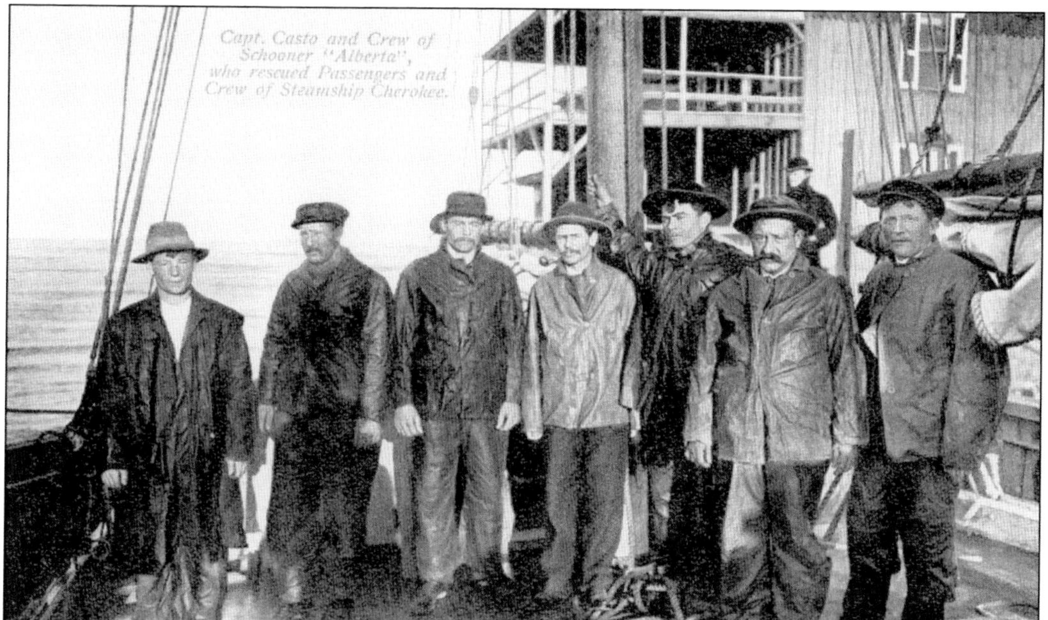

CAPTAIN CASTO AND CREW. Standing on the deck of their boat, moored to a wharf at the inlet, Capt. Mark Casto and his courageous crew pose for the camera after gaining fame for rescuing the passengers and crew from the steamer *Cherokee*. For his valiant efforts Casto was awarded two medals, as well as $1,500, from the Carnegie Hero Fund. Each member of his crew was presented with $500 in reward money as well. (Robbins Brothers, 1906.)

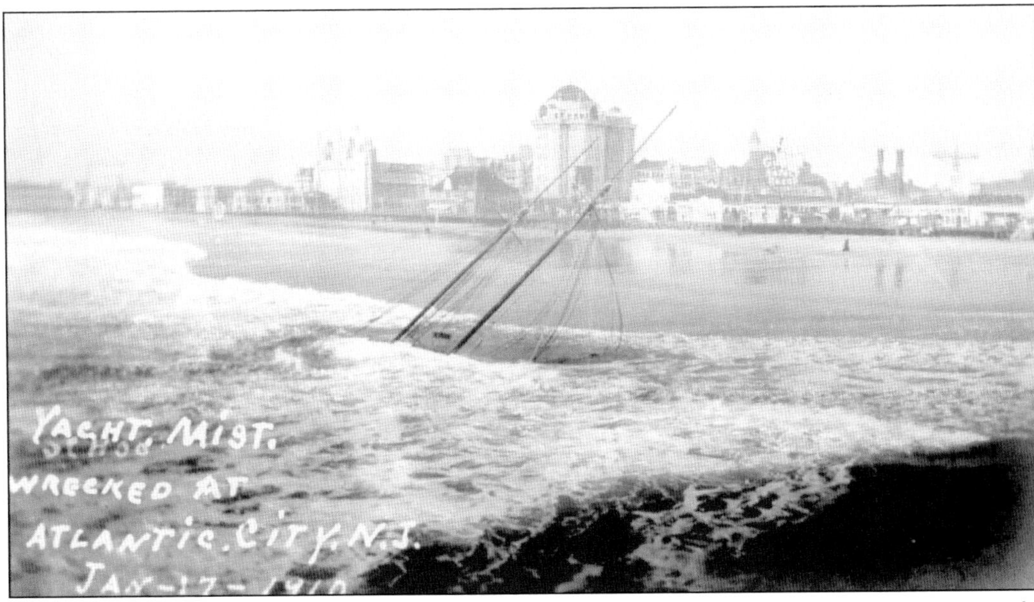

YACHT *MIST* WRECKED. The waters off Absecon Island have proven treacherous to many vessels, both large and small, over the years. This small sailing yacht, the *Mist*, meets its fate in the surf just off the beach, close to Young's Pier near New York Avenue. Capsized on January 17, 1910, only its masts are visible in this postcard view. (Hubin's Big Post Card Store, 1910.)

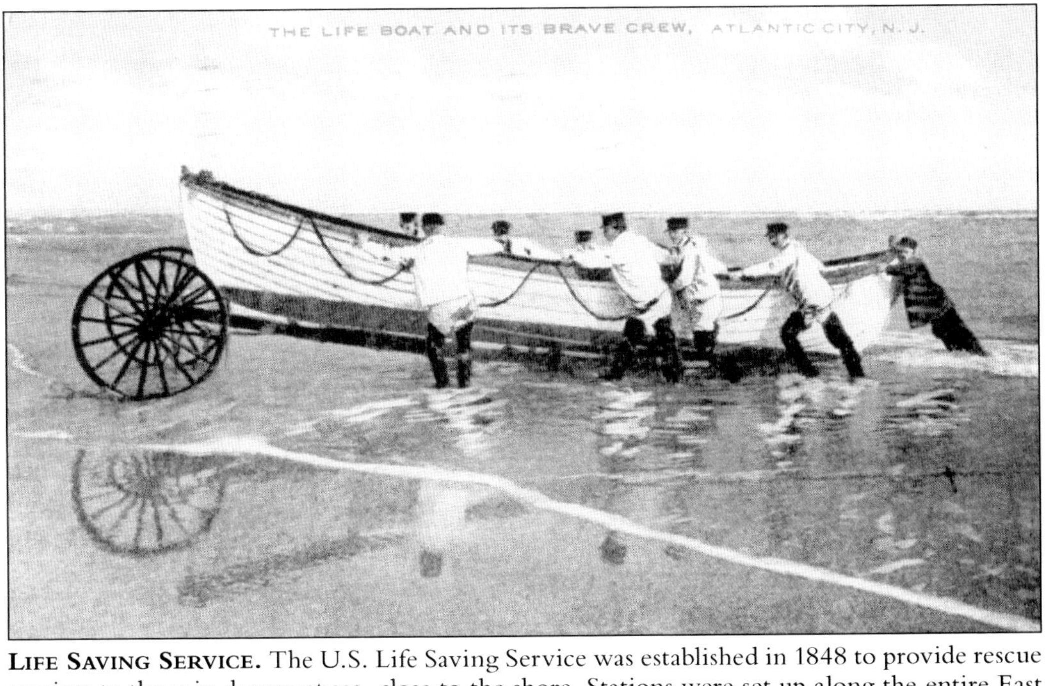

LIFE SAVING SERVICE. The U.S. Life Saving Service was established in 1848 to provide rescue services to those in danger at sea, close to the shore. Stations were set up along the entire East Coast, including Atlantic City. This organization later became part of the U.S. Coast Guard in 1915. Here a lifesaving crew, dressed in their white uniforms, loads a surfboat onto a wheeled boat carriage after a drill. (L. Beard, *c.* 1910.)

THE LIGHTHOUSE. The Absecon Lighthouse began operations on January 15, 1857. Towering 167 feet high with 228 steps, it took 598,634 bricks to construct upon a foundation of granite blocks. The cost for this guardian of the inlet was $52,187. Its beam, visible for 20 nautical miles, was helpful in preventing shipwrecks along the coast. This beacon of marine safety was decommissioned on July 11, 1933. (Publisher unknown, *c.* 1910.)

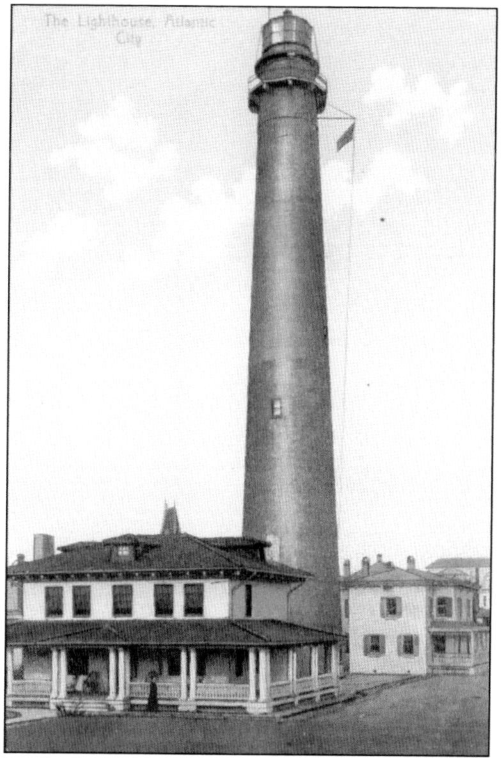

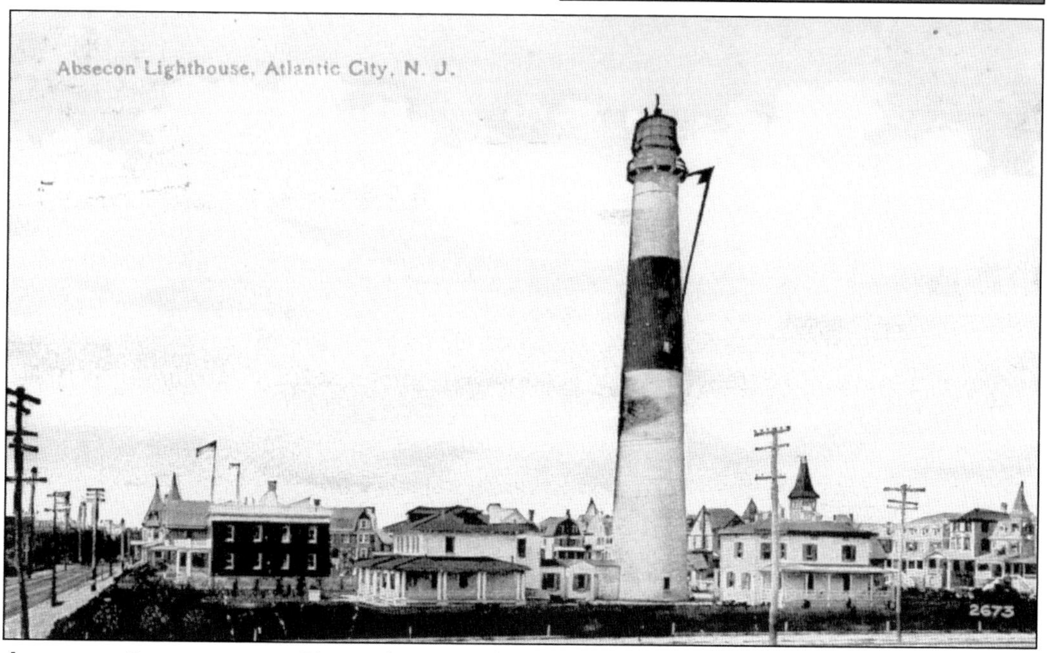

ABSECON LIGHTHOUSE. Situated on Pacific Avenue between Vermont and Rhode Island Avenues, the lighthouse is a major landmark in the area. In 1946, the lighthouse was deeded to the city for use as a public park but was later sold to the state in 1966 as a historical site. This important structure has been restored and is now open to the public. (Post Card Distribution Company, *c.* 1914.)